Hoddy (59- 11229) 4-29-65

Virginia Under the Stuarts

1607 - 1688

Virginia Under the Stuarts

1607 - 1688

By

THOMAS J. WERTENBAKER

New York
RUSSELL & RUSSELL
1959

PRINTED IN THE UNITED STATES OF AMERICA

Dedicated
to my mother

PREFACE

It was in May, 1910, that the author came to Princeton for an interview with President Woodrow Wilson concerning an appointment as Instructor in the Department of History, Politics, and Economics. He was elated when President Wilson engaged him, though not happy over the $1,000 salary. Yet with this sum to fall back on he borrowed $200, and took a trip to England.

In London he went treasure hunting, the treasure of old documents relating to the history of colonial Virginia. He sought out the British Public Record Office, off Chauncery Lane, and was soon immersed in the mass of letters, official reports, journal of the Assembly, and other papers.

The author was prepared to find valuable historical materials in London, for he had spent the summer of 1908 studying the William Noel Sainsbury and the McDonald abstracts and transcripts of the documents in the Record Office deposited in the Virginia State Library. But he was staggered at the extent of the manuscript collection on Virginia history alone. Among the scores of volumes are thirty-two devoted to the correspondence of the Board of Trade, seventeen to the correspondence of the Secretary of State, twenty-two to entry books, letters, commissions, warrants, etc.

When the summer waned he left for America taking with him many pages of closely written notes. But what he had learned served to whet his appetite for more, so that in 1912 and again in 1914 he was back, going over volume after volume, searching eagerly for fear some important point would escape him. The mass of abstracts and notes which he accumulated formed the basis of this volume .

In fact, any political history of Virginia in the colonial period must be based on the documents in the Public Record

Office, since most of the copies left in Virginia have been lost or destroyed. Today, however, colonial historians no longer have to visit London to consult them, since transcripts have been made and deposited in the Library of Congress.

In recent years the American Council of Learned Societies has made available other collections of manuscripts which have thrown new light on early Virginia history. The most important of these are the Coventry Papers at Longleat, the residence of the Marquess of Bath. Many of the letters deal with Bacon's Rebellion, and include the correspondence between Berkeley and Bacon, accounts of the Indian war, complaints of the misgovernment of Berkeley, the account of the evacuation of Jamestown written by Berkeley, accounts of Bacon's death and the collapse of the rebellion.

This new material adds new weight to the conclusions reached in this book—that the causes of Bacon's Rebellion were deep-seated, that it grew out of the discontent caused by the Navigation Acts, the heavy taxes, the corrupting of the Assembly by Berkeley, and the misuse of the courts. It in no way shakes the conviction expressed by Thomas Mathews, who himself was involved in the rebellion, that the Indian war was the excuse for it rather than the cause.

Yet certain recent historians have contended that this violent uprising was not a protest against injustice and misgovernment. One has gone so far as to call it merely a quarrel between a rash young man and an old fool. We could with equal justice call the American Revolution just a quarrel between George Washington and George III. Mathews tells us that it was the general opinion in Virginia at the time that it was not Bacon who was chiefly responsible for the uprising, but Thomas Lawrence. Bacon "was too young, too much a stranger there, and of a disposition too precipitate to manage things to that length they were carried," he pointed out, "had not thoughtful Mr. Lawrence been at the bottom."

But neither Lawrence's hatred of Berkeley, nor Bacon's rashness, nor Berkeley's folly, nor the Indian war suffice to explain the rebellion. When the news of the uprising reached Charles II, he thought it past belief that "so considerable body of men, without the least grievance or oppression, should rise up in arms and overthrow the government" He was quite right. Had there been no grievances and oppression there would have been no uprising.

That Bacon's Rebellion is explained in part by poverty and suffering is clear. Philip Ludwell said that the rebel army was composed of men "whose condition . . . was such that a change could not make worse." The men who fought so valiantly against the Indians and Berkeley's forces, braved the King's anger, faced death on the gallows were called in contempt "the bases of the people," "the rabble," the "scum of the people," "idle and poor people," "rag, tag, and bobtail." The Council reported that there were "hardly two amongst them" who owned estates, or were persons of reputation. Berkeley complained that his was a miserable task to govern a people "where six parts of seven at least are poor, indebted, discontented, and armed."

So when Bacon sent out his agents to every part of Virginia to denounce the governor for not permitting an election for a new Assembly, accusing him of misgovernment, and complaining of the heavy and unequal taxes, they "infested the whole country." Berkeley stated that the contaigion spread "like a train of powder." Never before was there "so great a madness as this base people are generally seized with." When, in panic, he dissolved the Long Assembly and called for a new election, all except eight of those chosen were pro-Bacon men.

One cannot but ask why. Surely the voters would not have sided with this young man who had been in Virginia but a few months had he not taken the lead in protesting against the many wrongs to which they had been subjected. And had those who rushed to arms, risking their property, if not their necks, done so merely because of a quarrel between Bacon and Berkeley, they would have been more than base, they would have been fools.

What these wrongs were Bacon and his followers tell us in what they called the Declaration of the People. Berkeley and his favorites they denounced "for having upon specious pretences of public works raised great unjust taxes upon the commonalty for the advancement of private favorites and other sinister ends . . . ; for having abused and rendered contemptible the magistrates of justice, by advancing to places of judicature scandalous and ignorant favorites . . . ."

In a burning manifesto, denouncing the injustice and corruption of the ruling group, Bacon said: "We appeal to the country itself what and of what nature their oppressions have been, and by what cabal and mystery the design of many of those whom we call great men have been transacted and carried on . . . . See what sponges have sucked up the public wealth and whether it hath not been privately contrived away by unworthy favorites, by vile juggling parasites, whose tottering fortunes have been repaired and supported by the charge." The constant breach of laws, unjust prosecutions, excuses, and evasions, proved that the men in power were conducting public affairs "as if it were but to play a booty, game, or divide a spoil."

In view of these statements recent attempts to prove that Bacon was no true patriot and not interested in righting the people's wrongs seem strange indeed. It is hardly credible that he was merely pretending when he wrote these fiery words, that he posed as the champion of the people to further his personal ambitions, that he trumped up charges against Berkeley because of the disagreement over the Indian war.

But, it has been said, Bacon showed no interest in the passage of the reform laws enacted by the Assembly of June 1676, refused to have them read before his army, and complained that the Burgesses had not lived up to his expectations. Had he been really interested in reform, would he not have gloried in these laws and have praised the Assembly for passing them?

Any such conclusion falls flat when we consider the conditions under which this session was held. The Burgesses had hardly taken their seats when Bacon, who had been elected as one of the members to represent Henrico County, was captured. Though Berkeley pardoned him and restored him to his seat in the Council, he was a virtual prisoner during the first few days of the session. So he looked on with growing resentment as the governor overawed the Burgesses and reform measures were set aside.

Then, suddenly, the entire situation changed. Bacon got permission to return to Henrico because his wife was ill. Once there he placed himself at the head of his army of enraged frontiersmen and marched rapidly on Jamestown. When this news reached the little capital, the governor, his Council, and the Burgesses were panic stricken. Since resistance was useless, every thought was of appeasement. A series of reform laws, which struck at the very roots of Berkeley's system of rule through placemen, was introduced in the Assembly, rushed through, and signed by the governor.

Not knowing what had happened during his absence, on his arrival Bacon mounted the steps to the Long Room of the State House where the Assembly met, to urge them to right the people's wrongs. Thomas Mathews, who was present, says that "he pressed hard, nigh an hour's harangue on preserving our lives from the Indians, inspecting the revenues, the exorbitant taxes, and redressing the grievances and calamities of that deplorable country." It was only when he had finished that someone spoke up to tell him that "they had already redressed their grievances." To contend that Bacon was not interested in laws which he himself had so passionately urged and which had obviously been passed to conciliate him and his followers is merely to attempt to disprove the obvious.

Philip A. Bruce, in a statement published in 1893, in the *Virginia Magazine of History and Biography*, points out that Bacon's Rebellion "preceded the American Revolution by a century, an event which it resembled in its spirit, if not in its causes and results. Bacon is known in history as the Rebel, but the fuller information which we have now as to the motives of his conduct shows that he can with more justice be described as Bacon the Patriot. He headed a powerful popular movement in which the sovereignty of the people was for the first time relied upon on American soil by a great leader as the justification of his acts. The spirit breathing through the Declaration of the People is the spirit of the Declaration of Independence." Nothing which has been brought out in the sixty-four years since Dr. Bruce wrote these words has shaken or can shake their truth. Bacon was the torchbearer of the Revolution.

Attempts to defend Sir John Harvey are as unconvincing as those to belittle Bacon. Certainly the Sackville Papers, recently made available to historians, contain nothing to warrant any change in the conclusion, long accepted by Virginia historians, that Harvey's expulsion was richly deserved.

Charles Campbell, in his *History of the Colony and Ancient Dominion of Virginia,* thus describes Harvey's administration: "He was extortionate, proud, unjust, and arbitrary; he issued proclamations in derogation of the legislative powers of the Assembly; assessed, levied, held, and disbursed the colonial revenue without check or responsibility; transplanted into Virginia exotic English statutes; multiplied penalties and exactions and appropriated fines to his own use; he added the decrees of the court of high commission of England to the ecclesiastical constitutions of Virginia." Could we have a more perfect description of a despot?

It remains to point out a few errors which crept into the original manuscript. On page 21 "the falls of the Appomattox" should be "the first bend of the Appomattox; on page 75 "John Pott" should be "Francis Pott"; on page 82 "Matthew Kemp" should be "Richard Kemp".

Princeton, New Jersey   THOMAS J. WERTENBAKER
    August, 1957

CONTENTS

ABBREVIATIONS USED IN NOTES

Arb. Smith, *Works of Captain John Smith,* Edward Arber.

Scobell, *Scobell's Collection of Acts and Ordinances of General Use.*

F. R., *The First Republic in America,* Alexander Brown.

Gen., *The Genesis of the United States,* Alexander Brown.

Force, *Tracts and Other Papers Relating to the Colonies in North America,* Peter Force.

Nar. of Va., *Narratives of Early Virginia,* Lyon G. Tyler.

Va. Car., *Virginia Carolorum,* E. D. Neill.

Hen., *The Statutes at Large,* W. W. Hening.

Proceedings of Va. Co., *Proceedings of the Virginia Company of London.*

Cradle of Rep., *The Cradle of the Republic,* Lyon G. Tyler.

Bruce, Inst. Hist., *Institutional History of Virginia in the Seventeenth Century,* P. A. Bruce.

Bruce, Ec. Hist., *Economic History of Virginia in the Seventeenth Century,* P. A. Bruce.

Miller, *The Legislature of the Province of Virginia,* E. I. Miller.

P. R. O., British Public Record Office.

Stith, *History of Virginia,* William Stith.

Osg., *American Colonies in the Seventeenth Century,* H. L. Osgood.

Neill, Va. Co., *History of the Virginia Company of London,* E. D. Neill.

Fiske, Old Va., *Old Virginia and her Neighbors,* John Fiske.

Burk, *History of Virginia,* John Burk.

Va. Hist. Reg., *Virginia Historical Register.*

Beverley, *History of Virginia,* Robert Beverley.

Va. Mag., *Virginia Magazine of History and Biography.*

Wise, *The Early History of the Eastern Shore of Virginia,* J. C. Wise.

Southern Lit. Mess., *Southern Literary Messenger.*

Campbell, *History of Virginia,* Charles Campbell.

McD., *McDonald Papers,* Virginia State Library.

Jour. H. of B., *Journals of the House of Burgesses.* Manuscript copies in the Virginia State Library.

Justice in Virginia, *Justice in Colonial Virginia,* O. P. Chitwood.

Sains., *Sainsbury Papers,* Virginia State Library.

Mass. S. IV., *Massachusetts Historical Collections, Series IV.*

T. M., *The Beginning, Progress and Conclusion of Bacon's Rebellion.*

W. & M. Q., *William and Mary Quarterly.*

Inds' Pros., *Indians' Proceedings.*

Bac's Pros., *Bacon's Proceedings.*

Ing's Pros., *Ingram's Proceedings.*

Cotton, *Our Late Troubles in Virginia,* Mrs. A. Cotton.

Va. Vet., *Virginia Vetusta,* E. D. Neill.

CHAPTER I

The Founding of Virginia

In December, 1606, three little vessels—the *Sarah Constant,*
the *Discovery* and the *Goodspeed*—set sail from England
under Captain Christopher Newport, for the distant shores
of Virginia.[1] After a long and dangerous voyage across the
Atlantic the fleet, on the sixth of May, 1607, entered the
Chesapeake Bay.[2] The adventurers spent several days exploring this great body of water, landing parties to investigate
the nature of the shores, and to visit the Indian tribes that
inhabited them. They were delighted with the "faire med-
dowes, . . . full of flowers of divers kinds and colours", and
with the "goodly tall trees" of the forests with "Fresh-waters
running" between, but they had instructions not to settle near
the coast, lest they should fall victims to the Spaniards.[3] So
they entered the broad mouth of a river which they called the
James, and made their way cautiously up into the country.
On the twenty-third of May they found a peninsula in the
river, which afforded a convenient landing place and was
easy to defend, both from the Indians and the Spaniards.
This place they called Jamestown. Landing their men, they
set immediately to work building houses and erecting fortifications. Thus did the English begin their first permanent
settlement in the New World.

The bold band of adventurers that came thus hopefully
into this beautiful and smiling country little realized that
before them lay only dangers and misfortunes. Could they
have foreseen the terrible obstacles to founding a colony in
this land, they would have hesitated before entering upon the
enterprise.

Four things conspired to bring misfortune and disaster upon

---

[1] F. R., pp. 21, 22.   [2] F. R., p. 23.
[3] Arb. Smith, lxi-lxii.

Virginia.   The form of government prescribed by the King
and the Company was unsuited to the infant settlement, and
its defects kept the colonists for many months in turmoil and
disorder.   The Indians proved a constant source of danger,
for they were tireless in cutting off stragglers, ambushing
small parties and in destroying the crops of the white men.
Famines came at frequent intervals to weaken the colonists
and add to their misfortunes.   But by far the most
terrible scourge was the "sicknesse" that swept over Virginia year after year, leaving in its wake horrible suffering
and devastation.

The charter that James I granted to the London Company
served as a constitution for Virginia, for it prescribed the
form of government and made regulations that none could
disregard.   It provided for a Council, resident in England, to
which was assigned the management of the colony and the
supervision of its government.[4]   This body was appointed by
the King and was strictly answerable to him through the
Privy Council for its every act.[5]   The immediate government
of the colony was entrusted to a local Council, selected by the
Council in England, and responsible to it.   The Virginia
Council exercised extraordinary powers, assuming all administrative, legislative and judicial functions, and being in no
way restrained by the wishes or demands of their fellow
colonists.[6]   Although they were restricted by the charter and
by the instructions of the Council in England, the isolation of
the settlement and the turbulent spirit of the adventurers made
them reckless in enforcing their own will upon the colonists.
More than once they were guilty of unpardonable harshness
and cruelty.

The charter did not provide for the appointment of a
Governor.   The nominal leadership of the colony was entrusted to a President, chosen by the local Council from among
its members.   This officer had no duty distinct from that of
the Councillors, other than to preside at their meetings and
to cast a double or deciding vote in case of deadlock.[7]   He

[4] Gen., p. 55.   [5] Gen., p. 56
[6] Gen., pp. 55, 70, 73.   [7] Gen., p. 77.

was to serve but one year and if at any time his administration proved unsatisfactory to his colleagues, they could, by a majority vote, depose him. In like manner, any Councillor that had become obnoxious could be expelled without specific charges and without trial.[8] These unwise provisions led naturally to disorder and strife, and added much to the misfortunes of the infant colony.[9]

The selections for the Council were made some days before the fleet sailed, but the Company, fearing a conflict of authority during the voyage, thought it best that they should be kept secret until the colonists had reached Virginia. The names of the appointees were embodied in "several instruments" which were entrusted to the commanders of the vessels, with instructions that they should be opened within twenty-four hours after they had arrived off the coast of America.[10] Upon entering the Chesapeake Bay the adventurers read the papers, and found that Christopher Newport, the commander of the fleet, Edward Wingfield, Bartholomew Gosnold, George Kendall, John Ratcliffe, John Martin and John Smith were those that had been chosen.[11]

After the landing the Council met, were sworn to office, and then elected Wingfield President.[12] Captain John Smith, who had been accused of mutiny during the voyage, was not allowed to take his seat, and was kept under restraint until the twentieth of June.[13]

Hardly had the founding of Jamestown been effected when the weakness of the constitution became apparent. The meetings of the Council were discordant and stormy. The mem-

[8] Gen., p. 67. [9] Gen., pp. 342, 411.
[10] Gen., p. 77. [11] Arb. Smith, p. 91.
[12] Arb. Smith, p. 91.
[13] Arb. Smith, p. 91; F. R., pp. 27, 32. Smith denied the justice of these charges. "Now Captaine Smith, who all this time from their departure from the Canaries, was restrained as a prisoner, upon the scandalous suggestions of some of the chiefe (envying his repute); who fained he intended to ursurpe the government, murder the Councell, and make himself king; that his confederats were dispearsed in all the three ships, and that divers of his confederats that revealed it, would affirme it: for this he was committed." Arb. Smith, p. 92.

bers were utterly unable to act with vigor and determination, or to agree upon any settled course of action in establishing the little colony. The President, because of the limitation of his powers, could do nothing to restore harmony or to enforce his own wishes and policies. Confusion and mismanagement resulted. In less than a month after the first landing the inefficiency of the government had created such discontent that the colonists petitioned the Council for redress.[14] It was only the tact and moderation of Captain Newport that appeased the anger of the settlers and persuaded them to submit to the decrees of the governing body.[15]

On the second of July, Newport, with his little fleet, sailed for England, leaving the ill-fated colonists to their own resources.[16] No sooner had he gone than the spirit of discord reappeared. The quarrels within the Council became more violent than ever, and soon resulted in the complete disruption of that body. Captain Kendall, who seems to have been active in fomenting ill feeling among his colleagues, was the first to be expelled. Upon the charge of exciting discord he was deprived of his seat and committed to prison.[17]

As Captain John Smith had, before the departure of Newport, been allowed to take his place in the Council, there were now five members of that body. The number was soon reduced to four by the death of Captain Gosnold, who fell a victim to the sickness.[18] One would imagine that the Council, thus depleted, would have succeeded in governing the colony in peace, but the settlers were given no respite from their wrangling and disputes. In September, Ratcliffe, Smith and Martin entered into an agreement to depose President Wingfield and to oust him from the Council. Before they proceeded against him, however, they pledged each other that the expulsions should then stop, and that no one of the three should be attacked by the other two.

The Councillors then appeared before Wingfield's tent with a warrant, "subscribed under their handes, to depose the

---

[14] Arb. Smith, liii.
[16] F. R., p. 39.
[18] Arb. Smith, lxxvi.

[15] Arb. Smith, liv.
[17] Arb. Smith, lxxvii.

President; sayeing they thought him very unworthy to be eyther President or of the Councell, and therefore discharged him of both".[19] They accused him of misappropriating funds, of improper division of the public stores, of being an atheist, of plotting to desert Virginia in the pinnace left at Jamestown by Captain Newport, of combining with the Spaniards for the destruction of the colony. Wingfield, when he returned to England, made a vigorous defense of his conduct, but it is now impossible to determine whether or not he was justly accused. After his expulsion from office, he was summoned before the court by the remnant of the Council to answer these numerous charges. It might have gone hard with him, had he not demanded a hearing before the King. As his enemies feared to deny him this privilege, they closed the court, and committed him to prison on board the pinnace, where he was kept until means were at hand to send him to England.[20]

The removal of the President did not bring peace to the colony. If we may believe the testimony of Wingfield, the triumvirate that now held sway ruled the settlers with a harsh and odious tyranny. "Wear," he says, "this whipping, lawing, beating, and hanging, in Virginia, known in England, I fear it would drive many well affected myndes from this honourable action."[21] One day Ratcliffe, who had been chosen to succeed Wingfield, became embroiled with James Read, the smith. Read forgot the respect due his superior, and struck the new President. So heinous a crime was this affront to the dignity of the chief officer of the infant colony, that the smith was brought to trial, convicted and sentenced to be hanged. But he saved his life, upon the very eve of his execution, by revealing to Ratcliffe a plot against the government, headed, he declared, by Captain Kendall.[22] Immediately Kendall, who had long been an object of suspicion, was tried for mutiny, found guilty and executed.[23]

In December, 1607, when the colony was suffering severely for the want of food, Captain Smith led an expedition into the

[19] Arb. Smith, lxxix.
[20] Arb. Smith, lxxxi.
[21] Arb. Smith, lxxxiv.
[22] Arb. Smith, lxxxiv.
[23] Arb. Smith, lxxxv.

territory of the Chickahominies in quest of corn.[24]   During
his absence the President, despite the protests of Martin,
admitted Captain Gabriel Archer to the Council.[25]   Archer,
who seems to have been a bitter enemy of Smith, had no
sooner attained this place of power, than he set to work to
ruin the adventurous captain.   "Being settled in his authority", he "sought to call Master Smythes lief in question,
and . . . indicted him upon a Chapter in Leviticus for the
death" of two men under his charge, that had been murdered
by the Indians.   He was to have had his trial upon the very
day of his return from his thrilling adventures with the
savages.   His conviction and immediate execution would
doubtless have resulted, had not the proceedings against him
been interrupted by the arrival of the First Supply from England.[26]   Captain Newport, whose influence seems always to
have been exerted in favor of moderation and harmony, persuaded the Council to drop the charges against Smith, to
release him from restraint, and to restore him to his seat in
the Council.

Of extraordinary interest is the assertion of Wingfield that
the arrival of the fleet "prevented a Parliament, which ye
newe Counsailour (Archer) intended thear to summon".[27]
It is not surprising that the settlers, disgusted as they were
with the violence and harshness of their rulers, should have
wished to share in the government.   But we cannot but wonder
at their boldness in attempting to set aside the constitution
given them by the King and the Company.   Had they succeeded in establishing direct government by the people, it
could not be supposed that James would have permitted it to
continue.   But the attempt is very significant, as indicating
that they were desirous, even at this early date, of having a
voice in the management of affairs.

Archer and the unfortunate Wingfield sailed with the fleet
when Captain Newport returned to England, and a few
months later Martin followed them.[28]   Since, with the First

---

[24] Arb. Smith, lxxxv.   [25] F. R., p. 54.
[26] Arb. Smith, lxxxvi.   [27] Arb. Smith, lxxxvi.
[28] F. R., p. 58.

Supply had come a new Councillor, Matthew Scrivener, the governing body once more numbered three.

During the summer of 1608 Smith was frequently away, chasing the phantom of the passage to the South Sea, but this did not prevent the usual quarrels. If we may believe the account in Smith's history, Ratcliffe was deposed from the Presidency because of "pride and unreasonable needlesse cruelty" and for wasting the public stores.[29] It is probable that for some weeks Scrivener conducted the government, while Ratcliffe was kept a prisoner.[30] In September, Captain Smith, returning from a voyage in the Chesapeake Bay, "received the letters patents, and took upon him the place of president".[31]

Smith was now supreme in the government, for the Council was reduced to two, and his casting vote made his will superior to that of Scrivener. But he was not long to enjoy this power. In October, 1608, Captain Newport, arriving with the Second Supply, brought with him two "antient souldiers and valient gentlemen"—Richard Waldo and Peter Wynne—both bearing commissions as Councillors.[32] Soon afterward Ratcliffe was restored to his seat. The Council, thus recruited, resumed its control over the colony, "so that although Smith was President yet the Council had the authority, and ruled it as they listed".[33]

Two months later, when Newport sailed again, Ratcliffe returned to England. Smith wrote the English Council, "Captaine Ratcliffe is . . . a poore counterfeited Imposture. I have sent you him home, least the company should cut his throat."[34] The next spring Waldo and Scrivener, with nine others, were caught in a small boat upon the James by a violent gale, and were drowned.[35] As Captain Wynne soon succumbed to the sickness, Smith became the sole surviving Councillor.[36] During the summer of 1609 the colony was governed, not, as the King and Company had designed, by a Council, but by the will of this one man.

[29] Arb. Smith, pp. 114, 115.
[30] Arb. Smith, p. 119.
[31] Arb. Smith, p. 121; F. R., p. 61.
[32] F. R., p. 68; Arb. Smith, p. 122.
[33] Arb. Smith, p. 122.
[34] Arb. Smith., p. 444.
[35] F. R., 70.
[36] F. R., 71.

In the meanwhile the London Company was becoming aware that a mistake had been made in entrusting the government of the colony to a body of Councillors. The reports of Wingfield, Archer, Newport and Ratcliffe made it evident that the lack of harmony in the Council had been a serious hindrance to the success of the enterprise.[37] Feeling, therefore, that this "error in the equality of the governors . . . had a little shaken so tender a body", the managers held an especial meeting to effect a change.[38] A new charter was drawn up by Sir Edwin Sandys, approved by the Company and assented to by the King.

In this document James relinquished into the hands of the Company not only the direct management of the colony, but the power of drawing up a new and more satisfactory system of government. Acting under this authority, Sandys and his associates abolished the Council and entrusted the entire control of the colony to an all-powerful Governor. The disorder that had so impeded the success of the enterprise was to be crushed under the iron hand of a despot. Doubtless Sandys would have attempted to establish representative government at once in Virginia, had conditions favored so radical a change. But the colony was too young and feeble, and James could hardly be expected to give his consent. Yet the many liberal members of the Company were deeply interested in Virginia and were determined, should a favorable opportunity occur, to establish there an Assembly similar in character to the English Parliament.

The granting of the new charter aroused extraordinary interest in the fortunes of the colony throughout England and stimulated the Company to renewed efforts.[39] Thousands of pounds were contributed to defray the expenses of another expedition, and hundreds of persons responded to the appeals for settlers. The first Governor was a man of ability and distinction—Thomas Lord De la Warr. Sir Thomas Gates was made Lieutenant-Governor, George Summers, Admiral, and Captain Newport, Vice-Admiral.[40] De la Warr found it

---

[37] F. R., p. 73.   [38] F. R., p. 73.
[39] F. R., p. 80.   [40] F. R., p. 84.

impossible to leave at once to assume control of his government, but the other officers, with nine vessels and no less than five hundred colonists, sailed in June, 1609.[41] Unfortunately, in crossing the Gulf of Bahama, the fleet encountered a terrific storm, which scattered the vessels in all directions. When the tempest abated, several of the ships reunited and continued on their way to Jamestown, but the *Sea Adventure,* which carried Gates, Summers and Newport, was wrecked upon an island in the Bermudas.[42] As a result of this misfortune none of the leaders of the expedition reached Virginia until May, 1610, ten months later.

The other vessels, with most of the settlers, arrived at Jamestown in August, 1609. The newcomers told Captain Smith of the Company's new plan of government, and requested him to relinquish the old commission. This the President refused to do. All the official papers relating to the change had been aboard the *Sea Adventure,* and he would not resign until he had seen them.[43] A long and heated controversy followed, but in the end Smith gained his point.[44] It was agreed that until the arrival of the *Sea Adventure* the colony should remain under the old charter, and that Smith should continue to act as President until the twentieth of September, when he was to relinquish the government to Captain Francis West.[45]

This arrangement did not restore harmony. West felt aggrieved that Captain Smith should insist upon continuing the old order of affairs despite the known wishes of the Company, and took occasion to ignore and slight his authority. This so angered the President that he is said to have plotted with the Indians to surprise and cut off a party of men that his rival was leading up the James. Before this could be accomplished, however, Smith met with a serious accident, which led to his immediate overthrow. "Sleeping in his Boate . . . accidentallie, one fired his powder-bag, which tore the flesh . . . in a most pittifull manner; but to quench the

[41] F. R., p. 84.

[42] Gen., pp. 1329, 1330, 346, 400; Force, III; Arb. Smith, p. 635.

[43] F. R., p. 93.   [44] Gen., pp. 331, 347.

[45] Gen., pp. 331, 332; F. R., p. 98.

tormenting fire . . . he leaped over-board into the deepe river, where ever they could recover him he was neere drowned."[46]   Three former Councillors—Ratcliffe, Archer and Martin—who had come over with the new fleet, availed themselves of the helplessness of their old foe to rid the colony of his presence.   Claiming, with some justice, that if Smith could retain his office under the old charter, they were by the same power still members of the Council, they held a meeting, deposed him from the Presidency and sent him back to England.[47]   Having thus disposed of the troublesome Captain, they looked about them for some man suitable to head the colony until the arrival of Gates.   Neglecting the claims of West, whom they probably considered too inexperienced for the place, they selected Captain George Percy.[48]

In the meanwhile, the crew and passengers of the *Sea Adventure* were stranded in the Bermudas, upon what was called Devil's Island.   Some of their number were daring enough to venture out into the ocean in the longboat, in an attempt to reach the colony, but they must have perished, for they were never heard from again.[49]   The rest of the company, seeing no other way of escape, built two pinnaces and, in May, 1610, sailed away in them for Jamestown.   A few days later, upon their arrival in Virginia, Gates received the old patent and the seal from the President and the period of the first royal government in Virginia came to an end.[50]

But the "faction breeding" government by the Council was by no means the only cause of trouble.   Far more disastrous was the "sicknesse".   When the first expedition sailed for Virginia, the Council in England, solicitous for the welfare of the emigrants, commanded them to avoid, in the choice of a site for their town, all "low and moist places".[51]   Well would it have been for the colonists had they obeyed these

---

[46] Arb. Smith, p. 484.

[47] Ratcliffe wrote the Earl of Salisbury, "This man is sent home to answere some misdemenors, whereof I perswade me he can scarcely clear himselfe from great imputation of blame." Gen., p. 334.

[48] F. R., p. 108.   [49] F. R., p. 115.
[50] F. R., p. 117.   [51] Gen., p. 84.

instructions. Captain Smith says there was in fact opposition on the part of some of the leaders to the selection of the Jamestown peninsula, and it was amply justified by the event. The place was low and marshy and extremely unhealthful.[52] In the summer months great swarms of mosquitoes arose from the stagnant pools of water to attack the immigrants with a sting more deadly than that of the Indian arrow or the Spanish musket ball.

Scarcely three months had elapsed from the first landing when sickness and death made their appearance. The settlers, ignorant of the use of Peruvian bark and other remedies, were powerless to resist the progress of the epidemic. Captain George Percy describes in vivid colors the sufferings of the first terrible summer. "There were never Englishmen," he says, "left in a forreign country in such miserie as wee were in this new discouvered Virginia. Wee watched every three nights, lying on the bare-ground, what weather soever came; . . . which brought our men to bee most feeble wretches. . . . If there were any conscience in men, it would make their harts to bleed to heare the pitifull murmurings and outcries of our sick men without reliefe, every night and day for the space of sixe weekes; in the morning their bodies being trailed out of their cabines like Dogges, to be buried."[53] So deadly was the epidemic that when Captain Newport brought relief in January, 1608, he found but thirty-eight of the colonists alive.[54]

Nor did the men that followed in the wake of the *Sarah Constant,* the *Discovery* and the *Goodspeed* fare better. In the summer of 1608, the sickness reappeared and once more wrought havoc among the unhappy settlers. Captain Smith, who probably saved his own life by his frequent exploring expeditions, on his return to Jamestown in July, "found the Last Supply al sicke".[55] In 1609, when the fleet of Summers and Newport reached Virginia, the newcomers, many of whom were already in ill health, fell easy victims to malaria and dysentery. Smith declared that before the end of 1610 "not

[52] Arb. Smith, p. 5.
[54] F. R., p. 55.
[53] Arb. Smith, lxxii.
[55] Nar. of Va., p. 146.

past sixtie men, women and children" were left of several hundred that but a few months before had sailed away from Plymouth.[56]   During the short stay of Governor De la Warr one hundred and fifty, or more than half the settlers lost their lives.[57]

Various visitors to Virginia during the early years of the seventeenth century bear testimony to the ravages of this scourge. A Spaniard named Molina, writing in 1613, declared that one hundred and fifty out of every three hundred colonists died before being in Virginia twelve months.[58]   DeVries, a Dutch trader to the colony, wrote, "During the months of June, July and August it is very unhealthy, then people that have lately arrived from England, die, during these months, like cats and dogs, whence they call it the sickly season."[59] This testimony is corroborated by Governor William Berkeley, who reported in 1671, "There is not now oft seasoned hands (as we term them) that die now, whereas heretofore not one of five escaped the first year."[60]

In 1623 a certain Nathaniel Butler, in an attack upon the London Company, called "The Unmasked Face of our Colony in Virginia", drew a vivid, though perhaps an exaggerated picture of the unhealthfulness of the climate.   "I found the plantations," he said, "generally seated upon meer salt marshes, full of infectious bogs and muddy creeks and lakes, and thereby subjected to all those inconveniences and diseases which are so commonly found in the most unsound and most unhealthy parts of England, whereof every country and climate hath some."   It was by no means uncommon, he declared, to see immigrants from England "Dying under hedges and in the woods", and unless something were done at once to arrest the frightful mortality Virginia would shortly get the name of a slaughter house.[61]

The climate of eastern Virginia, unhealthful as it undoubtedly was in the places where the first settlements were made,

---

[56] Many of these, however, died of starvation or were killed by the Indians. Nar. of Va., p. 200.

[57] Nar. of Va., p. 212.

[59] Va. Car.

[61] Proceedings of Va. Co., p. 171.

[58] Nar. of Va., p. 220; Gen., p. 648.

[60] Hen., Vol. I; Gen., p. 499.

cannot be blamed for all the epidemics that swept the colony. Much of the ill health of the immigrants was due to unwholesome conditions on board the ships which brought them from England. The vessels were usually crowded far beyond their real capacity with wretched men, women and children, and were foul beyond description.[62] Not infrequently great numbers died at sea. One vessel is reported to have lost a hundred and thirty persons out of a hundred and eighty-five. On the ships that left England in June, 1609, both yellow fever and the London plague appeared, doing fearful havoc, and making it necessary to throw overboard from two of the vessels alone thirty-two unfortunate wretches.[63] The diseases thus started, often spread after the settlers had reached their new homes, and under favoring conditions, developed into terrible epidemics.[64]

Less deadly than the "sicknesse", but still greatly to be dreaded, was the hostility of the Indians.[65] The natives, resentful at the attempt of the white men to establish themselves in their midst, proved a constant menace to the colony. Their superstitious awe of the strange newcomers, and their lack of effective weapons alone prevented untiring and open war. Jamestown was but a few days old when it was subjected to a violent assault by the savages. On the twentieth day of May, 1607, the colonists, while at work without their arms in the fields, were attacked by several hundred Indians. In wild dismay they rushed into the fort, while the savages followed at their heels. "They came up allmost into the ffort, shot through the tents, appeared in this Skirmishe (which lasted hott about an hower) a very valient people." The guns of the ships came to the aid of the English and their thunders struck dismay into the hearts of the savages. Yet they retired without panic, taking with them their dead and wounded. Four of the Council, standing in the front ranks, were wounded by the natives, and President Wingfield, while fighting valiently, had an arrow shot through his beard, "yet scaped hurte".[66]

[61] Gen., p. 489.
[64] F. R., p. 98.
[66] Arb. Smith, lii.

[63] Gen., p. 329.
[65] Gen., p. 503.

A few days after this event a gentleman named Clovell came running into the fort with six arrows sticking in him, crying, "Arm, arm". He had wandered too far from the town, and the Indians, who were still prowling near, shot him from ambush. Eight days later he died.[67] Thus at the very outset, the English learned the nature of the conflict which they must wage against the Indians. In open fight the savages, with their primitive weapons, were no match for them, but woe to any of their number that strayed far from the fort, or ventured into the long grass of the mainland. So frequently were small parties cut off, that it became unsafe for the English to leave their settlements except in bodies large enough to repel any attack.[68]

The epidemics and the wars with the Indians conspired to bring upon the colony still another horrible scourge. The constant dread of attack in the fields and the almost universal sickness made it impossible for the settlers to raise crops sufficient for their needs. During the summer of 1607 there were at one time scarce five able men at Jamestown, and these found it beyond their power even to nurse the sick and bury the dead. And in later years, when corn was planted in abundance, the stealthy savages often succeeded in cutting it down before it could be harvested. There can be no surprise then that famines came at frequent intervals to add to the misery of the ill-fated colonists. The most terrible of these visited Virginia in the winter of 1609-10. Smith's Historie gives a graphic account of the suffering during those fearful months. Those that escaped starvation were preserved, it says, "for the most part, by roots, herbes, acornes, walnuts, berries, now and then a fish: they that had starch in these extremities, made no small use of it; yea, even the very skinnes of our horses. Nay, so great was our famine, that a Salvage we slew and buried, the poorer sort took him up againe and eat him; and so did divers one another boyled and stewed with roots and herbs: And one amongst the rest did kill his wife, powdered her, and had eaten part of her before it was knowne; for which hee was

[67] Arb. Smith, liii.
[68] Force, Vol. III, Tract I, p. 17; Gen., p. 405, 419, 456.

executed, as hee well deserved. . . . This was the time, which to this day we call the starving time; it were too vile to say, and scarce to be believed, what we endured."[69]

The misery of the wretched settlers in time of famine is vividly described in a letter written in 1623 by a servant to his parents. The people, he said, cried out day and night, "Oh that they were in England without their limbs . . . though they begged from door to door". He declared that he had eaten more at home in a day than was now allowed him in a week, and that his parents had often given more than his present day's allowance to a beggar at the door. Unless the ship *Sea Flower* came soon, with supplies, his master's men would have but half a penny loaf each a day for food, and might be turned away to eat bark off the trees, or moulds off the ground. "Oh," he said, "that you did see my daily and hourly sighs, groans, tears and thumps that I afford mine own breast, and rue and curse the time of my birth and with holy Job I thought no head had been able to hold so much water as hath and doth daily flow from mine eyes."[70]

Thus was the immigrant to Virginia beset on all sides with deadly perils. If he escaped the plague, the yellow fever and the scurvy during his voyage across the Atlantic, he was more than apt to fall a victim to malaria or dysentery after he reached his new home. Even if he survived all these dangers, he might perish miserably of hunger, or be butchered by the savage Indians. No wonder he cursed the country, calling it "a miserie, a ruine, a death, a hell".[71]

It is remarkable that the enterprise, in the face of these stupendous difficulties, should ever have succeeded. The explanation lies in the great enthusiasm of all England for this attempt to extend the British domains to the shores of the New World, and in the devotion of a few brave spirits of the London Company, who would not be daunted by repeated failures. It mattered not to them that thousands of pounds were lost in the undertaking, that many hundreds of men

---

[69] Force, Vol. III, Tract I, p. 17; Nar. of Va., p. 295; Gen., pp. 330, 392, 401, 404, 456.

[70] Va. Vet.   [71] Nar. of Va., p. 117.

perished, the English flag and the English religion must gain a foothold upon the American continent.

Sir Thomas Gates found the colony in a pitiable condition. The tomahawk of the Indians, famine and pestilence had wrought terrible havoc with the settlers. A mere handful of poor wretched men were left to welcome the newcomers and to beg eagerly to be taken away from the ill-fated country. The town "appeared rather as the ruins of some auntient fortification, then that any people living might now in habit it: the pallisadœs he found tourne downe, the portes open, the gates from the hinges, the church ruined and unfrequented. . . . Only the block house . . . was the safetie of the remainder that lived: which yet could not have preserved them now many days longer from the watching, subtile, and offended Indians."[72]

Nor was it in the power of Gates to remedy these conditions, for he had brought with him from Devil's Island but a limited supply of provisions. So, with great reluctance, the Lieutenant-Governor decided to abandon Virginia rather than sacrifice his people. As the colonists climbed aboard the vessels which were to take them from the scene of their sufferings, they would have set fire to the town had not Gates prevented with his soldiers. He, himself, "was the last of them, when, about noon, giving a farewell with a peale of small shott, he set sayle, and that night, with the tide, fell down . . . the river."[73]

But it was not destined that this enterprise, which was of such importance to the English nation, should be thus abandoned. In April, 1610, De la Warr, the Lord Governor, had sailed for Virginia with three vessels, about a hundred and fifty immigrants and supplies for the relief of the colony.[74] Reaching Cape Comfort June the sixteenth, he learned from a small party there of the intended desertion of Jamestown. Immediately he sent a pinnace up the river to meet Gates, advise him of his arrival and to order his return to the aban-

[72] Gen., p. 405.
[73] Gen., p. 406; Force, Vol. III, Tract I, p. 18.
[74] F. R., p. 127.

doned town. Upon receiving these welcome tidings, Gates bore "up the helm" for Jamestown, and the same night landed all his men.[75] Soon after, the Governor reached the town and took formal possession of the government.

De la Warr began his administration by listening to a sermon from the good pastor, Mr. Buck. He then made an address to the people, "laying some blames on them for many vanities and their idleness", and promising, if occasion required, to draw the sword of justice.[76]

The Governor was not unrestrained in his authority over the colonists, for he was to "rule, punish, pardone and governe according to such directions" as were given him by the London Company. In case of rebellion or mutiny he might put into execution martial law. In matters not covered by his instructions he was to "rule and governe by his owne discretion or by such lawes" as he should think fit to establish.[77] The Council, which had formerly been all-powerful, was now but an advisory body, appointed by the Governor and removable at his discretion. De la Warr chose for his Council Sir Thomas Gates, Sir George Somers, Captain George Percy, Sir Ferdinando Weinman, Captain Christopher Newport and William Strachey, Esquire.[78]

Forgetting their former quarrels and factions, the people united in a zealous effort to serve their noble Governor. "You might shortly behold the idle and restie diseases of a divided multitude, by the unity and authority of the government to be substantially cured. Those that knew not the way to goodnes before, but cherished singularity and faction, can now chalke out the path of all respective dutie and service."[79]

For a while peace and prosperity seemed to have come at last to the little colony. All set to work with a good will to build comfortable houses and to repair the fort. The chapel was restored. The Governor furnished it with a communion table of black walnut and with pews and pulpit of cedar. The font was "hewn hollow like a canoa". "The church was so

---

[75] F. R., p. 128; Force, Vol. III, Tract I, p. 19; Gen., p. 407.
[76] Gen., p. 407.   [77] Gen., p. 379.
[78] F. R., p. 131.   [79] Force, Vol. III, Tract I, p. 20.

cast, as to be very light within and the Governor caused it to be kept passing sweet and trimmed up with divers flowers." In the evening, at the ringing of the bell, and at four in the afternoon, each man addressed himself to prayer.[80]   "Every Sunday, when the Lord Governor went to Church he was accompanied with all the Councillors, Captains, other officers, and all the gentlemen, and with a guard of fifty Halberdiers in his Lordships Livery, fair red cloaks, on each side and behind him.   The Lord Governor sat in the choir, in a green velvet chair, with a velvet cushion before him on which he knelt, and the Council, captains, and officers, on each side of him."[81]

But the misfortunes of the colony were far from being at an end.   The principal causes of disaster had not yet been removed.   Before many weeks had passed the "sickly season" came on, bringing the usual accompaniment of suffering and death.   "Not less than 150 of them died of pestilent diseases, of callentures and feavors, within a few months after" Lord De la Warr's arrival.[82]   So universal was the sickness among the newcomers that all the work had to be done by the old settlers, "who by use weare growen practique in a hard way of livinge".[83]

The war with the Indians continued without abatement, causing constant alarm to the settlers and keeping them closely confined to their forts.   At one time fourteen were treacherously massacred by the Queen of Appomattox.   The English revenged themselves by attacking the savages, burning their villages and destroying their crops, but they could not force them into friendly relations.[84]

Lord De la Warr, himself, was assailed by a series of maladies, that came near costing him his life.   "Presently after my arrival in James Town," he wrote, "I was welcomed by a hot and violent Ague, which held mee a time. . . . That disease had not long left mee, till . . . I began to be distempered with other greevous sickness, which successively & sev-

[80] F. R., pp. 129, 130.
[81] F. R., p. 130.
[82] F. R., p. 134.
[83] F. R., p. 134.
[84] F. R., pp. 135, 136.

erally assailed me: for besides a relapse into the former disease; . . . the Flux surprised me, and kept me many daies: then the cramp assaulted my weak body, with strong paines; & afterward the Gout afflicted me in such sort, that making my body through weaknesse unable to stirre, . . . drew upon me the disease called Scurvy . . . till I was upon the point to leave the world."[85] Realizing that it would be fatal for him to remain longer in Virginia, the Lord Governor set sail with Captain Argoll for the West Indies, where, he hoped, he would recover his health.[86] As Gates had left the colony some months before, the government fell into the experienced hands of Captain George Percy.[87]

In the meanwhile the London Company, undismayed by their former failures, were preparing a new expedition, which they hoped would establish the colony upon a firm footing. Three hundred immigrants, carefully selected from the better class of working men, were assembled under the command of Sir Thomas Dale, and, on March the twenty-seventh, 1611, embarked for Virginia. Upon the arrival of the fleet at Jamestown, Dale received the letters patent from Captain Percy, and assumed command of the colony as Deputy for Lord De la Warr.[88]

The new Governor seems to have perceived at once that the chief source of disaster had been the location of the settlement upon the Jamestown peninsula. The small area which this place afforded for the planting of corn, and the unhealthfulness of the climate rendered it most undesirable as the site for a colony. Former Governors had refused to desert the peninsula because of the ease with which it could be defended against the Indians. But Dale at once began a search for a spot which would afford all the security of Jamestown, but be free from its many disadvantages. This he succeeded in finding up the river, some fifty miles from Jamestown.[89] "I have surveyed," he wrote, "a convenient strong, healthie and sweet seate to plant the new towne in, from whence might be no

---

[85] Gen., p. 479.　　　　　　　[86] Gen., p. 480.
[87] F. R., p. 137.　　　　　　　[88] F. R., p. 137.
[89] Gen., p. 492; Arb. Smith, p. 507; F. R., p. 150.

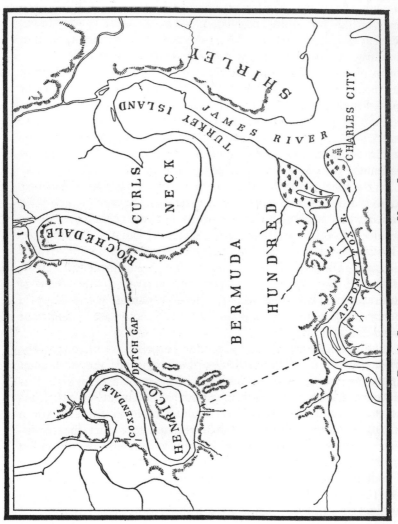

Dale's Settlements on the Upper James

more remove of the principall Seate." This place, which he
named Henrico, was located not far from the point of juncture of the James and the Appomattox, at what is now called
Farrar's Island. Here the river makes a sweeping curve,
forming a peninsula about one square mile in extent.

In August, 1611, Sir Thomas Gates, returning to assume
the command of the colony, pushed vigorously the work upon
the new settlement.[90] Dale was sent up the river with no less
than three hundred men, with directions to construct houses
and fortifications. The settlers, working with new life and
vigor in the more wholesome air of the upper James, soon
rendered the place almost impregnable to attack from the Indians. They cut a ditch across the narrow neck of the peninsula, and fortified it with high palisades. To prevent a sudden
raid by the savages in canoes from the other shore, five strong
block houses were built at intervals along the river bank.
Behind these defenses were erected a number of substantial
houses, with foundations of brick and frame superstructures.
Soon a town of three streets had been completed, more commo-
dious and far more healthful than Jamestown.[91]

When this work had been completed, Dale led a force of
men across to the south bank of the river and took possession of the entire peninsula lying between the Appomattox
and the James. An Indian settlement just below Turkey
Island bend was attacked and destroyed, and the savages driven
away. The English built a palisade over two miles long and
reinforced at intervals with forts and block houses, from the
James at Henrico to the falls of the Appomattox. These fortifications secured from the attacks of the savages "many miles
of champion and woodland", and made it possible for the
English to lay out in safety several new plantations or hundreds. Dale named the place Bermuda, "by reason of the
strength of the situation".

Here, for the first time, something like prosperity came to
the colony. Although the "sicknesse" was not entirely eliminated even at Henrico, the percentage of mortality was greatly

[90] Gen., p. 474.
[91] Arb. Smith, pp. 509, 510; F. R., p. 157; Cradle of Rep., p. 136.

reduced. Soon there were in Virginia several hundred persons that had lived through the fatal months of June, July and August and were thoroughly "seasoned" or immune to the native disorders. Not until 1618, when the settlers, in their greed for land suitable for the cultivation of tobacco, deserted their homes on the upper James for the marshy ground of the lower country, and new, unacclimated persons began arriving in great numbers, did the pestilence again assume its former proportions.

Thus protected from the ravages of disease and from the assaults of the savages, Dale's men were able to turn their attention to the cultivation of the soil. Soon they were producing an annual crop of corn sufficient to supply their more pressing needs. And it was well for them that they could become, to some extent, independent of England, for the London Company, at last discouraged by continued misfortune, was often remiss in sending supplies. Clothing became exceedingly scarce. Not only were the gaudy uniforms of De la Warr's time lacking, but many persons were forced to imitate the savages by covering themselves with skins and furs.[92] The Company, however, succeeded in obtaining for them from the King many suits of old armor that were of great value in their wars with the savages. Coats of mail and steel that had become useless on the battlefields of Europe and had for years been rusting in the Tower of London, were polished up and sent to Virginia. Thus, behind the palisades of Henrico or in the fort at Jamestown one might have seen at this time soldiers encased in armor that had done service in the days of Richard III and Henry VII.[93]

The London Company, when they sent Sir Thomas Gates to Virginia with the letters patent of 1609, gave directions that the utmost severity should be used in putting an end to lawlessness and confusion. Gates, who had fought against the Spaniards in the Netherlands and had the soldier's dislike of insubordination, was well suited to carry their wishes into effect. No sooner had he arrived from Devil's Island in 1610 than he posted in the church at Jamestown certain laws, orders

[92] F. R., p. 226.   [93] F. R., p. 172.

and instructions which he warned the people they must obey strictly.[94] These laws were exceedingly severe. It was, for instance, ordered that "every man and woman daly twice a day upon the first towling of the Bell shall upon the working daies repaire into the Church, to hear divine Service upon pain of losing his or her dayes allowance for the first omission, for the second to be whipt, and for the third to be condemned to the Gallies for six Months". Again, it was decreed that "no man shall give any disgracefull words, or commit any act to the disgrace of any person . . . upon paine of being tied head and feete together, upon the guard everie night for the space of one moneth. . . . No man shall dare to kill, or destroy any Bull, Cow, Calfe, Mare, Horse, Colt, Goate, Swine, Cocke, Henne, Chicken, Dogge, Turkie, or any tame Cattel, or Poultry, of what condition soever, . . . without leave from the Generall, upon paine of death. . . . There shall no man or woman . . . dare to wash any unclean linnen . . . within the Pallizadoes, . . . nor rench, and make clean, any kettle, pot or pan . . . within twenty foote of the olde well . . . upon pain of whipping."[95]

During the administration of Gates and De la Warr these laws seem not to have been enforce vigorously, but were utilized chiefly *in terrorem*.[96] Under Dale and Argoll, however, not only were they put into merciless operation, but were reinforced with a series of martial laws, drawn from the code in use among the armies of the Netherlands.

The Divine, Moral and Martial Laws, as they were called, undoubtedly brought about good order in the colony, and aided in the establishment of prosperity, but they were ill suited for the government of free-born Englishmen. They were in open violation of the rights guaranteed to the settlers in their charters, and caused bitter discontent and resentment.

At times they were enforced with odious harshness and injustice. Molina declared that the Governors were most cruel in their treatment of the people, often using them like

[94] F. R., p. 126; Gen., pp. 342, 345, 528, 529; Force, Vol. III, Tract II, pp. 9-19.
[95] Force, Vol. III, Tract II, pp. 9-10   [96] Bruce, Inst. Hist. Vol. I, p. 474.

slaves.[97] The Virginia Assembly of 1624 gives a vivid, though perhaps an exaggerated, picture of the severity of the government. "The Colony . . . remained in great want and misery under most severe and Cruell lawes sent over in printe," they said, "and contrary to the express Letter of the Kinge in his most gracious Charter, and as mercylessly executed, often times without tryall or Judgment." Many of the people fled "for reliefe to the Savage Enemy, who being taken againe were putt to sundry deathes as by hanginge, shooting and breaking uppon the wheele and others were forced by famine to filch for their bellies, of whom one for steelinge of 2 or 3 pints of oatmeale had a bodkin thrust through his tounge and was tyed with a chain to a tree untill he starved, if a man through his sicknes had not been able to worke, he had noe allowance at all, and soe consequently perished. Many through these extremities, being weary of life, digged holes in the earth and there hidd themselves till they famished."[98] In 1612, several men attempted to steal "a barge and a shallop and therein to adventure their lives for their native country, being discovered and prevented, were shot to death, hanged and broken upon the wheel".[99] There was some criticism in England of the harshness of the laws, but Sir Thomas Smith, then the guiding spirit of the London Company, declared that they were beneficial and necessary, "in some cases *ad terrorum,* and in others to be truly executed".[100]

As time passed and the population of the colony increased, it became necessary to extend beyond the confines of Jamestown and Henrico. The cultivation of tobacco, which was rapidly becoming the leading pursuit of the people, required more ground than was comprised within the fortified districts. Even the expansion of the settlement upon the upper James to other peninsulas along the "Curls of the River" could not satisfy the demand for arable land. At one time the very streets of Jamestown were planted with tobacco.[101] Soon the people, despite their dread of the savages, were deserting their palisades, and spreading out in search of fertile soil.

[97] Gen., p. 648.
[98] Nar. of Va., pp. 422, 423.
[99] F. R., pp. 148, 172.
[100] Gen., pp. 529, 530.
[101] Bruce, Ec. Hist., Vol. I, p. 222.

This recklessness brought upon the colony a renewal of the disastrous epidemics of the earlier period, and exposed the planters to imminent danger from the savages. Fortunately, however, at this very time the long sought peace with the Indians was brought about by the romantic marriage of Pocahontas, the daughter of the powerful chief Powhatan, with Captain John Rolfe.

In the spring of 1613 Sir Samuel Argoll, while cruising in the Rappahannock in quest of corn, learned from the natives that the princess was visiting Japazaws, a neighboring king, at his village upon the Potomac. Argoll at once resolved to capture the daughter of the greatest enemy of the white men, and to hold her until all the tools and weapons stolen by the Indians had been returned.[102] Hastening into the country of the Potomacs, he demanded the maid of Japazaws. The king, fearing the hostility of the English more than the anger of Powhatan, consented, although with great reluctance, and she was placed aboard Argoll's ship.

The news of the capture of his favorite child filled Powhatan with rage and grief. Imploring Argoll to do Pocahontas no harm, he promised to yield to all his demands and to become the lasting friend of the white men.[103] He liberated seven captives and sent with them "three pieces, one broad Axe, and a long whip-saw, and one canow of Corne".[104] Knowing that these did not constitute all the tools in the hands of the king, the English refused to relinquish Pocahontas, but kept her a prisoner at Jamestown.[105]

The young princess was treated with consideration and kindness by Governor Dale. Her gentle nature, her intelligence and her beauty won the respect and love of the sternest of her captors. Dale himself undertook to direct her education. "I was moved," he exclaimed, "by her desire to be taught and instructed in the knowledge of God, her capableness of understanding, her aptness and willingness to receive any good impression. . . . I caused her to be carefully instructed in the Christian religion, who, after she had made

[102] Gen., p. 642.
[104] Gen., pp. 643, 644.
[103] Gen., p. 643.
[105] Nar. of Va., p. 308.

some good progress therein, renounced publicly her Country's idolatry; openly confessed her Christian faith; and was, as she desired, baptized."[106]

Before many months had passed the charm of this daughter of the American forest had inspired a deep love in the breast of Captain John Rolfe. This worthy gentleman, after struggling long against a passion so strange and unusual, wrote Dale asking permission to wed the princess. I am not ignorant, he said "of the inconvenience which may . . . arise . . . to be in love with one whose education hath bin rude, her manners barbarous, her generation accursed".[107] But I am led to take this step, "for the good of the plantation, for the honour of our countrie, for the glory of God, for my owne salvation, and for the converting to the true knowledge of God and Jesus Christ, an unbeleeving creature, like Pokahuntas. To whom my heartie and best thoughts are, and have a long time bin so intangled, and inthralled in so intricate a laborinth, that I was awearied to unwinde myselfe thereout."[108]

Dale, overjoyed at this opportunity to secure the friendship of the Indians, consented readily to the marriage. Powhatan, too, when he learned of his daughter's affection for Captain Rolfe, expressed his approval of the union, and sent Apachisco, an uncle of the bride, and two of her brothers to represent him at the ceremony.

Both English and Indians regarded this wedding as a bond of friendship between the two races. Apachisco, acting as deputy for Powhatan, concluded with Governor Dale a peace which lasted eight years and was fairly well kept by both parties.[109] "Besides this," wrote Captain Ralph Hamor, "we became in league with our next neighbors, the Chicahamanias, a lustie and daring people, free of themselves. These people, as soone as they heard of our peace with Powhatan, sent two messengers with presents to Sir Thomas Dale and offered . . . their service."[110] Thus was one of the greatest menaces to

[106] Arb. Smith, p. 512.
[108] Nar. of Va., pp. 240, 241.
[110] Arb. Smith, p. 515.
[107] Nar. of Va., p. 241.
[109] F. R., p. 205; Arb. Smith, p. 514.

the prosperity of the colony removed. Now the settlers could cultivate the soil, or hunt and fish without fear of the treacherous savage, and leave their cattle to range in comparative safety. John Rolfe himself wrote, "The great blessings of God have followed this peace, and it, next to him, hath bredd our plentie—everie man sitting under his fig tree in safety, gathering and reaping the fruits of their labors with much joy and comfort."[111]

In 1616 Sir Thomas Dale, who had been in command of the colony since the departure of Gates in 1614, returned to England, leaving the government in the hands of Captain George Yeardley. Despite the harshness and cruelty of Dale and Gates, they must be credited with obtaining the final success of the colony. These two stern soldiers of the Dutch wars had found the settlers dispirited, reduced in numbers, fighting a losing battle against pestilence, starvation and the savages. By their rigid discipline and able leadership they had brought unity and prosperity, had taught the people how to resist the sickness, and had secured a long peace with the Indians.[112] Dale left about three hundred and fifty persons in Virginia, most of them thoroughly acclimated and busily engaged in building up prosperity for the colony.

Tobacco was already becoming the staple product of Virginia. As early as 1612 Captain Rolfe had been experimenting with the native leaf, in an effort to make it suitable for the English market.[113] In 1613 he sent a part of his crop to London, where it was tested by experts and pronounced to be of excellent quality.[114] The colonists were greatly encouraged at the success of the venture, for the price of tobacco was high, and its culture afforded opportunities for a rich return. Soon every person that could secure a little patch of ground was devoting himself eagerly to the cultivation of the plant. It even became necessary for Dale to issue an order that each man should "set two acres of ground with corn", lest the new craze should lead to the neglect of the food supply.[115] In

[111] F. R., p. 226.   [112] F. R., pp. 230, 236.
[113] Bruce, Ec. Hist., Vol. I, p. 211.
[114] F. R., p. 197; Bruce, Ec. Hist., Vol. I, p. 217.
[115] F. R., p. 228; Gen., p. 782.

1617 *The George* sailed for England laden with 20,000
pounds of tobacco, which found a ready market at five shillings and three pence a pound. John Rolfe's discovery was
opening for Virginia a veritable gold mine.

Fortunately the King, in 1612, had granted the Company an
exemption for seven years from custom duties upon goods
brought from the colony. So, for a while, at least, the Crown
could not appropriate to its own use the profits from the
Virginia tobacco. Since, however, the exemption had only a
few years more to run, the Company hastened to secure what
immediate returns were available. They took from the planters the entire crop, giving them for it three pence per pound,
while they themselves were able to obtain a much larger
price from the English dealers.

The profits thus secured were at once utilized in new measures for increasing and strengthening the colony. Encouraged by the discovery in Virginia of so profitable a
commodity, the Company became convinced that now at last
success was at hand. "Broadsides" were sent out to the
British people, depicting in glowing terms the advantages of
the country, and asking for immigrants and for financial support. Once more a wave of enthusiasm for the enterprise
swept over England. Money was contributed liberally. The
clergy, interested in the spread of the Anglican Church, and
in the conversion of the savages, worked ardently for the
success of the colony. Soon vessel after vessel was being
fitted out for the voyage across the Atlantic, and hundreds of
artisans and laborers were preparing to risk their all in the
New World.[116]

[116] F. R., p. 209.

CHAPTER II

The Establishment of Representative Government

King James I, from the beginning of his reign, was deeply desirous of planting the English nation upon the shores of the New World. It was with envy and alarm that he witnessed the extension of the power of Spain and of the Roman Catholic church across the Atlantic, while his own subjects were excluded from a share in the splendid prize. He must have perceived clearly that if the English wished to maintain their position as a great naval and mercantile people, the establishing of colonies in America was imperative. Peru, Mexico and the West Indies added greatly to the wealth and power of the Spanish King; why should England not attempt to gain a foothold near these countries, before it became too late?

But James had no desire to arouse the hostility of Philip III. Despite religious differences, despite the hatred of the English for the Spaniards, he had reversed the policy of Elizabeth by cultivating the friendship of these hereditary enemies. And so wedded was he to this design, that later, when his son-in-law, Frederick of the Palatinate, was being overwhelmed by a coalition of Catholic nations, he refused to affront Spain by coming to his rescue. Yet he knew that Philip considered America his own, and would resent any attempt of the English to establish colonies on its shores. So the crafty James resolved to disguise the founding of a royal colony under the guise of a private venture.[1] If the Spaniards complained of the occupation of their territory, he could free himself from blame by placing the responsibility upon the London Company. "If it take not success," his advisors told the King, "it is done by their owne heddes. It is but the attempt of private gentlemen, the State suffers noe losse, noe disreputa-

[1] F. R., p. 6.

tion.   If it takes success, they are your subjects, they doe it
for your service, they will lay all at your Majesty's feet and
interess your Majesty therein."[2]

James was quite liberal in granting charters to those that
had undertaken the settlement, and he encouraged them as
much as was consistent with his friendship for Spain.   It was
truly written of him after his death, "Amongst the . . .
workes of the late Kinge, there was none more eminent, than
his gracious inclination . . . to advance and sett forward a
New Plantation in the New World."[3]   That he was deeply
interested in the undertaking is shown most strikingly by his
consent to the establishment of the Puritans in America.   James
hated the tenets of Calvin from the depths of his soul, and
could have no desire to see them infect the English settlements
in America, yet his solicitude for the welfare of the colony
induced him to yield to the request of the Pilgrims for permission to settle there.   How much greater was his foresight
than that of Louis XIV, who, by refusing to allow the persecuted Huguenots to settle in any part of his domains, deprived
the French colonies of what might have been their most numerous and valuable recruits!   When some of the leading men of
the London Company pleaded with James for the Puritans,
the King lent a ready ear.   He was asked to allow them
"liberty of conscience under his . . . protection in America;
where they would endeavour the advancement of his Majesty's
dominions, and the enlargement of the interests of the Gospel".
James replied that it was "a good and honest motion".   He
refused to tolerate them by public authority and would not
confirm under the broad seal their petition for leave to worship
as they chose, but he let it be understood that they were not
to be molested in their new homes in any way.[4]   And in this
promise they finally decided to put their trust, feeling that "if
afterwards there should be a purpose or desire to wrong them,
though they had a seale as broad as ye house flore, it would
not serve ye turn; for ther would be means a new found to
recall or reverse it".[5]

[2] F. R., p. 76.
[4] F. R., p. 265.
[3] Gen., p. 1027.
[5] F. R., p. 271.

But the chief glory of the establishment of the English in America must be given to the patriotic and persevering men of the Virginia Company. It is erroneous and unjust to accuse them of mean and mercenary motives in founding and maintaining the colony at Jamestown. Some of them, perhaps, were dazzled with visions of a rich harvest of gold and silver, but most must have realized that there was small chance of remuneration. Many were merchants and business men of great foresight and ability, and it is quite evident that they were fully aware of the risks of the undertaking in which they ventured their money. What they did hope to gain from the colony was the propagation of the English Church, the extension of the English nation and its institutions, and the increase of British trade.

Over and over again it was asserted that the first object of the enterprise was to spread the Christian religion. In 1610 the London Company declared it their especial purpose "to preach and baptize . . . and by propagation of the Gospell, to recover out of the armes of the Divell, a number of poore and miserable soules, wrapt up unto death, in almost invincible ignorance".[6] The first draft of the Virginia charter of 1606 declared that the leading motive of this "noble work", was "the planting of Christianity amongst heathens".[7] The charter of 1609 asserted that the "principle effect, which we can desire or expect of this action, is the conversion and reduction of the people in those parts unto the true worship of God".[8]

That they were also actuated by a desire to extend the British possessions and trade is attested by numerous documents and letters. The Company declared it their purpose to promote the "honor and safety of the Kingdome, the strength of our Navy, the visible hope of a great and rich trade".[9] One of the leading shareholders wrote that the colony should be upheld for "ye Honor and profitt to our Nation, to make provinciall to us a land ready to supply us with all

[6] Gen., p. 339.   [7] F. R., p. 6.
[8] Gen. p. 236. Compare F. R., pp. 262, 263, 264, 31, 248, 80; Gen., pp. 49, 146.
[9] F. R., p. 80.

necessary commodytyes wanting to us: In which alone we suffer ye Spanish reputation and power to swell over us."[10] The colonists themselves declared that one of the objects of the settlement of America was the extension of British territory and the enriching of the kingdom, "for which respects many noble and well minded persons were induced to adventure great sums of money to the advancement of so pious and noble a worke".[11]

The Company, in fact, did no more than take the lead in the work. It was really the English nation that had decided to second their King in gaining a foothold in America, and it was they that insisted that this foothold should not be relinquished. Again and again the London Company appealed to the people for support, and never without success, for all classes of Englishmen felt that they were interested in this new venture. The spirit of the nation is reflected in the statement of the Council for Virginia in 1610, that the Company "are so farre from yielding or giving way to any hindrance or impeachment . . . that many . . . have given their hands and subscribed to contribute againe and againe to new supplies if need require".[12]

But although James I and his people were agreed as to the necessity of extending the English nation to America, they were not in accord in regard to the form of government which should be established there. The King, who was always restive under the restraint placed upon him by the English Parliament, had no desire to see the liberal institutions of the mother country transplanted to Virginia. He wished, beyond doubt, to build a colonial empire which should be dependent upon himself for its government and which should add to the royal revenues. In this way he would augment the power of the Crown and render it less subject to the restraint of Parliament. But to found colonies that would set up little assemblies of their own to resist and thwart him, was not at all his intention.

On the other hand, many of the leading spirits of the Lon-

[10] F. R., p. 49.   [11] Gen., p. 50.
[12] Gen., p. 355.

don Company hoped "to establish a more free government in Virginia".[13]   Some, perhaps, feared that the liberties of the English people might be suppressed by the King, and they looked hopefully to this new land as a haven for the oppressed. "Many worthy Patriots, Lords, Knights, gentlemen, Merchants and others . . . laid hold on . . . Virginia as a providence cast before them."[14]   In the meetings of the Company were gathered so many that were "most distasted with the proceedings of the Court, and stood best affected to Religion and Liberty", that James began to look upon the body as a "Seminary for a seditious Parliament".[15]

The leader of these liberals was Sir Edwin Sandys.   This man, who was widely known as an uncompromising enemy of despotism, was heartily detested by the King.[16]   In his youth he had gone to Geneva to study the reformed religion and while there had become most favorably impressed with the republican institutions of the little Swiss state.   He was afterwards heard to say that "he thought that if God from heaven did constitute and direct a forme of government on Earth it was that of Geneva".[17]   Returning to England, he had entered Parliament, where he had become known as an eminent advocate of liberal principles.   He had contended for the abolition of commercial monopolies; had demanded that all accused persons be given the assistance of counsel; had denounced many of the unjust impositions of the Crown; had raised "his voice for the toleration of those with whom he did not wholly agree"; and had aided in drawing up the remonstrance against the conduct of James towards his first Parliament.[18]

But Sandys and his friends were not without opposition in the London Company.   Many of the "adventurers", as the stockholders were called, were by no means willing to permit the liberal party to utilize the Company as an instrument for propagating their political tenets.   The great struggle between the forces of progress and reaction that was convulsing

[13] F. R., p. 558.

[14] F. R., p. 85.

[15] F. R., p. 237.

[16] F. R., vi.

[17] F. R., p. 251.

[18] F. R., p. 75.

Parliament and the nation, was fought over again in the Quarter Courts. At times the meetings resounded with the quarrels of the contending factions. Eventually, however, Sandys was victorious, and representative government in America was assured.

Sandys seems to have planned to secure from the King successive charters each more liberal than its predecessor, and each entrusting more fully the control of the colony to the Company. This could be done without arousing the suspicions of James under the pretext that they were necessary for the success of the enterprise. When at length sufficient power had been delegated, Sandys designed to establish in Virginia a representative assembly, modelled upon the British Parliament.

Under the provisions of the charter of 1606 Virginia had been, in all but form, a royal colony. The King had drawn up the constitution, had appointed the Council in England, and had controlled their policies. This charter had granted no semblance of self-government to the settlers. But it was declared "They shall have and enjoy all the liberties, franchises, and immunities . . . to all intents and purposes, as if they had been abiding and born, within . . . this realm of England".[19] This promise was not kept by the Kings of England. Several of the provisions of the charter itself were not consistent with it. In later years it was disregarded again and again by the royal commissions and instructions. Yet it was of the utmost importance, for it set a goal which the colonists were determined to attain. Throughout the entire colonial period they contended for all the rights of native Englishmen, and it was the denial of their claim that caused them to revolt from the mother country and make good their independence. Provision had also been made for trial by jury. James had decreed that in all cases the Council should sit as a court, but in matters of "tumults, rebellion, conspiracies, mutiny, and seditions . . . murther, manslaughter", and other crimes punishable with death, guilt or innocence was to be determined by a jury of twelve. To what extent the Council made use of the jury

[19] Gen., pp. 60, 61.

system it is impossible to say, but Wingfield states that on one occasion he was tried before a jury for slander, and fined £300.[20]

The second charter had been granted in 1609. This document is of great importance because through it the King resigned the actual control of the colony into the hands of the Virginia Company. And although this did not result immediately in the establishment of representative government, it strengthened the hands of Sandys and made it possible for him to carry out his designs at a future date. Under this charter the Company might have set up liberal institutions at once in Virginia, but conditions were not ripe, either in England or in America, for so radical a change.

In 1612 the third charter had been granted. This had still further strengthened the Company and made them more independent of the King. It gave them the important privilege of holding great quarterly meetings or assemblies, where all matters relating to the government of the colony could be openly discussed. Still Virginia remained under the autocratic rule of Dale and Gates.

In 1617 or 1618, however, when the liberals were in full control of the Company, it was decided to grant the colonists the privilege of a parliament.[21] In April, 1618, Lord De la Warr sailed for Virginia to reassume active control of affairs there, bringing with him instructions to establish a new form of government. What this government was to have been is not known, but it was designed by Sir Edwin Sandys, and beyond doubt, was liberal in form.[22] Possibly it was a duplicate of that established the next year by Governor Yeardley. Most unfortunately, Lord De la Warr, whose health had been shattered by his first visit to Virginia, died during the voyage across the Atlantic, and it became necessary to continue the old constitution until the Company could appoint a successor.[23]

In November, 1618, George Yeardley was chosen Governor-General of Virginia, and was intrusted with several documents by whose authority he was to establish representative govern-

[20] Arb. Smith, lxxxiii.
[22] F. R., p. 266.
[21] F. R., p. 266.
[23] F. R., pp. 281, 282.

ment in the colony.[24]   These papers, which became known as
the Virginia Magna Charta, were the very corner-stone of
liberty in the colony and in all America.   Their importance
can hardly be exaggerated, for they instituted the first representative assembly of the New World, and established a government which proved a bulwark against royal prerogative
for a century and a half.

Governor Yeardley sailed from England January, 1619, and
reached Virginia on the 29th of April.   After some weeks of
preparation, he issued a general proclamation setting in operation the Company's orders.   It was decreed, "that all those
who were resident here before the departure of Sir Thomas
Dale should be freed and acquitted from such publique services
and labors which formerly they suffered, and that those cruel
laws by which we had so long been governed were now abro-
gated, and that now we were to be governed by those free
laws which his Majesty's subjects live under in Englande. . . .
And that they might have a hand in the governing of themselves, it was granted that a General Assembly should be held
yearly once, whereat were to be present the Governor and
Counsell, with two Burgesses from each plantation freely to be
elected by the inhabitants thereof ; this Assembly to have power
to make and ordaine whatsoever lawes and orders should by
them be thought good and proffittable for our subsistence."[25]

The exact date of the election for Burgesses is not known.[26]
The statement that the representatives were to be "chosen by
the inhabitants" seems to indicate that the franchise was at
once given to all male adults, or at least to all freemen.   "All
principall officers in Virginia were to be chosen by ye ballot-
ing box."   From the very first there were parties, and it is
possible that the factions of the London Company were reflected at the polls in the early elections.   The Magna Charta
made provision for the establishment of boroughs, which were
to serve both as units for local government and as electoral districts.   No attempt was made to secure absolute uniformity of
population in the boroughs, but there were no glaring inequali-

[24] F. R., p. 293.   [25] F. R., p. 312.
[26] F. R., p. 315.

ties. With the regard for the practical which has always been characteristic of Englishmen, the Company seized upon the existing units, such as towns, plantations and hundreds, as the basis of their boroughs. In some cases several of these units were merged to form one borough, in others, a plantation or a town or a hundred as it stood constituted a borough. As there were eleven of these districts and as each district chose two Burgesses, the first General Assembly was to contain twenty-two representatives.[27]

The Assembly convened at Jamestown, August 9th, 1619. "The most convenient place we could finde to sitt in," says the minutes, "was the Quire of the Churche Where Sir George Yeardley, the Governor, being sett down in his accustomed place, those of the Counsel of Estate sate nexte him on both hands excepte onely the Secretary then appointed Speaker, who sate right before him, John Twine, the clerk of the General Assembly, being placed nexte the Speaker, and Thomas Pierse, the Sergeant, standing at the barre, to be ready for any service the Assembly shoulde comand him. But forasmuche as men's affaires doe little prosper where God's service is neglected, all the Burgesses tooke their places in the Quire till a prayer was said by Mr. Bucke, the Minister. . . . Prayer being ended, . . . all the Burgesses were intreatted to retyre themselves into the body of the Churche, which being done, before they were fully admitted, they were called in order and by name, and so every man tooke the oathe of Supremacy and entered the Assembly."[28]

The body at once claimed and made good its right to exclude Burgesses who they thought were not entitled to seats. The Speaker himself raised an objection to admitting the representatives of Warde's plantation, because that settlement had been made without a commission from the London Company. But Captain Warde promised to secure a patent as soon as possible, and the objection was waived. The Assembly refused absolutely, however, to seat the Burgesses from Martin's Hundred. Captain Martin had been one of the first Council for Virginia, and as a reward for his long services had been

[27] Nar. of Va., pp. 249, 250.   [28] Nar. of Va., p. 251.

granted privileges that rendered him almost independent of
the government at Jamestown.   He was summoned before
the Assembly and requested to relinquish these extraordinary
rights, but he refused to do so.   "I hold my patent," he said,
"for my service don, which noe newe or late comer can meritt
or challenge."[29]   So the Assembly, feeling that it would be
mockery to permit the Burgesses from Martin's Hundred to
assist in the making of laws which their own constituents,
because of their especial charter, might with impunity disobey,
refused to admit them.[30]

The legislative powers granted the Virginia Assembly in
the Magna Charta, and continued with slight alterations after
the revocation of the charter of the London Company, were
very extensive.   The Assembly could pass laws dealing with a
vast variety of matters appertaining to the safety and welfare
of the colony.   Statutes were enacted in the session of 1619
touching upon Indian affairs, the Church, land patents, the
relations of servants and landlords, the planting of crops, general morality in Virginia, the price of tobacco, foreign trade,
etc.   The collected laws of the entire colonial period fill many
volumes, and cover a vast variety of subjects.   But there were
three things which limited strictly the Assembly's field of
action.   They must pass no statutes contravening first, the
laws of England; secondly, the charters; thirdly, the instructions sent them by the London Company.   When the colony
passed into the hands of the King, all statutes were forbidden
that conflicted with the charters, or with the instructions of the
Crown.   These restrictions lasted during the entire colonial
period, but they were not always carefully regarded.   The
Company, and later the King, retained two ways of nullifying
legislation which was unauthorized, or was distasteful to them.
First, there was the veto of the Governor.   As the guardian
of the interests of England and his monarch, this officer could
block all legislation.   Secondly, the Company, and later the
King, could veto laws even though the Governor had consented
to them.

[29] F. R., p. 317.
[30] Nar. of Va., pp. 252, 253, 254, 255, 260, 261.

But the most important power exercised by the Assembly was its control over taxation in Virginia. In the very first session it made use of this privilege by ordering, "That every man and manservant of above 16 years of age shall pay into the handes and Custody of the Burgesses of every Incorporation and plantation one pound of the best Tobacco".[31] The funds thus raised were utilized for the payment of the officers of the Assembly.

The levy by the poll, here used, was continued for many years, and became the chief support of the government. As the colony grew, however, and the need for greater revenues was felt, customs duties and other forms of taxation were resorted to. Large sums were raised by an export duty upon tobacco. At times tariffs were placed upon the importation of liquors, slaves and other articles. But these duties had to be used with great care, for the carrying of the colony was done chiefly by English merchants, and Parliament would permit nothing detrimental to their interests.

The Assembly claimed the exclusive right to levy general taxes. The Governor and Council time and again tried to wrest this privilege from them, but never with success.[32] The Burgesses, realizing that their hold upon the exchequer was the chief source of their power, were most careful never to relinquish it. From time to time the Governors sought to evade this restraint by levying taxes under the guise of fees. But this expedient invariably excited intense irritation, and yielded a revenue so small that most Governors thought it best to avoid it entirely. Of more importance were the quit-rents, a tax on land, paid to the King by all freeholders. But this was frequently avoided, and, except at rare intervals, the funds raised by it were left in Virginia to be expended for local purposes. The greatest blow to the power of the Burgesses was struck by the King in 1680, when he forced through the Assembly a law granting to the government a perpetual income

[31] Nar. of Va., p. 276.

[32] In 1662 the Assembly granted power to the Governor and Council for three years to levy a small tax by the poll. The county taxes for defraying local expenses, were assessed and collected by the justices of the peace. The vestries controlled the raising of the parish dues.

from the export duty on tobacco. This revenue, although not large, was usually sufficient to pay the Governor's salary, and thus to render him less dependent upon the Assembly. Finally, it must not be forgotten that the English government, although it refrained from taxing the colony directly, imposed an enormous indirect tax by means of a tariff upon tobacco brought into England. These duties were collected in England, but there can be no doubt that the incidence of the tax rested partly upon the Virginia planters. Despite these various duties, all levied without its consent, the Assembly exercised a very real control over taxation in Virginia, and used it as an effective weapon against the encroachments of the Governors.

From the very first the General Assembly showed itself an energetic and determined champion of the rights of the people. Time and again it braved the anger of the Governor and of the King himself, rather than yield the slightest part of its privileges. During the decade preceding the English Revolution only the heroic resistance of this body saved the liberal institutions of the colony from destruction at the hands of Charles II and James II.

The General Assembly was not only a legislative body, it was also a court of justice, and for many years served as the highest tribunal of the colony. The judicial function was entrusted to a joint committee from the two houses, whose recommendations were usually accepted without question. Since this committee invariably contained more Burgesses than Councillors, the supreme court was practically controlled by the representatives of the people. During the reign of Charles II, however, the Assembly was deprived of this function by royal proclamation, and the judiciary fell almost entirely into the hands of the Governor and Council.

The General Assembly consisted of two chambers—the House of Burgesses and the Council. In the early sessions the houses sat together and probably voted as one body.[33] Later, however, they were divided and voted separately. The Burgesses, as time went on, gradually increased in numbers until they became a large body, but the Council was always small.

[33] Miller, p. 41.

The Councillors were royal appointees. But since the King could not always know personally the prominent men of the colony, he habitually confirmed without question the nominations of the Governor. The members of the Council were usually persons of wealth, influence and ability. As they were subject to removal by the King and invariably held one or more lucrative governmental offices, it was customary for them to display great servility to the wishes of his Majesty or of the Governor. It was very unusual for them to oppose in the Assembly any measure recommended by the King, or in accord with his expressed wishes. Although the Councillors were, with rare exceptions, natives of Virginia, they were in no sense representative of the people of the colony.

As the upper house of the Assembly, the Council exercised a powerful influence upon legislation. After the separation of the chambers their consent became necessary for the passage of all bills, even money bills. Their legislative influence declined during the eighteenth century, however, because of the growing spirit of liberalism in Virginia, and the increasing size of the House of Burgesses.

The executive powers entrusted to the Council were also of very great importance. The Governor was compelled by his instructions to secure its assistance and consent in the most important matters. And since the chief executive was always a native of England, and often entirely ignorant of conditions in the colony, he was constantly forced to rely upon the advice of his Council. This tendency was made more pronounced by the frequent changes of Governors that marked the last quarter of the seventeenth century. So habitually did the Council exercise certain functions, not legally within their jurisdiction, that they began to claim them as theirs by right. And the Governor was compelled to respect these claims as scrupulously as the King of England respects the conventions that hedge in and limit his authority.

Before the end of the seventeenth century the Council had acquired extraordinary influence in the government. With the right to initiate and to block legislation, with almost complete control over the judiciary, with great influence in administrative matters, it threatened to become an oligarchy of almost unlimited power.

But it must not be supposed that the influence of the Council rendered impotent the King's Governor. Great powers were lodged in the hands of this officer by his various instructions and commissions. He was commander of the militia, was the head of the colonial church, he appointed most of the officers, attended to foreign affairs, and put the laws into execution. His influence, however, resulted chiefly from the fact that he was the representative of the King. In the days of Charles I, in the Restoration Period and under James II, when the Stuarts were combating liberal institutions, both in England and in the colonies, the Governor exercised a powerful and dangerous control over affairs in Virginia. But after the English Revolution his power declined. As the people of England no longer dreaded a monarch whose authority now rested solely upon acts of Parliament, so the Virginians ceased to fear his viceroy.

The powers officially vested in the Governor were by no means solely executive. He frequently made recommendations to the Assembly, either in his own name or the name of the King, and these recommendations at times assumed the nature of commands. If the Burgesses were reluctant to obey, he had numerous weapons at hand with which to intimidate them and whip them into line. Unscrupulous use of the patronage and threats of the King's dire displeasure were frequently resorted to. The Governor presided over the upper house, and voted there as any other member. Moreover, he could veto all bills, even those upon which he had voted in the affirmative in the Council. Thus he had a large influence in shaping the laws of the colony, and an absolute power to block all legislation.

Such, in outline, was the government originated for Virginia by the liberal leaders of the London Company, and put into operation by Sir George Yeardley. It lasted, with the short intermission of the Commonwealth Period, for more than one hundred and fifty years, and under it Virginia became the most populous and wealthy of the English colonies in America.

The successful cultivation of tobacco in Virginia, as we have seen, put new life into the discouraged London Company. The shareholders, feeling that now at last the colony would grow and prosper, exerted themselves to the utmost to secure desirable settlers and to equip them properly. Soon fleets of considerable size were leaving the English ports for America, their decks and cabins crowded with emigrants and their holds laden with clothing, arms and farming implements.[34] During the months from March 1620 to March 1621 ten ships sailed, carrying no less than 1051 persons.[35] In the year ending March, 1622, seventeen ships reached Virginia, bringing over fifteen hundred new settlers.[36] And this stream continued without abatement until 1624, when disasters in Virginia, quarrels among the shareholders and the hostility of the King brought discouragement to the Company. In all, there reached the colony from November, 1619, to February, 1625, nearly five thousand men, women and children.[37]

Although tobacco culture was the only enterprise of the colony which had yielded a profit, it was not the design of Sandys and his friends that that plant should monopolize the energies of the settlers. They hoped to make Virginia an industrial community, capable of furnishing the mother country with various manufactured articles, then imported from foreign countries. Especially anxious were they to render England independent in their supply of pig iron. Ore having been discovered a few miles above Henrico on the James, a furnace was erected there and more than a hundred skilled workmen brought over from England to put it into operation. Before the works could be completed, however, they were utterly demolished by the savages, the machinery thrown into the river, all the workmen slaughtered,[38] and the only return the Company obtained for an outlay of thousands of pounds was a shovel, a pair of tongs and one bar of iron.[39] Efforts were made later to repair the havoc wrought by the Indians and to reëstablish the works, but they came to nothing. Not

[34] F. R., p. 376.
[35] F. R., p. 415.
[36] F. R., p. 464.
[37] F. R., p. 612.
[38] Bruce, Ec. Hist., Vol. II, pp. 448, 449.
[39] *Ibid.*

until the time of Governor Spotswood were iron furnaces
operated in Virginia, and even then the industry met with
a scant measure of success.

The Company also made an earnest effort to promote the
manufacture of glass in Virginia. This industry was threatened with extinction in England as a result of the great inroads
that had been made upon the timber available for fuel, and
it was thought that Virginia, with its inexhaustible forests,
offered an excellent opportunity for its rehabilitation. But
here too they were disappointed. The sand of Virginia proved
unsuitable for the manufacture of glass. The skilled Italian
artisans sent over to put the works into operation were in-
tractable and mutinous. After trying in various ways to dis-
courage the enterprise, so that they could return to Europe,
these men brought matters to a close by cracking the furnace
with a crowbar. George Sandys, in anger, declared "that
a more damned crew hell never vomited".[40]

In order to show that they were sincere in their professions
of interest in the spiritual welfare of the Indians, the Company
determined to erect a college at Henrico "for the training up
of the children of those Infidels in true Religion, moral virtue
and civility".[41] The clergy of England were enthusiastic
in their support of this good design, and their efforts resulted
in liberal contributions from various parts of the kingdom.[42]
Unfortunately, however, the money thus secured was expended
in sending to the college lands a number of "tenants" the
income from whose labor was to be utilized in establishing
and supporting the institution.[43] As some of these settlers
fell victims to disease and many others were destroyed in the
massacre of 1622, the undertaking had to be abandoned, and
of course all thought of converting and civilizing the savages
was given up during the long and relentless war that ensued.

Even more discouraging than these failures was the hostility
of the King to the cultivation of tobacco in Virginia, and his
restrictions upon its importation into England. Appeals were

[40] Bruce, Ec. Hist., Vol. II, pp. 442, 443.
[41] F. R., p. 322.   [42] F. R., p. 335.
[43] F. R., p. 336.

made to him to prohibit the sale of Spanish tobacco, in order that the Virginia planters might dispose of their product at a greater profit. This, it was argued, would be the most effective way of rendering the colony prosperous and self sustaining. But James, who was still bent upon maintaining his Spanish policy, would not offend Philip by excluding his tobacco from England. Moreover, in 1621, he issued a proclamation restricting the importation of the leaf from Virginia and the Somers Isles to fifty-five thousand pounds annually.[44] This measure created consternation in Virginia and in the London Company. The great damage it would cause to the colony and the diminution in the royal revenue that would result were pointed out to James, but for the time he was obdurate.[45] Indeed, he caused additional distress by granting the customs upon tobacco to a small association of farmers of the revenue, who greatly damaged the interests of the colony. In 1622, James, realizing that his policy in regard to tobacco was injuring the exchequer, made a compromise with the Company. The King agreed to restrict the importation of Spanish tobacco to 60,000 pounds a year, and after two years to exclude it entirely. All the Virginia leaf was to be admitted, but the Crown was to receive one third of the crop, while the other two thirds was subjected to a duty of six pence a pound.[46] This agreement proved most injurious to the Company, and it was soon abandoned, but the heavy exactions of the King continued. Undoubtedly this unwise policy was most detrimental to Virginia. Not only did it diminish the returns of the Company and make it impossible for Sandys to perfect all his wise plans for the colony, but it put a decided check upon immigration. Many that would have gone to Virginia to share in the profits of the planters, remained at home when they saw that these profits were being confiscated by the King.[47]

Yet the strenuous efforts of the London Company would surely have brought something like prosperity to the colony had not an old enemy returned to cause the destruction of hundreds of the settlers. This was the sickness. For some years

[44] Bruce, Ec. Hist., Vol. I, p. 264.　[45] Bruce, Ec. Hist., Vol. I, p. 265.
[46] Bruce, Ec. Hist., Vol. I, p. 269.　[47] P. R. O., CO1-3.

the mortality had been very low, because the old planters were acclimated, and few new immigrants were coming to Virginia. But with the stream of laborers and artisans that the Sandys régime now sent over, the scourge appeared again with redoubled fury. As early as January, 1620, Governor Yeardley wrote "of the great mortallitie which hath been in Virginia, about 300 of ye inhabitants having dyed this year".[48] The sickness was most deadly in the newly settled parts of the colony, "to the consumption of divers Hundreds, and almost the utter destruction of some particular Plantations".[49] The London Company, distressed at the loss of so many men, saw in their misfortunes the hand of God, and wrote urging "the more carefull observations of his holy laws to work a reconciliation".[50] They also sent directions for the construction, in different parts of the colony, of four guest houses, or hospitals, for the lodging and entertaining of fifty persons each, upon their first arrival.[51] But all efforts to check the scourge proved fruitless. In the year ending March, 1621 over a thousand persons died upon the immigrant vessels and in Virginia.[52] Despite the fact that hundreds of settlers came to the colony during this year, the population actually declined. In 1621 the percentage of mortality was not so large, but the actual number of deaths increased. During the months from March, 1621, to March, 1622, nearly twelve hundred persons perished. It was like condemning a man to death to send him to the colony. Seventy-five or eighty per cent. of the laborers that left England in search of new homes across the Atlantic died before the expiration of their first year. The exact number of deaths in 1622 is not known, but there is reason to believe that it approximated thirteen hundred.[53] Mr. George Sandys, brother of the Secretary of the London Company, wrote, "Such a pestilent fever rageth this winter amongst us: never knowne before in Virginia, by the infected people that came over in ye *Abigall,* who were poisoned with . . . beer and all falling sick & many dying, every where dispersed the contagion, and

[48] F. R., p. 372.   [49] F. R., p. 377.
[50] F. R., p. 377.   [51] F. R., p. 377.
[52] F. R., p. 415.   [53] F. R., p. 506.

the forerunning Summer hath been also deadly upon us."[54] Not until 1624 did the mortality decline.   Then it was that the Governor wrote, "This summer, God be thanked, the Colony hath very well stood to health".[55]   The dread sickness had spent itself for lack of new victims, for the immigration had declined and the old planters had become "seasoned".

History does not record an epidemic more deadly than that which swept over Virginia during these years.   It is estimated that the number of those that lost their lives from the diseases native to the colony and to those brought in from the infected ships amounts to no less than four thousand.[56]   When the tide of immigration was started by Sir Edwin Sandys in 1619, there were living in Virginia about nine hundred persons; when it slackened in 1624 the population was but eleven hundred.   The sending of nearly five thousand settlers to Virginia had resulted in a gain of but two hundred.   It is true that the tomahawk and starvation accounts for a part of this mortality, but by far the larger number of deaths was due to disease.

Yet hardly less horrible than the sickness was the Indian massacre of 1622.   This disaster, which cost the lives of several hundred persons, struck terror into the hearts of every Englishman in Virginia.   The colonists had not the least intimation that the savages meditated harm to them, for peace had existed between the races ever since the marriage of Rolfe and Pocahontas.   Considering the protection of their palisades no longer necessary after that event, they had spread out over the colony in search of the most fertile lands.   Their plantations extended at intervals for many miles along both banks of the James, and in the case of a sudden attack by the Indians it would obviously be difficult for the settlers to defend themselves or to offer assistance to their neighbors.

The apparent friendship of the Indians had created such great intimacy between the two races, that the savages were received into the homes of the white men and at times were fed at their tables.[57]   At the command of the London Company

[54] F. R., p. 506.
[56] P. R. O., CO1-36-37.
[55] F. R., p. 608.
[57] Stith, p. 210.

itself some of the Indian youths had been adopted by the settlers and were being educated in the Christian faith.   So unsuspecting were the people that they loaned the savages their boats, as they passed backward and forward, to formulate their plans for the massacre.[58]

The plot seems to have originated in the cunning brain of Opechancanough. This chief, always hostile to the white men, must have viewed with apprehension their encroachment upon the lands of his people. He could but realize that some day the swarms of foreigners that were arriving each year would exclude the Indians from the country of their forefathers. Perceiving his opportunity in the foolish security of the English and in their exposed situation, he determined to annihilate them in one general butchery.

His plans were laid with great cunning. Although thousands of natives knew of the design, no warning reached the white men until the very eve of the massacre. While Opechancanough was preparing this tremendous blow, he protested in the strongest terms his perpetual good will and love, declaring that the sky would fall before he would bring an end to the peace.[59]   In order to lull the suspicions of the planters, "even but two daies before the massacre", he guided some of them "with much kindnesse through the woods, and one Browne that lived among them to learne the language", he sent home to his master. The evening before the attack the Indians came as usual to the plantations with deer, turkeys, fish, fruits and other provisions to sell.[60]

That night, however, a warning was received, which although too late to save the most remote settlements, preserved many hundreds from the tomahawk. Chanco, an Indian boy who had been adopted by an Englishman named Race, revealed the entire plot to his master. The man secured his house, and rowed away before dawn in desperate haste to Jamestown, to give warning to the Governor. "Whereby they were prevented, and at such other plantations as possibly intelligence could be given."[61]

[58] Stith, p. 210.
[60] Arb. Smith, p. 573.
[59] Arb. Smith, p. 573.
[61] Arb. Smith, p. 578.

The assault of the savages was swift and deadly. In all parts of the colony they fell upon the settlers, and those that had received no warning were, in most cases, butchered before they could suspect that harm was intended. Sometimes the Indians sat down to breakfast with their victims, "whom immediately with their owne tooles they slew most barbarously, not sparing either age or sex, man woman or childe".[62]   Many were slain while working in the fields; others were trapped in their houses and butchered before they could seize their weapons.   The savages, "not being content with their lives, . . . fell againe upon the dead bodies, making as well as they could a fresh murder, defacing, dragging, and mangling their dead carkases into many peeces".[63]

That the plot was so successful was due to the completeness of the surprise, for where the English made the least resistance the savages were usually beaten off.   A planter named Causie, when attacked and wounded and surrounded by the Indians, "with an axe did cleave one of their heads, whereby the rest fled and he escaped; for they hurt not any that did either fight or stand upon their guard.   In one place where they had warning of it, (they) defended the house against sixty or more that assaulted it."[64]

At the plantation of a Mr. Harrison, where there were gathered seven men and eighteen or nineteen women and children, the savages set fire to a tobacco house and then came in to tell the men to quench it.   Six of the English, not suspecting treachery, rushed out, and were shot full of arrows.   Mr. Thomas Hamor, the seventh man, "having finished a letter he was writing, followed after to see what was the matter, but quickly they shot an arrow in his back, which caused him to returne and barricado up the dores, whereupon the Salvages set fire to the house.   But a boy, seizing a gun which he found loaded, discharged it at random.   At the bare report the enemy fled and Mr. Hamor with the women and children escaped."[65] In a nearby house, a party of English under Mr. Hamor's brother, were caught by the Indians without arms, but they

[62] Arb. Smith, p. 573.
[64] Arb. Smith, p. 575.
[63] Arb. Smith, p. 574.
[65] Arb. Smith, p. 576.

defended themselves successfully with spades, axes and brickbats.[66]

One of the first to fall was Reverend George Thorpe, a member of the Virginia Council, and a man of prominence in England.[67] Leaving a life of honor and ease, he had come to Virginia to work for the conversion of the Indians. He had apparently won the favor of Opechancanough, with whom he often discoursed upon the Christian religion. At the moment of his murder, his servant, perceiving the deadly intent of the savages, gave him warning, but his gentle nature would not permit him to believe harm of those whom he had always befriended, and he was cut down without resistance.[68]

The barbarous king failed in his design to destroy the English race in Virginia, but the massacre was a deadly blow to the colony. No less than three hundred and fifty-seven persons were slaughtered, including six Councillors. The news of the disaster brought dismay to the London Company. For a while they attempted to keep the matter a secret, but in a few weeks it was known all over England. Although the massacre could not have been foreseen or prevented, it served as a pretext for numerous attacks upon Sandys and the party which supported him. It discouraged many shareholders and made it harder to secure settlers for the colony. Even worse was the effect in Virginia. The system of farming in unprotected plantations, which had prevailed for some years, had now to be abandoned and many settlements that were exposed to the Indians were deserted. "We have not," wrote the Assembly, "the safe range of the Country for the increase of Cattle, Swyne, etc; nor for the game and fowle which the country affords in great plentye; besides our duties to watch and warde to secure ourselves and labor are as hard and chargeable as if the enemy were at all times present."[69]

The massacre was followed by a venomous war with the Indians, which lasted many years. The English, feeling that their families and their homes would never be safe so long as the savages shared the country with them, deliberately planned

[66] Arb. Smith, p. 576.   [67] Stith, p. 211.
[68] Stith, pp. 211, 212.   [69] F. R., pp. 576, 577.

the extermination of all hostile tribes in Virginia. Their conversion was given no further consideration. "The terms betwixt us and them," they declared, "are irreconcilable."[70] Governor Wyatt wrote, "All trade with them must be forbidden, and without doubt either we must cleere them or they us out of the Country."[71]

But it soon became apparent that neither people would be able to win an immediate or decisive victory. The Indians could not hope to destroy the English, now that their deeply laid plot had failed. In open battle their light arrows made no impression upon the coats of plate and of mail in which the white men were incased, while their own bodies were without protection against the superior weapons of their foes. On the other hand, it was very difficult for the colonists to strike the savages, because of the "advantages of the wood and the nimbleness of their heels".[72] Even though they "chased them to and fro", following them to their villages and burning their huts, they found it very difficult to do them serious harm.

Finally the English hit upon the plan of bringing distress upon the savages by destroying their corn. Although the Virginia tribes subsisted partly upon game, their chief support was from their fields of maize, and the entire failure of their crop would have reduced hundreds of them to the verge of starvation.[73] Each year the white men, in small companies, in various parts of the country, brought ruin to the corn fields. Sometimes the savages, in despair at the prospect of famine, made valiant efforts to defend their fields, but were invariably beaten off until the work of destruction was done.

The natives retaliated with many sudden raids upon the more exposed parts of the colony, where they burned, pillaged and murdered. The planter at work in his fields might expect to find them lurking in the high grass, while their ambushes in the woods made communication from plantation to plantation very dangerous. "The harmes that they do us," wrote the Assembly, "is by ambushes and sudden incursions, where they

---

[70] F. R., p. 576. [71] F. R., p. 508.
[72] F. R., p. 576.
[73] Bruce, Ec. Hist., Vol. I, pp. 155 to 159.

see their advantages."[74]   In 1625 Captain John Harvey declared that the two races were "ingaged in a mortall warre and fleshed in each others bloud, of which the Causes have been the late massacre on the Salvages parte. . . . I conceive that by the dispersion of the Plantations the Salvages hath the advantage in this warre, and that by their suddaine assaults they do us more harme than we do them by our set voyages".[75]

When the English had recovered from the first shock of the massacre, they planned four expeditions against the tribes living on the river above Jamestown.   Mr. George Sandys attacked the Tappahatomaks, Sir George Yeardley the Wyanokes, Captain William Powell the Chickahominies and the Appomatocks, and Captain John West the Tanx-Powhatans. The savages, without attempting to make a stand, deserted their villages and their crops and fled at the approach of the English.   Few were killed, for they were "so light and swift" that the white men, laden with their heavy armor, could not overtake them.[76]   In the fall Sir George Yeardley led three hundred men down the river against the Nansemonds and against Opechancanough.   The natives "set fire to their own houses, and spoiled what they could, and then fled with what they could carry; so that the English did make no slaughter amongst them for revenge.   Their Corne fields being newly gathered, they surprised all they found, burnt the houses (that) remained unburnt, and so departed."[77]

It is remarkable that the colonists could continue this war while the sickness was raging among them.   At the very time that Yeardley was fighting Opechancanough, hundreds of his comrades were dying "like cats and dogs".   "With our small and sicklie forces," wrote Mr. George Sandys, "we have discomforted the Indians round about us, burnt their houses, gathered their corn and slain not a few; though they are as swift as Roebucks, like the violent lightening they are gone as soon as perceived, and not to be destroyed but by surprise or famine."[78]

[74] F. R., p. 576.   [75] F. R., p. 611.
[76] Arb. Smith, p. 594.
[77] Arb. Smith, p. 559; F. R., pp. 475, 495.
[78] F. R., p. 510.

How bitter was the war is shown by an act of treachery by the English that would have shamed the savages themselves. In 1623, the Indians, discouraged by the destruction of their crops, sent messengers to Jamestown, asking for peace. The colonists determined to take advantage of this overture to recover their prisoners and at the same time to strike a sudden blow at their enemy. Early in June, Captain William Tucker with twelve well armed men was sent "in a shalope under colour to make peace with them". On the arrival of this party at the chief town of Opechancanough, the savages thronged down to the riverside to parley with them, but the English refused to consider any terms until all prisoners had been restored. Assenting to this, the savages brought forth seven whites and they were placed aboard the vessel. Having thus accomplished their purpose, the soldiers, at a given signal, let fly a volley into the midst of the crowd, killing "some 40 Indians including 3 of the chiefest".[79]

In 1624 the English won a great victory over the most troublesome of the Indian tribes, the Pamunkeys. Governor Wyatt, in leading an expedition against this people had evidently expected little resistance, for he brought with him but sixty fighting men. The Pamunkeys, however, had planted that year a very large crop of corn, which they needed for the support of themselves and their confederates, and they determined to protect it at all hazards. So Wyatt and his little band were surprised, on approaching their village to find before them more than eight hundred warriors prepared for battle. The English did not falter in the face of this army, and a fierce contest ensued. "Fightinge not only for safeguards of their houses and such a huge quantity of corn", but for their reputation with the other nations, the Pamunkeys displayed unusual bravery. For two days the battle went on. Whenever the young warriors wavered before the volleys of musketry, they were driven back into the fight by the older men. Twenty-four of the English were detached from the firing line and were employed in destroying the maize. In this they were so successful that enough corn was cut down "as by Estimation

[79] F. R., pp. 514, 515.

of men of good judgment was sufficient to have sustained fower thousand men for a twelvemonth". At last the savages in despair gave up the fight and stood nearby "rufully lookinge on whilst their Corne was cutt down". "In this Expedition," wrote the colonists, "sixteene of the English were hurte our first and seconde day, whereby nyne of the best shott were made unserviceable for that tyme, yett never a man slayne, nor none miscarried of those hurtes, Since when they have not greatly troubled us, nor interrupted our labours."[80]

The series of misfortunes which befel the London Company during the administration of Sir Edwin Sandys culminated in the loss of their charter. For some time King James had been growing more and more hostile to the party that had assumed control of the colony. It is highly probable that he had had no intimation, when the charter of 1612 was granted, that popular institutions would be established in Virginia, and the extension of the English parliamentary system to America must have been distasteful to him. The enemies of Sandys had been whispering to the King that he "aymed at nothing more than to make a free popular state there, and himselfe and his assured friends to be the leaders of them".[81] James knew that Sandys was not friendly to the prerogative of the Crown. It had been stated "that there was not any man in the world that carried a more malitious heart to the Government of a Monarchie".[82]

In 1621 the controlling party in the London Company was preparing a new charter for Virginia. The contents of this document are not known, but it is exceedingly probable that it was intended as the preface to the establishment of a government in the colony far more liberal than that of England itself. It was proposed to have the charter confirmed by act of Parliament, and to this James had consented, provided it proved satisfactory to the Privy Council.[83] But it is evident that when the Councillors had examined it, they advised the King not to assent to it or to allow it to appear in Parliament. Indeed the document must have stirred James' anger, for not

[80] P. R. O., CO1-3.
[82] F. R., p. 529.
[81] F. R., p. 530.
[83] F R., p. 393.

only did he end all hopes of its passage, but he "struck some terrour into most undertakers for Virginia", by imprisoning Sir Edwin Sandys.[84]

Even more distasteful to the King than the establishment of popular institutions in the little colony was the spreading of liberal doctrines throughout England by the Sandys faction of the Company. James could no longer tolerate their meetings, if once he began to look upon them as the nursery of discontent and sedition. The party that was so determined in its purpose to plant a republican government in Virginia might stop at nothing to accomplish the same end in England. James knew that national politics were often discussed in the assemblies of the Company and that the parties there were sometimes as "animated one against the other" as had been the "Guelfs and Gebillines" of Italy.[85] He decided that the best way to end these controversies and frustrate the designs of his enemies was to annul the charter of the Company and make Virginia a royal colony.

The first unmistakable sign of his hostility came in June 1622, when he interfered with the election of their treasurer. It was not, he told them, his intention "to infringe their liberty of free election", but he sent a list of names that would be acceptable to him, and asked them to put one of these in nomination. To this the Company assented readily enough, even nominating two from the list, but when the election was held, the King's candidates were overwhelmingly defeated.[86] When James heard this, he "flung himself away in a furious passion", being "not well satisfied that out of so large a number by him recommended they had not made any choice".[87] The incident meant that James had given the Company an unmistakable intimation that it would be well for them to place the management of affairs in the hands of men more in harmony with himself, and that they had scornfully refused.

The Company was now doomed, for the King decided that the charter must be revoked. He could not, of course, annul a grant that had passed under the Great Seal, without some pre-

[84] F. R., pp. 436, 437.
[85] F. R., p. 542.
[86] F. R., p. 477.
[87] F. R., p. 478.

tence of legal proceedings, but when once he had determined
on the ruin of the Company, means to accomplish his end were
not lacking. John Ferrar wrote, "The King, notwithstanding
his royal word and honor pledged to the contrary . . . was
now determined with all his force to make the last assault, and
give the death blow to this . . . Company."[88]

James began by hunting evidence of mismanagement and
incapacity by the Sandys party. He gave orders to Captain
Nathaniel Butler, who had spent some months in Virginia, to
write a pamphlet describing the condition of the colony. *The
Unmasking of Virginia,* as Butler's work is called was nothing
less than a bitter assault upon the conduct of affairs since the
beginning of the Sandys administration. Unfortunately, it
was not necessary for the author to exaggerate much in his
description of the frightful conditions in the colony; but it
was unfair to place the blame upon the Company. The misfortunes of the settlers were due to disease and the Indians
and did not result from incapacity or negligence on the part
of Sandys. The Company drew up "A True answer to a writing of Information presented to his Majesty by Captain Nathaniel Butler", denying most of the charges and explaining
others, but they could not efface the bad impression caused by
the *Unmasking.*[89]

In April, 1623, James appointed a commission to make enquiry into the "true estate of . . . Virginia".[90] This body
was directed to investigate "all abuses and grievances . . . all
wrongs and injuryes done to any adventurers or planters and
the grounds and causes thereof, and to propound after what
sort the same may be better managed".[91] It seems quite clear
that the commissioners understood that they were expected
to give the King "some true ground to work upon", in his
attack on the Company's charter.[92] In a few weeks they were
busy receiving testimony from both sides, examining records
and searching for evidence. They commanded the Company
to deliver to them all "Charters, Books, Letters, Petitions,

[88] F. R., pp. 531, 532.   [89] F R., p, 524.
[90] F. R., p. 520.   [91] F. R., p. 520.
[92] F. R., p. 521.

Lists of names, of Provisions, Invoyces of Goods, and all other writing whatsoever" They examined the clerk of the Company, the messenger and the keeper of the house in which they held their meetings.[93] They intercepted private letters from Virginia, telling of the horrible suffering there, and made the King aware of their contents.[94]

In July the commission made its report. It found that "the people sent to inhabit there . . . were most of them by God's visitation, sicknes of body, famine, and by massacres . . . dead and deceased, and those that were living of them lived in miserable and lamentable necessity and want. . . . That this neglect they conceived, must fall on the Governors and Company here, who had power to direct the Plantations there. . . . That if his Majesty's first Grant of April 10 1606, and his Majesty's most prudent and princely Instructions given in the beginning . . . had been pursued, much better effects had been produced, than had been by the alteration thereof, into so popular a course."[95] James was much pleased with the report, and it confirmed his determination to "resume the government, and to reduce that popular form so as to make it agree with the monarchial form".[96]

Before taking the matter to the courts, the King resolved to offer the Company a compromise. If they would give up the old charter, he said, a new one would be granted them, preserving all private interests, but restoring the active control of the colony to the Crown. The government was to be modelled upon the old plan of 1606, which had already given so much trouble. "His Majesty," the Company was told, "hath . . . resolved by a new Charter to appoint a Governor and twelve assistants, resident here in England, unto whom shall be committed the government. . . . And his Majesty is pleased that there shall be resident in Virginia a Governor and twelve assistants, to be nominated by the Governor and assistants here . . . whereby all matters of importance may be directed by his Majesty."[97] The Company was commanded

---

[93] F. R., p. 541.
[95] F. R., pp. 519, 520.
[97] F. R., p. 551.
[94] F. R., p. 535.
[96] F. R., p. 542.

to send its reply immediately, "his Majesty being determined, in default of such submission, to proceed for the recalling of the said former charters".[98]

A special meeting of the stockholders was called, October 30th, 1623, to consider the King's proposal. Every man present must have known that the rejection of the compromise would mean the loss of all the money he had invested in the colony, and that if the King's wishes were acceded to his interests would be preserved. But the Company was fighting for something higher than personal gain—for the maintenance of liberal institutions in America, for the defence of the rights of English citizens. After a "hot debate" they put the question to the vote, and the offer was rejected, there being "only nine hands for the delivering up of the Charters, and all the rest (being about three score more) were of a contrary opinion".[99]

As a last hope the Company resolved to seek the assistance of Parliament. A petition was drawn up to be presented to the Commons, and the shareholders that were members of that body were requested to give it their strenuous support when it came up for consideration. The petition referred to Virginia as a "child of the Kingdom, exposed as in the wilderness to extreme danger and as it were fainting and labouring for life", and it prayed the House to hear "the grievances of the Colony and Company, and grant them redress".[100] The matter was brought before the Commons in May, 1624, but before it could be considered, a message was received from the King warning them "not to trouble themselves with this petition as their doing so could produce nothing but a further increase Schisme and factions in the Company". "Ourself," he announced, "will make it our own work to settle the quiet, and wellfare of the plantations."[101] This was received with some "soft mutterings" by the Commons, but they thought it best to comply, and the Company was left to its fate.[102]

In the meanwhile the King had placed his case in the hands

[98] F. R., p. 542.
[99] F. R., p. 554.
[100] F. R., pp. 595, 596.
[101] F. R., pp. 597, 598.
[102] F. R., p. 598.

of Attorney-General Coventry, who had prepared a *quo warranto* against the Company.[103] Although all hope of retaining the charter was gone, the Sandys party were determined to fight to the end. They voted to employ attorneys and to plead their case before the King's Bench. The *quo warranto* came up June 26th, 1624, and "the Virginia Patent was overthrown", on a mistake in pleading.[104] With this judgment the London Company practically ceased to exist, and Virginia became a royal province.

[103] F. R., p. 587.　　　　　　　　[104] F. R., pp. 601, 602.

CHAPTER III

The Expulsion of Sir John Harvey

The people of Virginia sympathized deeply with the London Company in its efforts to prevent the revocation of the charter. The Governor, the Council and the Burgesses gave active assistance to Sandys and his friends by testifying to the wisdom of the management and contradicting the calumnies of their enemies. In the midst of the controversy the Privy Council had appointed a commission which they sent to Virginia to investigate conditions there and to gather evidence against the Company. This board consisted of John Harvey, John Pory, Abraham Piersey and Samuel Matthews, men destined to play prominent rôles in Virginia history, but then described as "certayne obscure persons".[1] When the commissioners reached the colony they made known to the Assembly the King's desire to revoke the charter and to take upon himself the direction of the government. They then asked the members to subscribe to a statement expressing their gratitude for the care of the King, and willingness to consent to the contemplated change. The Assembly returned the paper unsigned. "When our consent," they said, "to the surrender of the Pattents, shalbe required, will be the most proper time to make reply: in the mean time wee conceive his Majesties intention of changing the government hath proceeded from much misinformation."[2]

After this they ignored the commissioners, and addressed themselves in direct letters and petitions to the King and the Privy Council.[3] They apprehended, they wrote, no danger from the present government, which had converted into freedom the slavery they had endured in former times.[4] They prayed that their liberal institutions might not be destroyed

[1] F. R., p. 556; Osg., Vol. III, p. 47. [2] F. R., p. 574.
[3] F. R., p. 572. [4] Osg., Vol. III, p. 50.

or the old Smith faction of the Company placed over them again.[5] These papers they sent to England by one of their number, John Pountis, even refusing to let the commissioners see them. But Pory succeeded in securing copies from the acting secretary, Edward Sharpless.[6] The Council, upon learning of this betrayal, were so incensed against the secretary that they sentenced him to "stand in the Pillory and there to have his Ears nailed to it, and cut off".[7] His punishment was modified, however, so that when he was "sett in the Pillorie", he "lost but a part of one of his eares".[8] The King, upon learning of this incident, which was represented to him "as a bloody and barbarous act", became highly incensed against the Council.[9]

In the meanwhile James had appointed a large commission, with Viscount Mandeville at its head, "to confer, consult, resolve and expedite all affaires . . . of Virginia, and to take care and give order for the directing and government thereof".[10] This body met weekly at the house of Sir Thomas Smith, and immediately assumed control of the colony.[11] Their first act was to decide upon a form of government to replace the Virginia Magna Charta. In conformance with the wishes of the King they resolved to return to the plan of 1606. In their recommendations no mention was made of an Assembly. It seemed for a while that the work of Sandys was to be undone, and the seeds of liberty in Virginia destroyed almost before they had taken root. Fortunately, however, this was not to be. The commission, perhaps wishing to allay the fears of the colonists, reappointed Sir Francis Wyatt Governor, and retained most of the old Council. This made it certain that for a while at least the government was to be in the hands of men of lofty character and liberal views.[12] More fortunate still for Virginia was the death of James I. This event removed the most determined enemy of their Assembly, and placed upon the throne a man less hostile to the Sandys faction, less determined to suppress the liberal institutions of the colony.

[5] Osg., Vol. III, p. 50.
[7] F. R., p. 584.
[9] F. R., p. 584.
[11] Osg., Vol. III, p. 74.
[6] F. R., p. 584.
[8] P. R. O., CO1-3.
[10] F. R., p. 634 .
[12] F. R., p. 639 .

Soon after his accession Charles I abolished the Mandeville commission and appointed in its place a committee of the Privy Council.[13] For a while he seemed inclined to restore the Company, for he consulted with Sandys and requested him to give his opinion "touching the best form of Government".[14] But he finally rejected his proposals, declaring that he had come to the same determination that his father had held. He was resolved, he said, that the government should be immediately dependent upon himself and not be committed to any company or corporation.[15] But, like his father, he was "pleased to authorise Sir Francis Wyatt knight to be governor there, and such as are now employed for his Majesties Councell there to have authoritie to continue the same employment". No provision was made for a representative body, the power of issuing decrees, ordinances and public orders being assigned to the Council.

But the Assembly was saved by the unselfish conduct of Wyatt and Yeardley and their Councils.[16] Had these men sought their own gain at the expense of the liberty of their fellow colonists, they would have welcomed a change that relieved them from the restraint of the representatives of the people. The elimination of the Burgesses would have left them as absolute as had been Wingfield and the first Council. But they were most anxious to preserve for Virginia the right of representative government, and wrote to England again and again pleading for the reëstablishment of the Assembly.[17] "Above all," they said, "we humbly intreat your Lordships that we may retaine the Libertie of our Generall Assemblie, than which nothing can more conduce to our satisfaction or the publique utilitie."[18] In 1625 Yeardley himself crossed the ocean to present a new petition. He pleaded with Charles "to avoid the oppression of Governors there, that their liberty of Generall Assemblyes may be continued and confirmed, and that they may have a voice in the election of officers, as in other Corporations".[19] After the overthrow of the Company char-

[13] F. R., p. 640.
[15] F. R., pp. 641, 642.
[17] F. R., p. 648.
[19] P. R. O., CO1-3-7.

[14] F. R., p. 641.
[16] F. R., p. 647.
[18] F. R., p. 573.

ter, there could be no legal election of Burgesses and no legislation save by proclamation of the Governor and Council. Yet
Wyatt, in order to preserve as far as possible some form of
representative government, held conventions or informal
meetings of leading citizens, to confer with the Council on
important matters. They issued papers under the title of
"Governor, Councell and Collony of Virginia assembled together",[20] and it is possible that the people elected their dele-
gates just as they had formerly chosen Burgesses. Since,
however, acts passed by these assemblages could not be enforced in the courts, all legislation for the time being took the
form of proclamations.[21]

Finally Charles yielded to the wishes of the people, and, in
the fall of 1627, sent written instructions to the officials in
Virginia to hold an election of Burgesses and to summon a
General Assembly.[22] The King's immediate motive for this
important step was his desire to gain the planters' acceptance
through their representatives of an offer which he made to
buy all their tobacco. In the spring of 1628 the Council wrote,
"In obedience to his Majesties Commands wee have given
order that all the Burgesses of Particular Plantations should
shortly be assembled at James Citty that by the general and
unanimous voice of the whole Colony his Majesty may receave
a full answere."[23] Although the Assembly must have realized
that its very existence might depend upon its compliance with
the King's wishes, it refused to accept his proposition. The
planters were willing to sell their tobacco to his Majesty, but
only upon more liberal terms than those offered them. Charles
rejected the counter-proposals of the Virginians, with some
show of anger, but he did not abolish the Assembly, and in
ensuing years sessions were held with great regularity.[24]

The apprehensions of the colonists during this trying period
were made more acute by the resignation of Sir Francis
Wyatt. In the winter of 1625-26 the Council wrote the Virginia commissioners, "The Governor hath long expected a

[20] P. R. O., CO1-3-5.   [21] Hen., Vol. I, pp. 129, 130.
[22] F. R., p. 648; P. R. O., CO1-4.   [23] P. R. O., CO1-20.
[24] Bruce, Ec. Hist., Vol. I, p. 287.

Successor, and the necessity of his private estate compelling him not to put off any longer his return for England, wee hope it is already provided for."[25]   Great must have been the relief in the colony when it was learned that Sir George Yeardley had been chosen to succeed Governor Wyatt.   Yeardley had been the bearer of the Virginia Magna Charta, under which the first Assembly had been established, and his services had not been forgotten by the people.   But he was not destined to see the restoration of the Burgesses, for he died in November, 1627.[26]   We have lost, wrote the Council in great grief, "a main pillar of this our building & thereby a support to the whole body".[27]

By virtue of previous appointment, Captain Francis West, brother of the Lord De la Warr who had lost his life in the service of Virginia, at once assumed the reins of government. Captain West continued in office until March 5th, 1629, when he resigned in order to return to England.[28]   John Harvey, a member of the Virginia commission of 1624, was the King's next choice for Governor, but pending his arrival, the office fell to one of the Council—Dr. John Pott.   This man had long been a resident of Virginia, and had acted as Physician-General during the years when the sickness was at the worst. He is described as "a Master of Arts . . . well practiced in chirurgery and physic, and expert also in the distilling of waters, (besides) many other ingenious devices".[29]   He had made use of these accomplishments to poison large numbers of Indians after the massacre of 1622.[30]   This exploit caused the temporary loss of his place in the Council, for when James I settled the government after the fall of the Company, Pott was left out at the request of the Earl of Warwick, because "he was the poysoner of the salvages thear".[31]   In 1626 his seat was restored to him.   He seems to have been both democratic and convival, and is described as fond of the company of his inferiors, "who hung upon him while his good liquor lasted".[31]

[25] P. R. O., CO1-4.
[27] P. R. O., CO1-4-18.
[29] Neill, Va. Co., p. 221.
[31] F. R., p. 639.
[26] F. R., p. 647.
[28] Gen., p. 1047.
[30] F. R., p. 568.
[32] Fiske, Old Va., Vol. I, p. 252.

In the spring of 1630 Sir John Harvey arrived in Virginia.[33] This man proved to be one of the worst of the many bad colonial governors. Concerned only for his own dignity and for the prerogative of the King, he trampled without scruple upon the liberties of the people, and his administration was marked throughout by injustice and oppression.

His first efforts as Governor were to attempt to win the friendship and support of one of the Council and to bring humiliation and ruin upon another. He had been in Virginia but a few weeks when he wrote the King asking especial favors for Captain Samuel Matthews. "This gentleman," he said, "I found most readie to set forward all services propounded for his Majesties honor, . . . and without his faithful assistance perhaps I should not soe soon have brought the busines of this Country to so good effect." It would be a just reward for these services, he thought, to allow him for a year or two to ship the tobacco of his plantation into England free of customs.[34] At the same time Harvey seemed bent upon the utter undoing of Dr. Pott. Claiming that the pleasure loving physician while Governor had been guilty of "pardoninge wilfull Murther, markinge other mens Cattell for his owne, and killing up their hoggs", Harvey suspended him from the Council and, pending the day of his trial, confined him to his plantation.[35]

It seems quite certain that this treatment of the two Councillors was designed to impress upon the people a just appreciation of the Governor's power. Harvey felt keenly the restriction of the Council. It had been the intention of James and after his death Charles to restore the government of the colony to its original form, in which all matters were determined by the Council. "His Majesties . . . pleasure," wrote the Privy Council in 1625, "is that all judgements, decrees, and all important actions be given, determined and undertaken by the advice and voices of the greater part."[36] If these instructions were adhered to, the Governor would become no more than the presiding officer of the Council. To this posi-

[33] Bruce, Ec. Hist., Vol. I, p. 130. [34] P. R. O., CO1-5-29.
[35] P. R. O., CO1-5. [36] F. R., p. 644.

tion Harvey was determined never to be reduced. He would, at the very outset, show that he was master in Virginia, able to reward his friends, or to punish those that incurred his displeasure.

Dr. Pott could not believe that the proceedings against him were intended seriously, and, in defiance of the Governor's commands, left his plantation to come to Elizabeth City. "Upon which contempt," wrote Harvey, "I committed him close prisoner, attended with a guard." At the earnest request of several gentlemen, the Governor finally consented that he might return to his plantation, but only under bond. Pott, however, refused to avail himself of the kindness of his friends, and so was kept in confinement.[37] On the 9th of July he was brought to trial, found guilty upon two indictments, and his entire estate confiscated.[38]

That Pott was convicted by a jury of thirteen men, three of them Councillors, is by no means conclusive evidence of his guilt. The close connection between the executive and the courts at this time made it quite possible for the Governor to obtain from a jury whatever verdict he desired. In fact it became the custom for a new administration, as soon as it was installed in power, to take revenge upon its enemies by means of the courts.

Pott's guilt is made still more doubtful by the fact that execution of the sentence was suspended "untill his Majesties pleasure might be signified concerning him", while the Council united in giving their security for his safe keeping.[39] Harvey himself wrote asking the King's clemency. "For as much," he said, "as he is the only Physician in the Colonie, and skilled in the Epidemicall diseases of the planters, . . . I am bound to entreat" your Majesty to pardon him.[40] It would seem quite inexplicable that Harvey should go to so much trouble to convict Dr. Pott, and then write immediately to England for a pardon, did not he himself give the clue to his conduct. "It

[37] P. R. O., CO1-5-31.
[38] P. R. O., CO1-5-32; Hen., Vol. I., p. 145.
[39] P. R. O., CO1-5; Hen., Vol. I, p. 146.
[40] P. R. O., CO1-5.

will be," he said, "a means to bring the people to . . . hold a better respect to the Governor than hitherto they have done."[41] Having shown the colonists that he could humble the strongest of them, he now sought to teach them that his intercession with the King could restore even the criminal to his former position.

When Dr. Pott was at Elizabeth City his wife was reported to be ill, but this did not deter her from making the long and dangerous voyage to England to appeal to the King "touching the wrong" done her husband.[42] Charles referred the matter to the Virginia commissioners, who gave her a hearing in the presence of Harvey's agent. Finding no justification for the proceedings against him, they wrote Harvey that for aught they could tell Pott had demeaned himself well and that there seemed to have been "some hard usage against him".[43] The sentence of confiscation seems never to have been carried out, but Pott was not restored to his seat in the Council.[44]

This arbitrary conduct did not succeed in intimidating the other Councillors. These men must have felt that the attack upon Dr. Pott was aimed partly at the dignity and power of the Council itself. If Harvey could thus ruin those that incurred his displeasure, the Councillors would lose all independence in their relations with him. Soon they were in open hostility to the Governor. Claiming that Harvey could do nothing without their consent, and that all important matters had to be determined "by the greater number of voyces at the Councell Table", they entered upon a policy of obstruction. It was in vain that the Governor declared that he was the King's substitute, that they were but his assistants, and that they were impeding his Majesty's business; they would yield to him only the position of first among equals. Early in 1631 Harvey was filling his letters to England with complaints of the "waywardness and oppositions of those of the Councell". "For instead of giving me assistance," he declared, "they stand Contesting and disputing my authoritie, avering that I can doe nothinge but what they shall advise me, and that my power extendeth

[41] P. R. O., CO1-5-32.   [42] P. R. O., CO1-5-33.
[43] P. R. O., CO1-5-33.   [44] P. R. O., CO1-6.

noe further than a bare casting voice."[45]   He had received, he claimed, a letter from the King, strengthening his commission and empowering him to "doe justice to all men, not sparinge those of the Councell", which he had often shown them, but this they would not heed. "I hope," he wrote, "you never held me to be ambitious or vainglorious, as that I should desire to live here as Governor to predominate, or prefer mine owne particular before the generall good." My position in Virginia is most miserable, "chiefly through the aversions of those from whom I expected assistance". He had often tried to bring peace and amity between them, but all to no purpose, for he was scorned for his efforts. He would be humbly thankful if his Majesty would be pleased to strengthen his commission, "that the place of Governor and the duty of Councellors may be knowne and distinguished".[46]

It is probable that the Councillors also wrote to England, to place before the King their grievances against Harvey, for before the end of the year letters came from the Privy Council, warning both sides to end the dispute and to proceed peacefully with the government of the colony. In compliance with these commands they drew up and signed a document promising "to swallow up & bury all forepart Complainte and accusations in a generall Reconciliation". They thanked their Lordships for advice that had persuaded their "alienated & distempered" minds to thoughts of love and peace and to the execution of public justice. The Council promised to give the Governor "all the service, honor & due Respect which belongs unto him as his Majesties Substitute".[47] It is quite evident, however, that this reconciliation, inspired by fear of the anger of the Privy Council, could not be permanent. Soon the Council, under the leadership of Captain Matthews, who had long since forfeited Harvey's favor, was as refractory as ever.

A new cause for complaint against the Governor arose with the founding of Maryland. In 1623 George Calvert, the first Lord Baltimore, had received a grant of the great southeastern promontory in Newfoundland, and had planted there a

[45] P. R. O., CO1-6-34.   [46] P. R. O., CO1-6-35, 57.
[47] P. R. O., CO1-6-37.

colony as an asylum for English Catholics. Baltimore himself had been detained in England for some years, but in 1627 came with his wife and children to take personal control of his little settlement. His experience with the severe Newfoundland winter persuaded him that it would be wise to transfer his colony to a more congenial clime. "From the middle of October," he wrote Charles I, "to the middle of May there is a sad face of winter upon all the land; both sea and land so frozen for the greater part of the time as they are not penetrable . . . besides the air so intolerable cold as it is hardly to be endured. . . . I am determined to commit this place to fishermen that are able to encounter stormes and hard weather, and to remove myself with some forty persons to your Majesties dominion of Virginia; where, if your Majesty will please to grant me a precinct of land, with such privileges as the King your father . . . was pleased to grant me here, I shall endeavour to the utmost of my power, to deserve it."[48]

In 1629 he sailed for Virginia, with his wife and children, and arrived at Jamestown the first day of October. His reception by Governor Pott and the Council was by no means cordial. The Virginians were loath either to receive a band of Catholics into their midst, or to concede to them a portion of the land that they held under the royal charters. Desiring to be rid of Baltimore as speedily as possible, they tendered him the oath of supremacy. This, of course, as a good Catholic he could not take, for it recognized the English sovereign as the supreme authority in all ecclesiastical matters. Baltimore proposed an alternative oath of allegiance, but the Governor and Council refused to accept it, and requested him to leave at once. Knowing that it was his intention to apply for a tract of land within their borders, the Virginians sent William Claiborne after him to London, to watch him and to thwart his designs.

Despite Claiborne's efforts a patent was granted Baltimore, making him lord proprietor of a province north of the Potomac river, which received the name of Maryland. Baltimore, with his own hand, drew up the charter, but in April, 1632, before it had passed under the Great Seal, he died. A few weeks

---

[48] Fiske, Old Va., Vol. I, pp. 262, 263.

later the patent was issued to his eldest son, Cecilius Calvert. The Virginians protested against this grant "within the Limits of the Colony", claiming that it would interfere with their Indian trade in the Chesapeake, and that the establishment of the Catholics so near their settlements would "give a generall disheartening of the Planters".[49] But their complaints availed nothing. Not only did Charles refuse to revoke the charter, but he wrote the Governor and Council commanding them to give Lord Baltimore every possible assistance in making his settlement. You must, he said, "suffer his servants and Planters to buy and transport such cattle and comodities to their Colonie, as you may conveniently spare . . . and give them . . . such lawful assistance as may conduce to both your safetyes".[50]

The second Lord Baltimore appointed his brother, Leonard Calvert, Governor of Maryland, and sent him with two vessels and over three hundred men to plant the new colony. In February, 1634, the expedition reached Point Comfort, where it stopped to secure from the Virginians the assistance that the King had promised should be given them.

They met with scant courtesy. The planters thought it a hard matter that they should be ordered to aid in the establishment of this new colony. They resented the encroachment upon their territories, they hated the newcomers because most of them were Catholics, they feared the loss of a part of their Indian trade, and they foresaw the growth of a dangerous rival in the culture of tobacco. Despite the King's letter they refused to help Calvert and his men. "Many are so averse," wrote Harvey, "that they crye and make it their familiar talke that they would rather knock their Cattell on the heades than sell them to Maryland."[51] The Governor, however, not daring to disobey his sovereign's commands, gave the visitors all the assistance in his power. "For their present accomodation," he said, "I sent unto them some Cowes of myne owne, and will do my best to procure more, or any thinge else they stand in need of."[52] This action secured for Harvey the praise of the

[49] P. R. O., CO1-6-39.   [50] P. R. O., CO1-6-39.
[51] P. R. O., CO1-6-46.   [52] P. R. O., CO1-6-46.

Privy Council, but it made him more unpopular with his Council and the people of Virginia.

After a stay of several weeks at Point Comfort, Calvert sailed up the Chesapeake into the Potomac, and founded the town of Saint Mary's. This, however, was not the first settlement in Maryland. In 1631, William Claiborne, returning from England after his unsuccessful attempt to block the issuing of Baltimore's charter, had established a settlement upon Kent Island in the Chesapeake Bay. Here he had built dwellings and mills and store houses, and had laid out orchards and gardens. In thus founding a colony within Baltimore's territory he was sustained by the Council. When Calvert arrived in 1634 he sent word to Claiborne that he would not molest his settlement, but since Kent Island was a part of Maryland, he must hold it as a tenant of Lord Baltimore. Upon receipt of this message Claiborne laid the matter before his colleagues of the Virginia Council, and asked their commands. The answer of the Councillors shows that they considered the new patent an infringement upon their prior rights and therefore of no effect. They could see no reason, they told Claiborne, why they should render up the Isle of Kent any more than the other lands held under their patents. As it was their duty to maintain the rights and privileges of the colony, his settlement must continue under the government and laws of Virginia.

Despite the defiant attitude of the Virginians, it is probable that Calvert would have permitted the Kent Islanders to remain unmolested, had not a report spread abroad that Claiborne was endeavoring to persuade the Indians to attack Saint Mary's. A joint commission of Virginians and Marylanders declared the charge false, but suspicion and ill will had been aroused, and a conflict could not be avoided. In April, 1635, Governor Calvert, alleging that Claiborne was indulging in illicit trade, fell upon and captured one of his merchantmen. In great indignation the islanders fitted out a vessel, the *Cockatrice,* to scour the Chesapeake and make reprisals. She was attacked, however, by two pinnaces from Saint Mary's and, after a severe conflict in which several men were killed, was forced to surrender. A few weeks later Claiborne gained revenge by defeating the Marylanders in a fight at the mouth of the Potomac.

In these encounters the Kent Islanders had the sympathy of the Virginia planters. Excitement ran high in the colony, and there was danger that an expedition might be sent to Saint Mary's to overpower the intruders and banish them from the country. Resentment against Harvey, who still gave aid and encouragement to Maryland, became more bitter than ever. His espousal of the cause of the enemies of Virginia made the planters regard him as a traitor. In 1635 Samuel Matthews wrote to Sir John Wolstenholme, "The Inhabitants also understood with indignation that the Marylanders had taken Capt. Claibournes Pinnaces and men . . . which action of theirs Sir John Harvey upheld contrary to his Majesties express commands."[53] The Councillors held many "meetings and consultations" to devise plans for the overthrow of the new colony, and an active correspondence was carried on with Baltimore's enemies in England in the vain hope that the charter might yet be revoked.[54]

Matters were now moving rapidly to a crisis. Harvey's administration became more and more unpopular. Sir John Wolstenholme, who kept in close touch with the colony, declared that the Governor's misconduct in his government was notorious at Court and in the city of London.[55] When, in the spring of 1635, he was rudely thrust out of his office, the complaints against him were so numerous that it became necessary to convene the Assembly to consider them.[56]

To what extent Harvey usurped the powers of the General Assembly is not clear, but it seems very probable that he frequently made use of proclamations to enforce his will upon the people.[57] It was quite proper and necessary for the Governor, when the houses were not in session, to issue ordinances of a temporary character, but this was a power susceptible of great abuse. And for the Governor to repeal statutes by proclamation would be fatal to the liberties of the people. That Harvey was guilty of this usurpation seems probable from the fact that a law was enacted declaring it the duty of the people

[53] P. R. O., CO1-6-52.
[55] P. R. O., CO1-8-60.
[57] Bruce, Inst. Hist., Vol. II, p. 324.
[54] P. R. O., CO1-6-46.
[56] Hen., Vol. I, p. 223.

to disregard all proclamations that conflicted with any act of Assembly.[58]

Also there is reason to believe that Harvey found ways of imposing illegal taxes upon the people. John Burk, in his *History of Virginia,* declares unreservedly that it was Harvey's purpose "to feed his avarice and rapacity, by assessing, levying, and holding the public revenue, without check or responsibility".[59]

In 1634 an event occurred which aroused the anger of the people, widened the breach between the Governor and the Council, and made it evident to all that Harvey would not hesitate upon occasion to disregard property rights and to break the laws of the colony. A certain Captain Young came to Virginia upon a commission for the King. Wishing to build two shallops while in the colony and having need of a ship's carpenter, Young, with the consent of Harvey, seized a skilled servant of one of the planters. This arbitrary procedure was in direct defiance of a statute of Assembly of March, 1624, that declared that "the Governor shall not withdraw the inhabitants from their private labors to any service of his own upon any colour whatsoever".[60]

Upon hearing of the incident Captain Samuel Matthews and other members of the Council came to Harvey to demand an explanation. The Governor replied that the man had been taken because Young had need of him "to prosecute with speed the King's service", and "that his Majesty had given him authority to make use of any persons he found there".[61] This answer did not satisfy the Councillors. Matthews declared "that if things were done on this fashion it would breed ill bloude in Virginia", and in anger "turning his back, with his truncheon lashed off the heads of certain high weeds that were growing there".[62] Harvey, wishing to appease the Councillors, said, "Come gentlemen, let us goe to supper & for the night leave this discourse", but their resentment was too great to be smoothed over, and with one accord rejecting his invitation,

[58] Hen., Vol. I, p. 264.
[60] Hen., Vol. I, p. 124.
[62] P. R. O., COI-8.

[59] Burk, Vol. II, pp. 28, 29.
[61] P. R. O., COI-8.

"they departed from the Governour in a very irreverent manner".[63]

Harvey, in his letters to the English government tried to convey the impression that he was uniformly patient with the Council, and courteous in all the disputes that were constantly arising. That he was not always so self restrained is shown by the fact that on one occasion, he became embroiled with one of the Councillors, Captain Stevens, and knocked out some of his teeth with a cudgel.[64] Samuel Matthews wrote that he had heard the Governor "in open court revile all the Councell and tell them they were to give their attendance as assistants only to advise with him". The Governor attempted, he declared, to usurp the whole power of the courts, without regard to the rights of the Councillors, "whereby justice was now done but soe farr as suited with his will, to the great losse of many mens estates and a generall feare in all".[65]

In 1634 the King once more made a proposal to the colonists for the purchase of their tobacco, and demanded their assent through the General Assembly. The Burgesses, who dreaded all contracts, drew up an answer which was "in effect a deniall of his Majesties proposition", and, in order to give the paper the character of a petition, they all signed it. This answer the Governor detained, fearing, he said, that the King "would not take well the matter thereof, and that they should make it a popular business, by subscribing a multitude of hands thereto. as thinking thereby to give it countenance".[66] The Governor's arbitrary action aroused great anger throughout the colony. Matthews wrote Sir John Wolstenholme, "The Consideration of the wrong done by the Governor to the whole Colony in detayning the foresaid letters to his Majesty did exceedingly perplex them whereby they were made sensible of the condition of the present Government."[67]

The crisis had now come. During the winter of 1634-35 the Councillors and other leading citizens were holding secret meetings to discuss the conduct of the Governor. Soon Dr.

[63] P. R. O., CO1-8.
[65] P. R. O., CO1-8.
[67] P. R. O., CO1-8.

[64] P. R. O., CO1-8-63.
[66] P. R. O., CO1-8.

John Pott, whose private wrongs made him a leader in the popular discontent, was going from plantation to plantation, denouncing the Governor's conduct and inciting the people to resistance. Everywhere the angry planters gathered around him, and willingly subscribed to a petition for a redress of grievances. In April, 1635, Pott was holding one of these meetings in York, at the house of one William Warrens, when several friends of the Governor presented themselves for admission. "A servant meeting them told them they must not goe in . . . whereupon they desisted and bended themselves to hearken to the discourse among them." In the confusion of sounds that came out of the house they could distinguish many angry speeches against Harvey and cries against his unjust and arbitrary government. When Pott read his petition, and told the assemblage that it had the support of some of the Councillors, they all rushed forward to sign their names.

When Harvey heard of these proceedings he was greatly enraged. Summoning the Council to meet without delay, he issued warrants for Dr. Pott and several others that had aided in circulating the petition. "After a few days Potts was brought up prisoner, having before his apprehending bin in the lower parts of the Country there also mustering his names at a meeting called for that purpose."[68] He does not seem to have feared the angry threats of the Governor, for when put in irons and brought before the Council, he readily consented to surrender the offending petition. At the same time he asserted "that if he had offended he did appeal to the King, for he was sure of noe justice from Sir John Harvey". When some of the other prisoners, in their hearing before the Council, asked the cause of their arrest, the Governor told them they should be informed at the gallows.

Shortly after this the Council was summoned to deliberate on the fate of the accused. The Governor, fearing that he might not secure conviction from a jury, "declared it necessary that Marshall law should be executed upon" them. When the Councillors refused to consent to any other than a legal trial, Harvey flew into a furious passion. For a while he paced

[68] P. R. O., CO1-8-48.

back and forth in the room hardly able to contain himself. At length he sat down in his chair, and with a dark countenance commanded his colleagues to be seated. A long pause ensued, and then he announced that he had a question that they must answer each in his turn, without deliberation or consultation. "What," he enquired, "doe you think they deserve that have gone about to persuade the people from their obedience to his Majesties substitute?" "And I begin with you," he said, turning to Mr. Minifie. "I am but a young lawyer," Minifie replied, "and dare not uppon the suddain deliver my opinion." At this point Mr. Farrar began to complain of these strange proceedings, but Harvey commanded him to be silent. Captain Matthews also protested, and the other Councillors soon joined him in refusing to answer the Governor's question. "Then followed many bitter Languages from him till the sitting ended."

At the next meeting Harvey asked what the Council thought were the reasons that the petition had been circulated against him, and demanded to know whether they had any knowledge of the matter. Mr. Minifie replied that the chief grievance of the people was the detaining of the letter of the Assembly to the King. This answer seems to have aroused the Governor's fury, for, arising from his seat, and striking Mr. Minifie a resounding blow upon the shoulder, he cried, "Doe you say soe? I arrest you upon suspicion of treason to his Majesty." But Harvey found that he could not deal thus arbitrarily with the Councillors. Utie and Matthews rushed up and seizing him cried, "And we you upon suspicion of treason to his Majestie". Dr. Pott, who was present and had probably been waiting for this crisis, held up his hand as a signal to confederates without, "when straight about 40 musketiers . . . which before that time lay hid, came . . . running with their peeces presented" towards the house. "Stay here," commanded Pott, "until there be use of you."

In the meanwhile the Councillors crowded around Harvey. "Sir," said Matthews, "there is no harm intended you save only to acquaint you with the grievances of the Inhabitants and to that end I desire you to sit downe in your Chayre."

And there, with the enraged Governor seated before him, he poured out the recital of the people's wrongs. When he had finished there came an ominous pause. Finally Matthews spoke again. "Sir," he said, "the peoples fury is up against you and to appease it, is beyond our power, unless you please to goe for England, there to answer their complaints." But this Harvey refused to do. He had been made Governor of Virginia by the King, he said, and without his command he would not leave his charge.

But before many days the Governor changed his mind. He found himself deserted by all and entirely in the power of the Councillors. As sentinals were placed "in all wayes & passages so that noe man could travell or come from place to place", he could make no effort to raise troops. Dr. Pott and the other prisoners were set at liberty. A guard was placed around Harvey, ostensibly to protect him, but really with the purpose of restraining him. A letter came from Captain Purifee, a Councillor then in the "lower parts" of the colony, which spoke of designs of the people to bring Harvey to account for his many wrongs. In alarm the Governor consented to take the first ship for England. He endeavored, however, to name his successor, to induce Matthews, Pierce, and Minifie to go with him to England, and to secure a promise from the Council not to molest Maryland. But they would consent to none of these things.

In the meantime an Assembly had been called to consider the innumerable grievances against the Governor. When they met at Jamestown, Harvey sent them a letter, declaring the session illegal and ordering them to disperse to their homes. "Notwithstanding his threats . . . the assembly proceeded according to their former intentions." Harvey then dispatched a letter to the Council, ordering them to send him his royal commission and instructions, but these documents had been intrusted to the keeping of Mr. Minifie with directions not to surrender them. The Council then turned themselves to the task of selecting a successor to Harvey. Their unanimous vote was given to Captain Francis West, the senior member of the board and formerly Governor. Feeling that since the expulsion of Harvey had been primarily a movement to protect the rights of the people, the Burgesses should have some voice in the election of the new Governor, they appealed to the Assembly for the ratification of their choice. West was popular in the colony, and "the people's suffrages" were cast for him as willingly as had been those of the Council. The Assembly then drew up resolutions setting forth the misconduct of Harvey and justifying their course in sending him back to England. These documents were entrusted to one Thomas Harwood, who was to deliver them to the King. Of what happened after Harvey's departure we have little record, but it is probable that the colonists revenged themselves upon the deposed Governor by confiscating all his ill gotten possessions.

It was decided that Dr. Pott should go to England to stand trial as his appeal to the King had taken the case beyond the jurisdiction of the Virginia courts. He and Harwood sailed upon the same vessel with Sir John. It is not hard to imagine with what dark looks or angry words Pott and Harvey greeted each other during their long voyage across the Atlantic. Doubtless Harwood and Pott held many a consultation upon what steps should be taken when they reached England to secure a favorable hearing for the colony, and to frustrate Harvey's plans for revenge. It was Harwood's intention to hasten to London, in order to forestall the Governor and "to make friends and the case good against him, before he could come".[69] But Sir John was too quick for him. Hardly had the ship touched the dock at Plymouth, than he was off to see the mayor of the city. This officer, upon hearing of the "late mutiny and rebellion" in Virginia, put Pott under arrest, "as a principal author and agent thereof", and seized all the papers and letters that had been entrusted to Harwood. Having thus gotten his hands upon the important documents, Harvey proceeded to London to complain of the indignities shown him and to ask for the punishment of his enemies.

When Charles I learned that the Virginians had deposed his Governor and sent him back to England, he was surprised

[69] P. R. O., CO1-8-61.

and angered. It was, he said, an assumption of regal power to oust thus unceremoniously one of his officers, and he was resolved to send Harvey back, if for one day only. And should the Governor acquit himself of the charges against him, he was to be inflicted upon the colony even longer than had at first been intended. The case came before the Privy Council in December 1635.[70] In the charges that were made against Harvey nothing was said of the illegal and arbitrary measures that had caused the people to depose him. All reference was omitted to the detaining of the Assembly's letter, to the support given Maryland, to the abuse of the courts, to illegal taxes and proclamations. Possibly the agents of the Virginians felt that such accusations as these would have no weight with the ministers of a monarch so little in sympathy with liberal government, so they trumped up other charges to sustain their cause. Despite the assertion of Harwood that Harvey "had so carryed himself in Virginia, that if ever hee retourned back thither hee would be pistolled or Shott", he was acquitted and restored to his office. West, Utie, Matthews, Minifie and Pierce, whom Harvey designated as the "chief actors in the munity", were ordered to come to England, there to answer before the Star Chamber the charge of treason.[71]

As the time approached for him to return to Virginia, Harvey began to show symptoms of nervousness. Feeling possibly that the threats of "pistolling" were not to be taken lightly, he requested the King to furnish him a royal vessel in which to make the journey. The appearance of one of the King's own ships in the James, he thought, would "much abate the bouldness of the offenders". This request was granted, and, after some months of delay, Harvey set forth proudly in the *Black George*. But Charles had not cared to send a really serviceable vessel to Virginia, and for a while it seemed that the *Black George* would relieve the colonists of their troubles by taking Sir John to the bottom. The vessel, it would appear, sprank a leak before it had been many hours at sea, and was forced to return to port. The Governor then decided that a merchant vessel would suffice for his purposes, and set sail again, upon a ship of the Isle of Wight.

He reached Point Comfort in January, 1637. Not wishing to wait until his ship reached Jamestown before asserting his authority, he landed at once and established a temporary capital at Elizabeth City. He had received instructions to remove from the Council all the members that had taken part in the "thrusting out", and he brought with him commissions for several new members. Orders were issued immediately for this reconstructed Council to convene in the church at Elizabeth City. There, after the oath had been administered, he published a proclamation of pardon to all persons implicated in the "mutiny", from which, however, West, Matthews, and the other leaders were excluded. The Governor then proceeded to displace all officials whom he considered hostile to his administration. "Before I removed from Elizabeth City," he wrote, "I appointed Commissioners and sheriffs for the lower counties, and for the plantation of Accomack, on the other side of the Bay."

The "thrusting out" did not cause Harvey to become more prudent in the administration of the government. His restoration, which Charles had meant as a vindication of the royal authority, the Governor seems to have interpreted as a license for greater tyranny. If the accusations of his enemies may be credited, he went to the greatest extremes in oppressing the people and in defying their laws. With the Council now completely under his control, he was master of the courts, and inflicted many great wrongs by means of "arbitrary and illegal proceedings in judgment". Confiscations and other "most cruel oppressions", it was declared, were used to punish all that showed themselves hostile to his government. He and his officers did not scruple to impose many unjust fines, which they converted "to their own private use", nor to strike terror into the people with whippings and "cutting of ears".[72]

Nor did Sir John neglect to take revenge upon those old enemies that had so defied and humiliated him. West, Utie, Matthews and Pierce were sent at once to England, and their

[72] Report of Com. on Hist. Mans. 3.

goods, cattle and servants seized. Beyond doubt it was against Samuel Matthews that Harvey bore the most bitter animosity, and it was his estate that suffered most. The Governor had been heard to say that if one "stood, tother should fall, and if hee swomme, the other should sinke". Matthews was one of the wealthiest men of the colony, his property consisting largely of cattle, but Sir John now swore that he would not leave him "worth a cow taile". At the next session of the Quarter Court, suit was entered against Matthews by one John Woodall, for the recovery of certain cattle. The learned judges, upon investigation, found that in the year 1622 Matthews held two cows rightfully belonging to Woodall. It was their opinion that the increase of these cows "unto the year 1628 . . . might amount unto the number of fifteen". "Computing the increase of the said fifteen head from the year 1628 to the time of their inquiry, they did return the number of fiftye head to the said Woodall."[73]

When Matthews heard that his estate had been seized and "havoc made thereof", he entered complaint with the Privy Council and secured an order requiring Harvey to restore all to his agents in Virginia. But the Governor was most reluctant to give up his revenge upon his old enemy. For seven months he put off the agents and at last told them that he had received new orders from the Privy Council, expressing satisfaction with what had been done and bidding him proceed.[74] Thereupon Secretary Kemp and other friends of the Governor entered Matthews' house, broke open the doors of several chambers, ransacked all his trunks and chests, examined his papers, and carried away a part of his goods and eight of his servants.[75] Soon after, however, Harvey received positive commands from the Privy Council to make an immediate restoration of all that had been taken. In January, 1639, he wrote that he had obeyed their Lordships exactly, by calling a court and turning over to Matthews' agents many of his belongings.[76] But Harvey denied that he had ever appropriated the estate to his own use, and claimed that he had been

[73] P. R. O., CO1-10-14.   [74] P. R. O., CO1-9-121.
[75] P. R. O., CO1-9-121.   [76] P. R. O., CO1-10-6.

misrepresented by "the Cunning texture of Captain Mathews, his complaint".[77]

Among those that felt most keenly the Governor's resentment was a certain clergyman, Anthony Panton. This man had quarrelled with Harvey's best friend and chief advisor in the stormy days of the expulsion, Secretary Matthew Kemp. Panton had incurred Kemp's undying resentment by calling him a "jackanapes", "unfit for the place of secretary", and declaring that "his hair-lock was tied up with ribbon as old as St. Paul's".[78] The belligerent parson was now brought to trial, charged with "mutinous speeches and disobedience to Sir John Harvey", and with disrespect to the Archbishop of Canterbury. His judges pronounced him guilty and inflicted a sentence of extreme rigor. A fine of £500 was imposed, he was forced to make public submission in all the parishes of the colony, and was banished "with paynes of death if he returned, and authority to any man whatsoever to execute him."[79]

In the meanwhile the Governor's enemies in England had not been idle. Matthews, Utie, West and Pierce, upon landing in 1637, had secured their liberty under bail, and had joined with Dr. Pott in an attempt to undermine Harvey's influence at Court. Had Sir John sent witnesses to England at once to press the charges against them before the Star Chamber, while the matter was still fresh in the memory of the King, he might have brought about their conviction and checked their plots. But he neglected the case, and Charles probably forgot about it, so the whole matter was referred to the Lord Keeper and the Attorney-General where it seems to have rested.[80] The exiles had no difficulty in finding prominent men willing to join in an attack upon Harvey. Before many months had passed they had gained the active support of the "sub-committee" of the Privy Council to which Virginia affairs were usually referred.[81] Harvey afterwards complained that members of this committee were interested in a

[77] P. R. O., CO1-10-6.
[79] P. R. O., CO1-10-32.
[81] P. R. O., CO1-10-10.

[78] Fiske, Old Va., Vol. I, p. 295.
[80] P. R. O., CO1-10-73.

plan to establish a new Virginia Company and for that reason were anxious to bring discredit upon his government.[82]   It was not difficult to find cause enough for removing Sir John. Reports of his misconduct were brought to England by every vessel from the colony.   Numerous persons, if we may believe the Governor, were "imployed in all parts of London to be spyes", and to "invite the meanest of the planters newly come for England into Taverns", where they made them talkative with wine and invited them to state their grievances.[83]

The English merchants trading to Virginia also entered complaint before the Privy Council against Harvey's administration.   They sought relief from a duty of two pence per hogshead on all tobacco exported from the colony, from a fee of six pence a head on immigrants, and a requisition of powder and shot laid upon vessels entering the James.[84]   The Privy Council, always careful of the welfare of British trade, wrote the Governor and the Council, demanding an explanation of these duties and requiring an account of the powder and shot. Harvey replied at great length, justifying the duties and begging their Lordships not to credit "the malitious untruths of such who by all means do goe about and studie to traduce us".

But the Privy Council, not waiting to receive all of Harvey's defense, decided to remove him and to appoint in his place Sir Francis Wyatt.[85]   The new Governor was directed to retain the old Council and to confirm Kemp as Secretary.[86]   But he was authorized to restore to Matthews any part of his estate yet withheld from him, and to reopen in the Virginia courts the case against Anthony Panton.[87]   The day of reckoning had now arrived.   When Wyatt reached Virginia, he lost no time in bringing Harvey to account for his misdeeds.   He was arraigned before the courts, where he was forced to answer countless complaints of injustice and oppression, and to restore to their owners his ill gotten gains.   Kemp wrote, in March, 1640, that Sir John was being persecuted with great rigor, that most of his estate had been confiscated, and at the

[82] P. R. O., CO1-10-10.   [83] P. R. O., CO1-10-15.
[84] P. R. O., CO1-10-5.   [85] P. R. O., CO1-10-3.
[86] P. R. O., CO1-10-43.   [87] P. R. O., CO1-10-26, 32.

next court would assuredly be swept away.[88] A few weeks later Harvey wrote to Secretary Windebank, to relate his misfortunes. "I am so narrowly watched," he complained, "that I have scarce time of priviledge for these few lines, which doe humbly crave of you to acquaint his Majesty how much I groan under the oppressions of my prevayling enemies, by whom the King's honor hath soe much suffered and who are now advanced to be my judges, and have soe farr already proceeded against me as to teare from me my estate by an unusuall way of inviting my creditors to clamour." He wished to return to England, there to repair his fortunes and seek revenge upon his enemies, but for some time he was detained in Virginia. The new Governor thought best to keep him in the colony where it would be difficult for him to plot against the administration. Harvey wrote, "I am denied my passage for England notwithstanding my many infirmities and weaknesses of body doe crave advice and help beyond the skill and judgment which this place can give."[89]

"Sir John being . . . layed flatt," the Governor next turned his attention to Kemp.[90] Sir Francis, who had strong reasons for hating the Secretary, summoned him into court to explain his offenses against Anthony Panton. Realizing that he had little hope of clearing himself, Kemp sought to leave for England, but his enemies restrained him. "I am extremely injured," he wrote in April, 1640, "and shall suffer without guilt, unless my friends now assist me, . . . the Governor and Council here . . . aim at my ruin."[91]

But Wyatt feared to retain Harvey and Kemp permanently in Virginia. Both had powerful friends who might take the matter before the King or the Privy Council. So, in the end, both made their way to England, taking with them the charter and many important letters and records.[92] It was now their turn to plot and intrigue to overthrow the party in power.[93] And so quickly did their efforts meet success that before Wyatt had been in office two years he was recalled and Sir William Berkeley made Governor in his place.

[88] P. R. O., COI-10-61.
[90] P. R. O., COI-10-64. I.
[92] Report of Com. on Hist. Man., 3.
[89] P. R. O., COI-10-67.
[91] P. R. O., COI-10-64.
[93] Report of Com. on Hist. Man., 3.

CHAPTER IV

Governor Berkeley and the Commonwealth

Sir William Berkeley, who succeeded Governor Wyatt in 1642, is one of the striking figures of American colonial history. Impulsive, brave, dogmatic, unrelenting, his every action is full of interest. He early displayed a passionate devotion to the house of Stuart, which remained unshaken amid the overthrow of the monarchy and the triumph of its enemies. When the British Commons had brought the unhappy King to the block, Berkeley denounced them as lawless tyrants and pledged his allegiance to Charles II. And when the Commonwealth sent ships and men to subdue the stubborn Governor, they found him ready, with his raw colonial militia, to fight for the prince that England had repudiated. Throughout his life his chief wish was to win the approbation of the King, his greatest dread to incur his censure.

Berkeley did not know fear. When, in 1644, the savages came murdering through the colony, it was he that led the planters into the forests to seek revenge. In 1666, when a Dutch fleet sailed into the James and captured a number of English vessels, the Governor wished to sally out in person with a few merchantmen to punish their temerity.

He possessed many of the graces of the courtier, and seems to have charmed, when he so desired, those with whom he came in contact. His friends are most extravagant in his praises, and their letters refer to him as the model soldier, statesman and gentleman.

The overthrow of Sir Francis Wyatt was a severe blow to the enemies of the old Harvey faction. Anthony Panton entered a protest against the change of administration, claiming that it had been brought about by surreptitious means and that no just complaint could be made against Governor Wyatt.[1] At

---

[1] Report of Commission on Hist. Manuscripts. 3.

his petition Berkeley was ordered to postpone his departure for Virginia until the matter could be investigated further. Upon signing an agreement, however, to protect the interests of Wyatt and his friends, he was allowed to sail and reached the colony in 1642.

The new Governor soon showed that he had no intention of persecuting Harvey's enemies, or of continuing the bitter quarrels of the preceding administrations. In his first Council we find Samuel Matthews, William Pierce and George Minifie, all of whom had been implicated in the "thrusting out".[2] Whether proceeding under directions from the English government, or actuated by a desire to rule legally and justly, he conferred a priceless blessing upon the colony by refusing to use the judiciary for political persecution. So far as we can tell there was no case, during his first administration, in which the courts were prostituted to personal or party ends. Thomas Ludwell afterwards declared that it was a convincing evidence of Berkeley's prudence and justice that after the surrender to the Commonwealth, when his enemies might easily have hounded him to his ruin, "there was not one man that either publickly or privately charged him with injustice".[3] In March, 1643, he affixed his signature to a law allowing appeals from the Quarter Courts to the Assembly. This right, which seems not to have been acknowledged by Sir John Harvey, was of the very highest importance. It gave to the middle class a share in the administration of justice and afforded an effectual check upon the abuse of the courts by the Governor and Council.

Berkeley greatly endeared himself to the poor planters by securing the abolition of a poll tax that contributed to the payment of his own salary.[4] "This," the Assembly declared, "is a benefit descending unto us and our posterity which we acknowledge contributed to us by our present Governor."[5] Berkeley also made an earnest effort to relieve the burden of the poor by substituting for the levy upon tithables "assessments proportioning in some measure payments according

[2] Hen., Vol. I, p. 235.
[3] P. R. O., CO1-20.
[4] Hen., Vol. I, pp. 236, 237.
[5] Hen., Vol. I, pp. 236, 237.

to mens abilities and estates"   But the colonial legislators soon found a just distribution of the taxes a matter of great difficulty, and we are told that the new measures, "through the strangeness thereof could not but require much time of controverting and debating".[6]   In 1648 the experiment was abandoned and the old oppressive tax upon tithables revived.[7]

During the first administration of Berkeley numerous other measures were adopted tending to augment the liberty and prosperity of the people.   In 1643 a law was passed prohibiting the Governor and Council from imposing taxes without the consent of the Assembly.[8]   At the same session Berkeley assented to a statute exempting the Burgesses from arrest during sessions of Assembly and for ten days after dissolution.[9]   The fees of the Secretary of State were limited and fixed in order to prevent excessive and unjust charges by that officer.[10]

That the colonists were not insensible of the Governor's liberal conduct is shown by their generosity to him on more than one occasion.   In 1642 they presented him with an "orchard with two houses belonging to the collony . . . as a free and voluntary gift in consideration of many worthy favours manifested towards the collony".[11]   In 1643, when the war in England caused the suspension of Berkeley's pensions and allowances from the King, the Assembly voted a tax of two shillings per poll on all tithable persons as a temporary relief.[12]

When Sir William assumed the government in 1642 he was conscious that an effort was being made in England to restore the old London Company of Virginia, and it became his first care to thwart this design.   In 1639 George Sandys had been sent to England as the agent of the Assembly and had presented a petition in the name of the Virginia planters, to the House of Commons, for the restoration of the old corporation.[13]   The Assembly of April, 1642, called together by Berkeley, repudiated entirely the action of their agent, declaring

[6] Hen., Vol. I, p. 237.   [7] Hen., Vol. I, p. 356.
[8] Hen., Vol. I, p. 244.   [9] Hen., Vol. I, p. 263.
[10] Hen., Vol. I, p. 265.   [11] Hen., Vol. I, p. 267.
[12] Hen., Vol. I, pp. 280, 281.   [13] Hen., Vol. I, p. 230.

that he had misunderstood his instructions.   The renewal of
the Company, they said, was never "desired, sought after or
endeavoured to be sought for either directly or indirectly by
the consent of any Grand Assembly or the common consent of
the people".   They drew up a petition to the King, expressing
their desire to remain under his immediate care and protection,
citing the many blessings of the present order of government,
and drawing the most melancholy picture of their sufferings
before the revocation of the charter.   "The present happiness,"
they said, "is exemplified to us by the freedom of yearly assemblies warranted unto us by his majesties gratious instructions, and the legal trial per juries in all criminal and civil
causes where it shall be demanded."[14]

This declaration of loyalty and contentment, reaching
Charles at a time when so many of his subjects were rising in
rebellion against his authority, was most pleasing to the unfortunate monarch.   "Your acknowledgement," he replied
to the Governor and the Assembly, "of our grace, bounty, and
favour, towards you, and your so earnest desire to continue
under our immediate protection, is very acceptable to us."
"And," he continued, "as we had not before the least intention
to consent to the introduction of any company over that our
Colony, we are by it much confirmed in our resolution, as
thinking it unfit to change a form of government wherein
our   subjects   there . . . receive   much   contentment   and
satisfaction.[15]

In the early years of Berkeley's administration the colony
experienced another horrible Indian massacre.   As in 1622
the blow came without warning.   The cruel and barbarous war
that followed the first massacre had long since come to an end
and for many years there had been peace between the two
races.   It is true that the friendly relations that resulted from
the marriage of Rolfe and Pocahontas had not been restored,
that the Indians were not allowed to frequent the English
settlements, that no weapons were sold them, but the peace
was fairly well observed and there was no reason to suspect
the savages of treachery.

[14] Hen., Vol. I, p. 231.   [15] Va. Hist. Reg., Vol. I, p. 160.

The plot originated in the brain of Opechancanough. This remarkable savage was long supposed to have been the brother of Powhatan, but newly discovered evidence tends to show that this was not the case. It is known that he belonged to a foreign tribe that came from the far southwest. Having, it is supposed, been defeated in a battle with the Spaniards, he had led his people to Virginia and united them with the tribes under the command of Powhatan. This tremendous march must have consumed many months, and have been beset with countless dangers, but Opechancanough overcame them, and "conquered all along from Mexico" to Virginia.[16] He was now an extremely aged man. Being unable to walk he was carried from place to place upon a litter. His eyelids were so heavy that he could not of his own volition move them, and attendants stood always ready to raise them whenever it became necessary for him to see.[17] But his mind was clear, his force of will unshaken, and the Indians paid him the reverent obedience that his able leadership demanded.

Opechancanough planned the massacre for April 18th, 1644, and it was carried out upon that date with the utmost ferocity.[18] The slaughter was even greater than in 1622, and no less than five hundred Christians are said to have been destroyed.[19] But this calamity fell almost entirely upon the frontier counties at the heads of the great rivers, and upon the plantations on the south side of the James. The savages could not penetrate to the older and more populous communities of the lower peninsula. For this reason the disaster, horrible as it was, did not overwhelm the entire colony and threaten its destruction as had the massacre of 1622.

Another deadly war with the savages ensued immediately. Sir William Berkeley several times placed himself at the head

---

[16] P. R. O., CO5-1371-6 to 16.   [17] Beverley.

[18] The Assembly, in 1645, ordered that the 18th of April be celebrated ever afterwards for the deliverance of the colony from the savages. Hen., Vol. I, p. 290. The year is fairly well determined by the fact that mention of an Indian war occurs for the first time, during this period, in the statutes of the session of Assembly of October, 1644. Hen., Vol. I, p. 285.

[19] Beverley.

of large expeditions and carried fire and destruction to many Indian villages.[20]   As in the former war, the naked and poorly armed natives could not withstand the English, and, deserting their homes, they usually fled into the woods at their approach. And again the white men brought famine upon them by going out each year in the months of July and August to cut down their growing maize.[21]   In order to protect the isolated frontier plantations the Governor ordered the people to draw together in fortified camps, strong enough to resist the assaults of a large body of the savages.[22]   "He strengthened the weak Families," it was said, "by joining two or three . . . together and Palizaded the houses about."[23]

Despite these wise measures the savages would probably have continued the war many years had not Opechancanough fallen into the hands of the English. The old king was surprised by Sir William Berkeley, and, because of his decrepitude, was easily captured.[24] He was taken in triumph to Jamestown, where the Governor intended to keep him until he could be sent to England and brought before Charles I. But a few days after the capture, a common soldier, in revenge for the harm done the colony by Opechancanough, shot the aged and helpless prisoner in the back.[25]

Soon after this event the Indians sued for peace. Discouraged and starving, they promised to become the friends and allies of the whites forever, if they would cease their hostility and grant them their protection. A treaty was drawn up and ratified by the Assembly and by the new Indian king Necotowance.[26] It provided that the savages should acknowledge the King of England as their sovereign and overlord; that Necotowance and his successors should pay as tribute "the number of twenty beaver skins at the goeing of the Geese yearly"; that all the land between the York and the James from the falls of both rivers to Kecoughtan should be ceded to the English; that all white prisoners and escaped negroes should be returned. In compensation the English agreed to protect

[20] P. R. O., CO1-30-71; CO1-41-111.   [21] P. R. O., CO5-1371-6 to 16.
[22] CO5-1371-6 to 16.   [23] CO5-1371-6 to 16.
[24] P. R. O., CO1-41-111.   [25] Beverley.
[26] Hen., Vol. I, p. 323.

the savages from the attacks of their enemies and to resign to them as their hunting ground the territory north of the York River.[27] This peace, which was most beneficial to the colony, was not broken until 1676, when the incursions of the wild Susquehannocks involved the native Virginia tribes in a new conflict with the white men.[28]

During the civil war that was at this time convulsing England most of the influential Virginia planters adhered to the party of the King. They were, with rare exceptions, members of the established church, and could have little sympathy with a movement that was identified with dissenters. If the triumph of Parliament was to bring about the disestablishment of the Church, or even the toleration of Presbyterians and Independents, they could not give them their support. Moreover, loyalty to the House of Stuart was strong in Virginia. The very remoteness of the planters from the King increased their reverence and love. They could not be present at court to see the monarch in all his human weakness, so there was nothing to check their loyal imaginations from depicting him as the embodiment of princely perfection. Nor had the wealthy families of the colony aught to anticipate of economic or political gain in the triumph of Parliament. Possessed of large estates, monopolizing the chief governmental offices, wielding a great influence over the Assembly and the courts, and looking forward to a future of prosperity and power, they could not risk their all upon the uncertain waters of revolution. Some, no doubt, sympathized with the efforts that were being made in England to limit the King's power of taxing the people, for the colony had always contained its quota of liberals, but the dictates of self-interest must have lulled them into quiescence. And the Governor, in this hour of need, proved a veritable rock of loyalty for the King. None that showed leanings towards the cause of Parliament could expect favors of any kind from Sir William Berkeley. Moreover, if they spoke too loudly of the rights of the people and of the tyranny of monarchs, they might find themselves under arrest and charged with treason.

[27]Hen., Vol. I, p. 323.   [28] P. R. O., CO1-30-71.

But there was another faction in Virginia, composed largely of small planters and freedmen, which sympathized with the aims of their fellow commons of the mother country. Prominent among these must have been a small number of Virginia Puritans, who had for some years been subjected to mild persecution. The overwhelming sentiment of the colony had long been for strict uniformity in the Church "as neere as may be to the canons in England", and several statutes had been passed by the Assembly to suppress the Quakers and Puritans.[29] In 1642, Richard Bennett and others of strong Calvinistic leanings, sent letters to Boston requesting that Puritan ministers be sent to Virginia, to minister to their non-conformist congregations.[30] The New Englanders responded readily, despatching to their southern friends three ministers of distinction—William Thompson, John Knowles and Thomas James. Despite the laws against non-conformity these men anticipated little interference with their work and even brought letters of introduction from Governor Winthrop to Sir William Berkeley.[31] Little did they know the temper of the new Virginia Governor. So far from welcoming this Puritan invasion Berkeley determined to meet it with measures of stern repression. A bill was put through the Assembly requiring all ministers within the colony to conform to the "orders and constitutions of the church of England", both in public and in private worship, and directing the Governor and Council to expel all dissenters from the country.[32] Disheartened at this unfriendly reception, James and Knowles soon returned to New England, leaving Thompson to carry on the work. This minister, in defiance of the law, lingered long in Virginia, preaching often and making many converts.

Among those that embraced the Calvinistic tenets at this time was Thomas Harrison, formerly Berkeley's chaplain. Harrison seems to have regarded the massacre of 1644 as a judgment of God upon the colonists for their persecution of the Puritans. His desertion of the established Church aroused both the anger and the alarm of the Governor and in 1648 he

[29] Hen., Vol. I, p. 123, 149, 277.   [30] Bruce, Inst. Hist., Vol. I, p. 254.
[31] Bruce, Inst. Hist., Vol. I, p. 254.   [32] Hen., Vol. I, p. 277.

was expelled from his parish for refusing to use the Book of Common Prayer. Later he left the colony for New England.

This persecution, although not severe enough to stamp out dissent in Virginia, could but arouse among the Puritans a profound dissatisfaction with the existing government, and a desire to coöperate with their brethren of England in the great contest with the King. Although not strong enough to raise the Parliamentary standard in the colony and to seek religious freedom at the sword's point, the Puritans formed a strong nucleus for a party of opposition to the King and his Governor.

Moreover, in addition to the comparatively small class of Puritans, there must have been in the colony hundreds of men, loyal to the established church, who yet desired a more liberal government both in England and in Virginia. A strong middle class was developing which must have looked with sympathy upon the cause of the English Commons and with jealousy upon the power of the Virginia Governor and his Council. There is positive evidence that many poor men had been coming to Virginia from very early times, paying their own passage and establishing themselves as peasant proprietors. Wills still preserved show the existence at this period of many little farms of five or six hundred acres, scattered among the great plantations of the wealthy. They were tilled, not by servants or by slaves, but by the freemen that owned them. Depending for food upon their own cattle, hogs, corn, fruit and vegetables, and for the other necessities of life upon their little tobacco crops, the poor farmers of Virginia were developing into intelligent and useful citizens. They constituted the backbone of a distinct and powerful middle class, which even at this early period, had to be reckoned with by aristocracy and Governor and King.

This section of the population was constantly being recruited from the ranks of the indentured servants. The plantations of the rich were tilled chiefly by bonded laborers, brought from the mother country. So long as land was plentiful in Virginia the chief need of the wealthy was for labor. Wage earners could not supply this need, for the poor man would not till the fields of others when he could have land of his own almost for the asking.   So the planters surmounted this difficulty by bringing workmen to the colony under indenture, to work upon their farms for a certain number of years.   Many a poor Englishman, finding the struggle for existence too severe at home, thus surrendered for a while his liberty, that in the end he might acquire a share in the good things of the New World. After serving his master five or six years the servant usually was given his liberty and with it fifty acres of land and a few farm implements.   Thus equipped, he could, with industry and frugality, acquire property and render himself a useful citizen in his adopted country.   There can be no doubt that many hundreds of former servants, become prosperous, did unite with the free immigrants of humble means to form a vigorous middle class.

Nothing could be more natural than that the small farmers should regard Parliament as the champion of the poor Englishman at home and in the colony.   They knew full well that if Charles should triumph over the Commons, his victory would mean greater power for their Governor, greater privilege for the wealthy planters.   On the other hand, the King's defeat might bring increased influence to the middle class and to the Burgesses.

It is not possible to determine how numerous was the Parliamentary party in Virginia, but the faction was powerful enough to cause serious apprehension to the loyalists.   So bitter was the feeling that fears of assassination were entertained for Sir William Berkeley, and a guard of ten men was granted him.   We are "sensible", declared the Assembly, in 1648, "of the many disaffections to the government from a schismaticall party, of whose intentions our native country of England hath had and yet hath too sad experience".[33]

But the commons of Virginia were not prepared to raise the standard of revolt.   They must have lacked organization and leaders.   Most of the aristocracy and wealth of Virginia was arrayed against them, while the government was in the hands of a man noted for his passionate attachment to the Throne.

[33] Hen., Vol. I, p. 355.

The Parliamentary party must have felt it best to await the event of the struggle in England, pinning their hopes upon the success of their comrades there.   But even after Parliament had won the victory, after the King had been executed, they were not strong enough to overthrow Berkeley's government and force Virginia into obedience to the Commonwealth.

The news of the death of Charles I filled the royalists of Virginia with grief and anger.   It seemed to them that the cause of law and order and religion in the unhappy kingdom had fallen with their monarch.   Moreover, they could but expect the victorious party, after settling all at home, to extend their arms to the little colony and force upon them a reluctant obedience to the new government.   But the intrepid Berkeley was determined never to submit until compelled to do so by force of arms.   Charles II was proclaimed King.   The Assembly was called together and a law enacted declaring it high treason to question, even by insinuation, the "undoubted & inherent right of his Majesty . . . to the Collony of Virginia, and all other his majesties dominions".[34]   The Assembly referred to Charles I in terms of reverence and affection, as their late blessed and sainted King, and, unmindful of consequences, denounced his executioners as lawless tyrants.   For any person to cast dishonor or censure upon the fallen monarch, or to uphold in any way the proceedings against him, or to assert the legality of his dethronement, was declared by the Assembly high treason.   "And it is also enacted," they continued, "that what person soever, by false reports and malicious rumors shall spread abroad, among the people, any thing tending to change of government, . . . such persons, not only the authors of . . . but the reporters and divulgers thereof, shall be adjudged guilty."[35]

Even before the news of these events reached England, Sir William had aroused the anger of Parliament by his persecution of the Puritans.   Some of the people of Nansemond county had written, complaining of the banishment of Mr. Harrison, whom they described as an able minister and a man of splendid character.   The English Council wrote Berkeley

[34] Hen., Vol. I, p. 360.   [35] Hen., Vol. I, p. 361.

commanding him to restore Mr. Harrison to his parish. "Wee know," they said, "you cannot be ignorant that the use of the common prayer book is prohibited by the parliament of England."[36] And when they learned that the colony had refused to acknowledge the Commonwealth, and still adhered to the House of Stuart, they were determined to punish the Virginians for their temerity. Since it would be exceedingly inconvenient at this time of uncertainty and change to send an expedition across the Atlantic, it was decided to bring the colonists to their senses by cutting off their foreign trade. An act was passed by Parliament in October, 1650, declaring that since the colony had been settled by the English at great cost to the nation, it should rightly be under the authority of the present government; that divers persons in Virginia had committed open treason, "traytorously by force and Subtilty" usurping the government and defying the Commonwealth; and in order to repress speedily the rebellious colonists and to inflict upon them a merited punishment, they were to be forbidden all "Commerce or Traffique with any people Whatsoever". The full force of the English navy was to be used in carrying out this act, and all commanders were directed to seize and bring in foreign vessels found trading with the colony. No English ships were to sail for Virginia without special license from the Council of State.[37]

This was a dire threat indeed. To cut off all commerce with England and foreign countries would bring utter ruin upon the planters, for their tobacco crop would then be without a market. Even now, however, the Governor did not falter in his loyalty. He felt, no doubt, that Parliament would have difficulty in enforcing this act, and he looked to the Dutch merchantmen to take off the tobacco.

Before an Assembly called together in March, 1651, Berkeley delivered an address ringing with defiance of Parliament. "Gentlemen," he said, "you perceave by the Declaration that the men of Westminster have set out, . . . how they meane to deale with you hereafter. . . . Indeed me thinks they might have proposed something to us which might have strengthened

---

[36] Sp. Dom. Inter., 1-94.   [37] Scobell, Vol. II, p. 132.

us to beare those heavy chaines they are making ready for us, though it were but an assurance that we shall eat the bread for which our owne Oxen plow, and with our owne sweat we reape; but this assurance (it seems) were a franchise beyond the Condition they have resolv'd on the Question we ought to be in: For the reason why they talk so Magisterially to us is this, we are forsooth their worships slaves, bought with their money and by consequence ought not to buy, or sell but with those they shall Authorize with a few trifles to Coszen us of all for which we toile and labour. . . . The strength of their argument runs onely thus: we have laid violent hands on your Land-lord, possessed his Manner house where you used to pay your rents, therefore now tender your respects to the same house you once reverenced. . . . They talke indeed of money laid out in this country in its infancy. I will not say how little, nor how Centuply repaid, but will onely aske, was it theirs? They who in the beginning of this warr were so poore, & indigent, that the wealth and rapines of three Kingdomes & their Churches too cannot yet make rich."

The Governor then began an impassioned appeal to the Assembly to remain firm in their loyalty to the Crown. "Surely Gentlemen," he cried, "we are more slaves by nature, than their power can make us if we suffer ourselves to be shaken with these paper bulletts, & those on my life are the heaviest they either can or will send us. . . . You have heard under what heavy burthens the afflicted English Nation now groans, and calls to heaven for relief: how new and formerly unheard of impositions make the wifes pray for barrenness and their husbands deafnes to exclude the cryes of their succourles, starving children. . . . Consider your selves how happy you are and have been, how the Gates of wealth and Honour are shut to no man, and that there is not here an Arbitrary hand that dares to touch the substance of either poore or rich: But that which I woud have you chiefly consider with thankfullnes is: That God hath separated you from the guilt of the crying bloud of our Pious Souveraigne of ever blessed memory: But mistake not Gentlemen part of it will yet stain your garments if you willingly submit to those murtherers hands that shed it; I tremble to thinke how the oathes they will impose will make those guilty of it, that have long abhor'd the traiterousnesse of the act. . . . Gentlemen by the Grace of God we will not so tamely part with our King, and all these blessings we enjoy under him; and if they oppose us, do but follow me, I will either lead you to victory, or lose a life which I cannot more gloriously sacrifice then for my loyalty, and your security."[38]

When the Governor had completed his appeal the obnoxious act of Parliament was read aloud. The Assembly then passed a series of resolutions, reiterating their loyalty to the Crown, denouncing the Commons as usurpers and regicides, and defending themselves against the charge of treachery and rebellion. They had, they declared, adhered always to the "Lawes of England", which enjoined upon them the oaths of allegiance and supremacy, and they refused now, at the bidding of Parliament, to break their word by renouncing their King. They could not be expected to give passive obedience to every party that possessed themselves of Westminster Hall, where the heads of divers factions had followed each other in quick succession. They had been accused of usurping the government of the colony, but their records would show that they had never swerved from their allegiance. And it ill became the Parliament that had overthrown the English constitution to bring such accusations. Finally, they declared, "we are resolv'd to Continue our Allegeance to our most Gratious King, yea as long as his gratious favour permits us, we will peaceably trade with the Londoners, and all other nations in amity with our Soveraigne: Protect all forraigne Merchants with our utmost force in our Capes: Allwaies pray for the happy restoration of our King, and repentance in them, who to the hazard of their soules have opposed him."[39]

As Berkeley had foreseen, the English found it impossible to enforce a strict blockade. The government could not spare war vessels enough to close the Virginia capes, and foreign merchantmen continued to sail unmolested into the James and the York, bringing goods to the planters and taking off their tobacco. Indeed the Dutch took advantage of this quarrel

[38] Va. Mag., Vol. I., p. 77.   [39] Va. Mag., Vol. I, pp. 75 to 81.

between colony and mother country to extend their American trade at the expense of the English merchants. The Council of State was soon made to realize by the complaints that poured in from the London shippers, that the "Blockade Act" was injuring England more than the refractory colony.

At this moment, several leaders of the Virginia Parliamentary party came to the Council at Westminster and represented to it the necessity of fitting out an expedition to overthrow the Berkeley government. They could plead that the blockade had proved ineffective, that the honor of the Commonwealth demanded the prompt subjection of the impudent Governor, that the coöperation of the Virginia commons would make the task easy. Nor could they omit to remind the Councillors that it was their duty to bring relief to their fellow Puritans of Virginia.

At all events the Council, seeing the necessity of prompt action, sent forth a well armed expedition under the command of Captain Robert Denis to subdue both the Barbadoes and Virginia. But wishing to avoid, if possible, open hostilities, at the same time they sent commissioners to treat with the colonists and persuade them to submit peaceably to the Commonwealth. The Council of State evidently expected active assistance from the Parliamentary party in the colony in these efforts to establish the new political order, for they gave directions to the commissioners to raise troops in the plantations, to appoint captains and other officers, and to guarantee freedom to all servants that volunteered to fight with the Commonwealth forces. They were given power to grant pardon to all that submitted, making such exceptions as they thought proper, and were directed to establish a new government in accord with the present constitution of England.

When, in the spring of 1652, the British fleet sailed up the James river, Captain Denis found the intrepid Berkeley prepared for a strenuous resistance. With the guns of the warships approaching his capital, with English soldiers ready for a landing, with a strong party in the colony in sympathy with the invaders, he might well have despaired. Resistance would certainly entail enormous misfortunes upon the colony—

bloodshed, devastation, civil strife—and success could be but temporary. Should he beat off the present expedition, others too powerful to be resisted would undoubtedly follow, and the punishment of the colony would be but the more severe.

Yet the Governor did not falter. He called around him the full strength of the colonial militia, posted them to good advantage, and himself took active command. Several Dutch vessels that had been trading in the James were pressed into service, filled with men and moored in close to Jamestown, with their guns trained upon the approaching enemy. Behind them were several land batteries. The whole made an imposing appearance, and might well have given apprehension to the invaders.

Fortunately, however, the threatened conflict was averted by the persuasion of the Parliamentary commissioners. These men, anxious to avoid civil war, availed themselves of the authority given them by the Council of State, to offer very lenient terms of surrender. Some of them seem to have preceded the fleet to Virginia, to consult with their friends and to formulate plans to render the Governor's resistance ineffectual. It is not improbable that these efforts were seconded by some of the most prominent men of the colony. Two members of the Council itself, it is said, who possessed goods of great value upon vessels in the fleet, received warning that their property would be at once confiscated, if they gave their support to the Governor. They therefore were constrained to advocate submission. With division in the ranks of the colonists and with the invaders ready for action, even Berkeley was at last forced to give way and consent to a capitulation.

The terms of surrender were drawn up at Jamestown and agreed to by the commissioners on the one hand, and by the Governor, Council and Burgesses on the other. It was agreed first, that Virginia should acknowledge its due allegiance to the Commonwealth of England, and "to the lawes there established". This submission, it was declared, was "a voluntary act, not forced nor constrained by a conquest upon the country".[40] It was also stipulated "that the people of Virginia have

[40] Hen., Vol. I, p. 363.

free trade as the people of England do enjoy to all places and with all nations according to the lawes of that commonwealth". Even more interesting was the agreement "that Virginia shall be free from all taxes, customs and impositions whatsoever, and none to be imposed on them without consent of the Grand Assembly, and soe that neither fforts nor castles bee erected or garrisons maintained without their consent". When these terms of surrender were reported to the English government, Parliament thought that the commissioners had been too liberal in their concessions, and some of the articles were not ratified.

The commissioners granted full pardon and indemnity for all "acts, words or writeings done or spoken against the parliament" and any persons refusing to take the oath of allegiance to the new government were given "a yeares time . . . to remove themselves and their estates out of Virginia". The use of the Book of Common Prayer was permitted for one year in the parishes that so desired, and no ministers were deprived of their charges or their livings.[41]

Separate articles were drawn up between the commissioners and the Governor and Council. Neither Berkeley nor the Councillors were to be compelled, during the ensuing twelve months, to take the oath of allegiance. They were not to be censured for speaking well in private of the King. They were given leave to sell all their property and to quit the country without molestation. They were permitted to send a message to Charles II, giving an account of the surrender.[42]

The commissioners were now confronted with the all-important task of establishing a new government. They had been given power by the Council of State to hold an election of Burgesses granting the franchise to all who had taken the oath of allegiance. Feeling, doubtless, a reluctance to assume the entire responsibility of moulding a new constitution, they resolved to wait until the Burgesses assembled and to consult with them in all their measures. The election was held without delay, and the members were sworn in on April 26th, 1652.

The Burgesses and the commissioners then entered upon a long and serious debate concerning "the settling and govern-

[41] Hen., Vol. I, pp. 363-365.   [42] Hen., Vol. I, pp. 365-367.

ing of Virginia".[43]   The English Council had not, it would
seem, given specific directions in regard to this work, so the
members of the little constitutional convention were practically
at liberty to do what they chose.   Realizing, however, that all
might be changed if it proved unsatisfactory to Parliament,
they proceeded cautiously.   Their chief concern was to establish a tentative government that would prevent present confusion and could later be perfected by the Council of State.
It so happened, however, that the English, amid the confusion
of the times, neglected to attend to this matter, and the work of
the convention remained essentially unaltered throughout the
Commonwealth period.

The House of Burgesses, since it had been officially recognized by the Council of State, was made the chief governing
body of the colony.   Except for the veto of the English government its power was to be unlimited.   It was to elect the
Governor and to specify his duties.   If his administration
proved unsatisfactory it might remove him from office.   The
Burgesses were also to elect the Council, to prescribe its
functions and limit its power.   This proud body, which had
formerly been so powerful, was now to exist only on the suffrage of the House.   It was even debated whether Councillors
should be admitted to membership in the General Assembly.
The appointment of all officials was also to "appertain to the
Burgesses, the representatives of the people", but it was agreed
that for the present most of the first nominations should be
left to the Governor and the commissioners.[44]

Thus did Virginia become in all but name a republic.   In
England, the long cherished hope of the patriots for liberty
was to be disappointed by the usurpation of Oliver Cromwell,
and the victory of Parliament over the stubborn Charles was
to result only in the substitution of one despot for another.
But the commons of Virginia, although they had played an
insignificant role in the great drama of the times, were to reap
the reward which was denied their cousins of England.   Their
government for the next eight years was to be truly representative of the people.   Nor did the English government often

[43] Hen., Vol. I, p. 371.   [44] Hen., Vol. I, pp. 371, 373.

interfere with their affairs. Busy with his numerous wars and with the cares of administration, the Protector never found time to acquaint himself thoroughly with what was happening in Virginia. In 1653, and again in 1658, Cromwell promised to make some definite regulations for the government of the colony, but he was interrupted on each occasion before he could put his resolutions into effect. That it was his intention, however, to keep the appointment of the Governor in his own hands seems certain. In 1654 the Assembly received word that his Highness had decided then to continue Colonel Bennett, of whose good character he had heard, in the execution of his office, until he could further signify his pleasure. In 1657, the Council of State requested Cromwell to appoint some person to go to Virginia as its Governor, but this he failed to do.[45] With the exception of such spasmodic interruptions as these, and the partial enforcement of the Navigation Acts, the colony was left almost to its own devices throughout the Commonwealth period.

By the unanimous vote of the commissioners and the Burgesses Mr. Richard Bennett was made Governor. This choice must have been satisfactory both to the English government and the Parliamentary party in the colony. Mr. Bennett had been one of the few prominent Virginia Puritans and had left the colony during the persecution of dissenters by Sir William Berkeley. As a member of the commission he had been instrumental in bringing about the surrender and saving the colony from civil war. It was agreed that he should serve for one year, "or untill the next meeting of the Assembly", but as his administration proved most satisfactory he was continued in office by Cromwell until March 31st, 1655.[46]

The new government, however, was not to be established entirely without disorder and strife. In the interval between the surrender and the assembling of the Burgesses affairs on the Eastern Shore assumed a threatening aspect. The people of Northampton, many of whom seem formerly to have been favorable to the Commonwealth, became ill affected to the new

[45] Sp. Dom. Int., 1-75; Hen., Vol. I, p. 510; Bruce, Inst. Hist., Vol. II, p. 302.
[46] Hen., Vol. I, pp. 371, 408.

régime, even before it was well begun.   A number of things
conspired to bring about this change.   Among the inhabitants
of Northampton were a number of Dutch who had settled there
during the preceding decade.   When war broke out between
Holland and England in 1652 it was rumored that these people
were conspiring with the Indians to bring about another
massacre in Virginia.   Groundless as these suspicions were,
they infuriated the English and caused grave fears for the
safety of the Dutch planters.   When the justices of the peace
took precautions to protect the unfortunate foreigners their
action caused discontent and bitterness against the new government.   Moreover, the Navigation Acts, recently passed by
Parliament, restricting foreign trade would, if enforced, prove
especially damaging to the people of the Eastern Shore.   Finally, Northampton had not been represented in the Assembly
since 1647, except for one Burgess in 1651, and the belief
had sprung up that the county was to become independent of
the government at Jamestown.   For various reasons, therefore,
Northampton was hostile to the government.   And when the
Parliamentary commissioners imposed upon them a tax of
forty-six pounds of tobacco per poll, the people of the county
voiced their anger in no uncertain terms, and selected a committee of six to draw up a statement of their grievances and
present it to the new Assembly.

"Wee," they protested, "the Inhabitants of Northampton
Countie doe complanye that from tyme to tyme wee have been
submitted & bine obedient unto the paymt of publeq taxacons.
Butt after ye yeare 1647, since yt tyme wee Conceive & have
found that ye taxes were very weightie.   But in a more es-
petiall manner . . . the taxacon of fforty sixe pounds of
tobacco p. poll (this present yeare).   And desire yt ye same bee
taken off ye charge of ye Countie; furthermore wee alledge
that after 1647, wee did understand & suppose or Countie or
Northampton to be disioynted & sequestered from ye rest of
Virginia.   Therefore that Llawe wch requireth & inioyneth
Taxacons from us to bee Arbitrarye & illegall; fforasmuch
as wee had neither summons for Ellecon of Burgesses nor
voyce in their Assemblye (during the time aforesd) but only

the Singular Burgess in September, Ano., 1651. Wee conceive that wee may Lawfullie ptest agt the pceedings in the Act of Assemblie for publiq Taxacons wch have relacon to Northmton Countie since ye year 1647."[47]

Thus early in the history of the colony was enunciated the principle that taxation without representation is unjust and illegal. The men of Northampton do not speak of the doctrine as something new, but as a thing understood and recognized. Certain it is that the people of Virginia, in all periods of their colonial history, realized the vast importance of confining the power of taxation to their own Assembly.

But the leaders of the new government did not receive the petition with favor. They were willing to give Northampton her due quota of Burgesses, but they were angered at the suggestion of separation. Moreover, the disorders on the Eastern Shore became more pronounced and the justices were compelled to seek aid from the Council in protecting the Dutch. In June, 1653, the turbulent people met and, amid scenes of disorder, denounced the action of the authorities. When a voice from the crowd cried out that the justices were a "company of asses and villyanes", the people roared out their approval. The Assembly, at its meeting in June, 1653, was forced to take active steps to suppress the agitation and to restore order upon the peninsula. Mr. Bennett with several members of the Assembly, was sent to Northampton, "for the settlement of the peace of that countie, and punishinge delinquents". In this he seems to have been entirely successful, for we hear no more of disorders upon the Eastern Shore during this period.[48]

When the commissioners and the Burgesses, in 1652, established anew the gubernatorial office, they were somewhat vague in defining the duties belonging to it. They first declared that Mr. Bennett was to exercise "all the just powers and authorities that may belong to that place lawfully".[49] But that it was not their intention to give the new officer the prerogatives enjoyed by the royal Governor is shown by their further statement that he was to have such power only as should

[47] Wise, p. 139.   [49] Hen., Vol. I, p. 371.
[48] Wise, pp. 114, 115; Hen., Vol. I, p. 380.

be granted him from time to time by the Assembly.[50]   This
lack of clearness led, quite naturally, to several clashes between
the legislative and executive branches of the government.

At the session of Assembly of July, 1653, the Burgesses
showed that they would brook no interference from the Governor with their affairs.   On the eve of the election of the
Speaker, they received a message from Mr. Bennett and the
Council advising them not to choose a certain Lieutenant-
Colonel Chiles.   Although it was clearly shown that this gentleman could not serve with propriety, the Burgesses gave
him the election, merely, it would seem, as a rebuke to the
presumption of the Governor.[51]

Edward Digges, who succeeded Mr. Bennett, seems to have
had no clash with the Assembly, but during the next administration, when Samuel Matthews was Governor, the executive
made a determined effort to break the power of the Burgesses.
At the session of 1658, the Governor and the Council sent a
message to the Assembly declaring that body dissolved.[52]   This
move startled the Burgesses.   The royal Governors had always
possessed the right of dissolving the House, but no such authority had been delegated to the new executive.   Moreover,
it was inconsistent with the theory, upon which everyone had
acted since the surrender in 1652, that all power resided in
the representatives of the people.   "The said disolution,"
replied the House, "as the case standeth is not presidentall
neither legall according to the lawes, now in force, Therefore
wee humbly desire a revocation of the said declaration."[53]

Although the Burgesses replied thus courteously they were
deeply angered.   Rightly judging this to be a challenge to
their power, they resolved to show once more that they were
supreme in the government.   They voted, therefore, to ignore
the dissolution.   And it was ordered that if any member left
his seat he was to be censured "as a person betraying the trust
reposed in him by his country".[54]   An oath of secrecy was
administered to all present, while the Speaker was directed to

[50] Hen., Vol. I, p. 372.   [51] Hen., Vol. I, pp. 377, 378.
[52] Hen., Vol. I, p. 499.   [53] Hen., Vol. I, p. 499.
[54] Hen., Vol. I, p. 500.

"sign nothing without the consent of the major part of the house".

Staggered by the determined attitude of the Burgesses, the Governor and Council at once showed signs of weakening. They were willing, they said, to allow the Assembly to continue its deliberations, provided the work were brought to a speedy conclusion. The "dispute of the power of disolving and the legality thereof" they wished to refer to the Lord Protector. But the House resolved unanimously that this answer was unsatisfactory. The withdrawal of the dissolution was not enough, the Governor and Council must acknowledge that their act was illegal and therefore had never taken effect. "The House, unsatisfied with these answers, appointed a committee to draw up a report for the manifestation and vindication of the Assembly's power which after presentation to the House to be sent to the Governour and Councell."[55] This committee recommended the immediate dismissal of the Council, and proposed resolutions declaring the "power of government to reside in such persons as shall be impowered by the Burgesses (the representatives of the people) who are not dissolvable by any power now extant in Virginia, but the House of Burgesses". Upon receiving this report the House proceeded to annul "all former election of Governour and Councill". Since the executive had presumed to abuse its authority by defying the body that had appointed it to office, it must be removed to evince to all the supremacy of the House. The Burgesses seem not to have laid the blame for this crisis upon the Governor, but upon some of the Councillors, who were endeavoring to make their own power supreme in the government. Colonel Matthews was, therefore, reëlected, and invested with "all just rights and privileges belonging to the Governour and Captain Generall of Virginia".[56]

Fearing that the Council might offer resistance to their decrees, the Burgesses commanded the serjeant-at-arms of the Assembly and the sheriffs of James City county not to execute any warrant, precept or command" from any other person than the Speaker of the House. The Secretary of State,

[55] Hen., Vol. I, p. 501.   [56] Hen., Vol. I, pp. 502, 503.

Colonel William Claiborne, was directed to deliver up the public records. But the Governor and Council seem not to have thought of resistance, and submitted to the recall and to a new election   by the Assembly. Although they had just resolved that "for the future none bee admitted a councellor but such who shall be nominated, appointed and confirmed by the house", the Burgesses now allowed the Governor to propose to them a list of names for the new Council. It would seem that Nathaniel Bacon and Francis Willis were regarded as the instigators of the dissolution, for they were the only members of the Council which had signed the offensive order who were not now reëlected.[57]

When the Assembly met again, in March, 1659, it found that its supremacy was once more threatened. A letter had been received from Henry Lawrence, President of the Council of State in the home government, which seemed to imply that the Governor and his Council and not the Burgesses, were to hold the chief power in Virginia. Lawrence declared that the "looseness" of affairs in the colony had induced Cromwell to take active steps for the settlement of its constitution, but that these measures had been brought to a sudden halt by the Lord Protector's death. The matter was, however, still before the Council of State, and the colony might soon expect some definite orders from its deliberations. In the meanwhile, he wrote, "their Lordships do will and require you the present Governour and Councill there to apply yourselves . . . to the peaceable and orderly management of the affairs of that collony, according to such good lawes and customes as have been heretofore used and exercised among you".[58]

The Burgesses were deeply agitated by this letter. They at once passed resolutions promising to obey the commands of the Council of State, but they determined to write the new Lord Protector, Richard Cromwell, asking that the privileges of the Burgesses be confirmed. In this crisis the Governor gave striking evidence of his liberal inclinations by coming before the House to promise them his support. "He acknowledged the supream power of electing officers to be by the

[57] Hen., Vol. I, pp. 499, 505.   [58] Hen., Vol. I, p. 510.

present lawes resident in the Grand Assembly", and offered to "joyne his best assistance with the countrey in makeing an addresse to his Highnesse for confirmation of their present priviledges".[59]

In the meanwhile an act was prepared making some important changes in the constitution, but confirming the power of the Burgesses. It was proposed, first, that Colonel Matthews "bee the Governour and Captain Gennerall of Virginia for two yeares ensueing, and then the Grand Assembly to elect a Governour as they think fitt, the person elect being then one of the Councell". The personnel of the Council was to remain unchanged and for the future its members were to serve for life, "except in case of high misdemanors". Lastly the Governor was to have the privilege of nominating the Councillors, but the Burgesses could confirm or reject at their discretion.[60] The Council at first assented to these proposals, "till the pleasure of his Highness be further signified", but later, it seems, they "expressly declined the said act", and declared the Assembly dissolved.[61] Whether or not the Burgesses submitted to this dissolution and left the Governor and Council to govern the colony as they chose, does not appear. It is quite probable that the executive, in the interval between the sessions of Assembly of March 1659 and March 1660, based its right to rule, not upon the commission of the Burgesses, but upon the authority given it in Lawrence's letter.

In May, 1659, Richard Cromwell resigned the reigns of government, and England was left a prey to confusion and uncertainty. The Virginians did not know to what government to give their allegiance. None could tell whether military despotism would be established in England, or another Cromwell would arise, or the House of Stuart be restored. To add to their troubles, in January, 1660, Colonel Matthews died, leaving them without a Governor. March 13th, the Assembly convened.

The Burgesses at once took steps to reëstablish their questioned prerogatives. An act was passed declaring that

[59] Hen., Vol. I, p. 512.　　[60] Hen., Vol. I, p. 517.
[61] Hen., Vol. I, p. 537.

"whereas by reason of the late frequent distractions there being in England noe resident absolute and gen'll confessed power; Be it enacted and confirmed, That the supreame power of the government of this country should be resident in the Assembly, And that all writts issue in the name of the Grand Assembly of Virginia, until such a comand and comission come out of England as shall be by the Assembly adjudged lawfull".[62]

Their next care was to elect a new Governor. Strangely enough their choice fell upon that staunch advocate of royalty, Sir William Berkeley. When the surrender had been made to the parliamentary commissioners in 1652, the Governor had secured for himself the right to quit the colony any time within the ensuing year. But circumstances had prevented his sailing during this period, and later he resolved to remain in Virginia. During the eight years of the Commonwealth period he had lived in retirement, obedient to the new government, but longing for the restoration of the Stuarts. Why he was now called forth by the Assembly to take once more the most important office in Virginia, cannot be certainly determined. It seems strange that the Burgesses in one act should assert their own sovereignty in the most emphatic terms, and in the next elect as their Governor this ardent servant of the Crown. If it had been their only aim to choose a leader of executive ability, they did not lack men of power and experience whose love of popular government was unquestioned. Berkeley had in his first administration ruled justly and well, but there is no reason to think that Virginia had been more prosperous and happy under him than under the Commonwealth Governors. It seems then most probable that the Assembly was actuated in its choice by an apprehension that the monarchy might be restored. If the English should invite Charles to reclaim his lost inheritance, it would be of much advantage to the colony to have at its head the former royal Governor. It would make the restoration in Virginia easy and peaceful, for the staunchest republican would not dare resist, with Charles II on his throne and Sir William Berkeley ruling at Jamestown. Moreover, it could but please

[62] Hen., Vol. I, p. 530.

the King and recommend the colony to his favor. On the other hand, the Assembly was careful to reserve all real authority to itself. Sir William was to be its servant, not its master. If, out of the confusion in England, should emerge a real republic, they could force the Governor either to acknowledge the new power or to resign his commission. In fact the office was at first proffered him only upon condition that he would submit to any power, whatever it might be, that succeeded in fixing itself over the English people.[63]

But to this requirement Berkeley would by no means consent. He was willing, during the present interregnum, to hold office from the people of Virginia, but never from any English power save that of the Crown. In an address to the Assembly, outlining his conduct during the troubles of the past eleven years, he made it quite clear that his sympathies had undergone no change. "When I came first into this Countrie," he said, "I had the Commicon and Commands of my most gracious master King Charles of ever blessed memory. . . . When God's wrath lay heavie upon us for the sins of our nation, my ever honoured Master was put to a violent death, and immeadiately after his Royall Sonne . . . sent me a Commicon to governe here under him. . . . But the Parliament, after the defeat at Worcester, (by the instigation of some other intent) sent a small power to force my submission to them, which finding me defenceless, was quietly (God pardon me) effected. But this parliament continued not long after this, but another supream power outed them, whoe remained not long neither, nor his sonne after him. . . . And now my intelligence is not enough to tell me what incorporate, mixt, or individuall power there is. . . . Under all these mutable governments of divers natures and constitutions, I have lived most resigningly submissive : But, Mr. Speaker, it is one duty to live obedient to a government, and another of a very different nature to Command under it. . . . You have, Mr. Speaker, with great wisdome and providence taken care of my obedient prostrating to the Supreame power the authoritie you would entrust me with,

[63] Southern Lit. Mess., Jan. 1845.

for which I give you my humble thanks; for this wisdome of yours hath animated my caution of assumeing this burden, which is so volatile, slippery and heavy, that I may justly feare it will breake my Limbs." It might be thought by some, he said, that the emergency would excuse his accepting this authority, but the King would judge him, and if his information were prejudiced, his punishment might be severe. He did not fear death, he was too old for that, but an imprudent, criminal death he abhorred. In conclusion he declared that these and other considerations must dissuade him from accepting the proffered office.

But the Assembly persisted in its determination to make him Governor. If he scrupled to promise to serve under the enemies of the Crown, that promise would not be required of him. Let him be Governor of Virginia, by their authority only, and only so long as the confusion in England continued. If a new Protector, or a new Commonwealth gained the ascendency, and demanded Virginia's submission, he might resign. If England returned to its obedience to the Throne, he could petition the King for a new commission. To this Berkeley assented. "Wee have all," he said, in another short address, "had great and pressing feares of offending a Supreame power which neither by present possession is soe, nor has a publiquely confessed politique capacity to be a Supream power. I alsoe, Mr. Speaker, have my pressing feares too, and I am seriously afraid to offend him, who by all Englishmen is confessed to be in a naturall politique capacity of being a Supreame power." He therefore, he said, made this declaration in the presence of God, that if any government became fixed in London, he would immediately lay down his commission. When this was recorded and they were still of the same mind, he was ready most thankfully to serve them.[64]

Thus did Sir William Berkeley a second time become Governor of Virginia. It must have been with trepidation that this man, who had so often denied the right of any officer to serve save by the King's commands, accepted now this commission from the hands of the people. The stern hater of

[64] Southern Lit. Mess., Jan. 1845.

republicanism was becoming the head of an independent little republic. For such Virginia was and must continue to be until there should appear in England some fixed government to which it could submit. "I am," Berkeley wrote Governor Stuyvesant of New Amsterdam, "but a servant of the assembly's; neither do they arrogate any power to themselves, further than the miserable distractions of England force them to. For when God shall be pleased in his mercy to take away and dissipate the unnatural diversions of their native country, they will immediately return to their own professed obedience."[65]

The restoration of the monarchy took place May 29th, 1660. When the news reached Virginia some weeks later, the people accepted the change without opposition, and probably with relief, for they were weary of uncertainty and confusion. Berkeley's unaffected joy was mingled with a deep apprehension that the King might be angered at his accepting office without his consent. But Charles was not so unmindful of his staunch support at a time when the fortunes of the monarchy were at their lowest ebb as to reproach him for this act, which might, and probably did, redound to his advantage. He soon relieved the Governor's fears by sending a new commission. In a passion of joy and gratitude Berkeley wrote his thanks. "I . . . doe most humbly throwe myselfe at your Ma'ties feet," he said, "in a dutifull thankfullness to your Majestie, that you yett think me worthy of your Royall Commands. It is true, . . . I did something, which if misrepresented to your Majestie, may cause your Majestie to think me guilty of a weakness I should ever abhor myself for. But it was noe more . . . than to leape over the fold to save your Majesties flock, when your Majesties enemies of that fold had barred up the lawfull entrance into it, and enclosed the Wolves of Scisme and rebellion ready to devour all within it. Nor did I adventure on this, without the advice and impulsion of your Majesties best Subjects in these parts. . . . I always in all conditions had more fear of your Majesties ffrownes than the Swords or Tortures of your Enemies."[66]

[65] Campbell, p. 74.   [66] Southern Lit. Mess., Jan., 1845.

And so the Commonwealth period in Virginia came to an end. The colony had benefited greatly by the eight years of semi-independence and self-government. The population had increased rapidly. In 1649, there had been about 15,000 people in Virginia, while six years after the Restoration, the Governor estimated their number at 40,000. This great gain was due chiefly to accelerated immigration from England. The overthrow and execution of the King had sent many of his followers to seek shelter with Sir William Berkeley, others had come to escape the confusion and horrors of civil war, while the numerous prisoners taken in battle had furnished abundant material for the never-ending stream of indentured servants. Gentleman and tradesman and laborer alike were welcome, for land was abundant and the colony's only need was men. Nor was prosperity yet strangled by the strict enforcement of the Navigation Acts. Dutch vessels continued to sail through the capes in defiance of England and to carry off the planters' tobacco. Not until the closing years of the Commonwealth period did the increasing freight rates and the decreasing price of tobacco indicate that the "Hollanders" were being more strictly excluded.[67]

Equally important was the training received by the people in self-government. For eight years they had been their own masters, enacting such laws as they chose, and free from the restraining hand of the King. There had been no royal Governor to veto their bills, or threaten the Burgesses, or intimidate the voters, or overawe the Council, or sway the courts of justice. And the experience was priceless. It schooled them in governmental affairs and taught them self-reliance, patience and stubbornness to oppose oppression. Having tasted the sweets of freedom, they were ill prepared ever again to tolerate injustice and misgovernment. If there had been no Commonwealth period in Virginia, possibly there had never been a Bacon's Rebellion.

[67] Bruce, Ec. Hist., Vol. I, pp. 357.-360.

CHAPTER V

The Causes of Bacon's Rebellion

There were many who hailed the restoration of the monarchy as the dawn of an era of prosperity and happiness for Virginia. The colony, despite the efforts of some of its people, had remained loyal to the Crown until overpowered by force of arms. It might well expect especial favor and care from its prince, now that he was firmly established upon his throne.[1] Of the ability and justice of the Governor Virginia had had ample experience during the ten years of his first administration.

Never was a people doomed to more bitter disappointment. The years which followed the Restoration were crowded with misfortunes greater than any that had befallen the colony since the ghastly days of the Great Sickness. Charles II, far from showing gratitude to his Old Dominion, overwhelmed it with injustice and oppression. The Virginians were crushed with tremendous duties on their tobacco and with ruinous restrictions upon their trade. The titles to their plantations were threatened by a grant of the entire colony to two unworthy favorites of the King. Governor Berkeley, embittered by the humiliation of the Commonwealth period, and growing avaricious and crabbed with advancing years, soon forfeited that respect and love which his former good conduct had gained him. His second administration was marred by partiality, oppression and inefficiency. The people were deprived of their right of suffrage by continued prorogation of the Assembly. Local government fell into the hands of small aristocratic cliques, while the poor were ground down with unequal and excessive taxes. Two wars with Holland added to the misfortunes of the colonists. Even the Heavens seemed to join with their enemies, for the country was visited

[1] P. R. O., CO1-34-95.

by a terrific hurricane which swept over the plantations, destroying crops and wrecking houses. These accumulated misfortunes brought such deep suffering upon the colony that hundreds of families were reduced to poverty and many were forced into debt and ruin. No wonder that the commons, finally driven to desperation, should have risen in insurrection against the Governor and the King.

First among the causes of distress during this unhappy period must be placed the Navigation Acts. England, in the middle of the 17th century, was engaged in an unsuccessful contest with Holland for the carrying trade of the world. The merchantmen of Amsterdam and Flushing found their way even to Maryland and Virginia, where their low freight rates and the liberal prices they gave for tobacco, assured them a hearty welcome. The exports of the colonies to England itself were not infrequently carried in Dutch bottoms. This was a source of much anxiety and annoyance to the British government. It seemed unjust that the American colonies, which had been founded at such tremendous cost, should now prove as great a source of wealth to Holland as to the mother country. And it could not but anger the English shippers to find themselves elbowed by these foreigners in the ports of the Bermudas or the rivers of Virginia.

In 1651, the British Parliament, thinking it necessary to give their merchants some protection from this lively competition, passed the first of the Navigation Acts. Under its provisions no goods of the growth or manufacture of Asia, America or Africa should be introduced into England in any but English ships, of which the owner, master and three-fourths of the sailors were English subjects; and all foreign commodities imported to England should be conveyed directly thither from the place of growth or manufacture.[2] This law injured the Virginians by excluding the Dutch carriers from the tobacco trade with England and thus causing a sharp rise in freight rates. During the early years of the Commonwealth period it was frequently avoided, but before 1660 the English government began to enforce it more strictly.

[2] Scobell, Vol. II, p. 132.

Nor did the people get relief with the restoration of the monarchy. Charles II proved more solicitous that Parliament for the welfare of the English merchants; even more indifferent to the complaints of the colonists. A new Navigation Act was passed in 1660 which struck a deadly blow at the prosperity of Virginia. Under its provisions all goods sent to the colonies, even though of foreign growth or manufacture, were to be exported from England, and all tobacco, sugar, wool, etc., produced in the colonies, must be shipped only to England or to her dominions.[3]

Thus were the colonies sacrificed upon the altar of greed. The new act injured the Virginia planters in several ways. Since all their tobacco must now be brought to English ports, they could no longer seek the most advantageous markets. Had the demand for the commodity in England been more elastic, the consequences of this provision might not have been disastrous. Declining prices would have so stimulated the demand that the English could have consumed the entire crop. But the King's customs kept up the price to the consumer, and made it impossible for the merchants to dispose of the vast quantities of the leaf that had formerly gone to Holland and other countries.[4] Moreover, the varieties sold to the Dutch were not popular in England, and could not be disposed of at any price. Soon the market became so glutted that the merchants refused to take more than half the crop, leaving the remainder to rot upon the hands of the planters.

There followed in Virginia a sharp decline in prices. The Dutch had given the colonists three pence a pound for their tobacco.[5] A few years after the Restoration the planters considered themselves fortunate if they could dispose of their crops at a half penny a pound. Much was sold at a farthing.[6] Now since tobacco was the staple product of Virginia and the main support of the people, this rapid decline in its value was disastrous. Frequent complaints were sent to England that

[3] Bruce, Ec. Hist., Vol. I, p. 357.
[4] Governor Berkeley wrote in 1666 that the King's customs from the Virginia and Maryland tobacco would amount "unto about £100,000".
[5] Bruce, Ec. Hist., Vol. I, p. 354.   [6] P. R. O., CO1-21.

the colonists could not maintain themselves and their families upon the meagre returns from their tobacco. "Twelve hundred pounds is the medium of men's yearly crops," wrote Secretary Ludwell in 1667, "and a half penny per pound is certainly the full medium of the price given for it." This made an average income for each planter of but fifty shillings. When the poor man had paid his taxes for the necessary support of the government, very little remained to him to clothe his wife and children. "So much too little," he adds, "that I can attribute it to nothing but the mercy of God, that he has not fallen into mutiny and confusion."[7] In 1673 the Governor and the Council declared that the colony was full of indigent persons, who could barely support themselves with their utmost exertions.[8]

Not only did the act of 1660 depress the price of tobacco, but it increased the already excessive freight rates. Since the bulk of the colonial exports had now to be brought directly to England, in English ships, the masters of Plymouth or London could double or triple their charges. Simultaneously there occurred a pronounced rise in the cost of manufactured goods. The far-famed skill of the Dutch workmen had made it possible for them to produce many articles more cheaply than the English, and to underbid them in their own colonies. But now that all foreign goods were excluded, the planters were forced to purchase the more expensive product of the English workshops.

Thus were the Virginians cut with a two-edged sword. At the very time that their incomes were being diminished, they were confronted by an increase in the cost of living. Nor could they, as Lord Baltimore declared they might, alleviate these evils by industry and thrift. For the more strenuous were their efforts to increase the tobacco crop, the greater would be the glut in the English market and the more disastrous the drop in prices.

The poor colonists found an able, but an unsuccessful ad-

[7] P. R. O., CO1-21.
[8] P. R. O., CO1-30-51. Compare Petition of Governor Berkeley, Aug. 22, 1662, CO1-16.

vocate, in a London merchant named John Bland. "If the Hollanders," he wrote in a paper addressed to the King, "must not trade to Virginia how shall the Planters dispose of their Tobacco? The English will not buy it, for what the Hollander carried thence was a sort of Tobacco, not desired by any other people, . . . the Tobacco will not vend in England, the Hollanders will not fetch it from England; what must become thereof?" But Charles II, who knew little of economic matters, and cared nothing for the welfare of the colonists, ignored Bland's convincing appeal. No alleviation was given Virginia, and she was allowed to drift on through poverty and desperation to rebellion.

In a vain attempt to make the colony independent of the English manufacturers and to turn the people from the excessive planting of tobacco, the Assembly passed a series of acts designed to encourage local industrial establishments. It was especially desired that Virginia should make her own cloth, for the cost of the English fabrics was excessive.[9] To stimulate the art of spinning and weaving the Assembly offered rewards for the best pieces of linen and woollen goods produced in the country. A bounty was placed on the manufacture of silk.[10] In 1666, the establishment of cloth works in each county was made compulsory by act of Assembly.[11] "Whereas," it was declared, "the present obstruction of trade and the nakedness of the country doe suffitiently evidence the necessity of provideing supply of our wants by improveing all meanes of raysing and promoteing manufactures amonge ourselves, . . . Be it enacted . . . that within two yeares at furthest . . . the commissioners of each county court shall provide and sett up a loome and weaver in each of the respective counties."[12] Nor were other industries neglected. Tanhouses were erected in various places "to tanne, curry and make the hides of the country into leather and shoes".[13] Bounties were offered for the construction of vessels, in the

[9] Hen., Vol. II, pp. 120, 121.
[10] P. R. O., CO1-19; Hen., Vol. II, p. 272.
[11] Hen., Vol. II, p. 238.
[12] Ibid.   [13] Hen., Vol. II, p. 123.

hope that Virginia might rival the prosperous ship-builders of New England.[14]

These experiments added a heavy burden to the poor taxpayer, while they accomplished little for the relief of the colony. Virginia, with its scattered plantations and its lack of skilled artisans, could not hope to compete with the workshops of England. The commissioners, whether from corruption or from lack of ability, proved poor business managers, and their ill success occasioned loud and bitter complaints.

In May, 1661, Governor Berkeley sailed for England to combat a new design to revive the Virginia Company. It is quite probable that he took occasion during his stay at court to protest against the Navigation Acts.[15] But he found it impossible to turn the King and Parliament from what had become their settled colonial policy. Ten years later, when the Lords of Trade and Plantations asked him what impediments there were to the improvement of trade in the colony, the Governor blurted out the truth with his accustomed vigor. "Mighty and destructive by that severe act of Parliament which excludes us from haveing any Commerce with any Nacon in Europe but our owne, Soe that wee cannot add to our plantacon any Comodity that growes out of itt . . . ffor it is not lawfull for us to carry a pipe-staff or a Bushel of Corne to any place in Europe out of the King's dominions. If this were for his Majesty's Service or the good of his Subjects wee should not repine what ever our Sufferings are for it. But on my Soule it is the Contrary for both."[16]

In seeking relief from the evil consequences of the Navigation Acts the Virginians turned to their cousins of New England.[17] And the hardy sailors of Massachusetts and Connecticut, tempted by the high prices of manufactured goods in the southern colonies, brought their wares into the James, the York and the Potomac, where they entered into lively competition with the English merchants. Nor did they hesitate,

[14] P. R. O., CO1-19; Hen., Vol. II, p. 178.
[15] P. R. O., CO1-16; Hen., Vol. II, p. 17.
[16] P. R. O., CO1-26-77; Hen., Vol. II, p. 315.
[17] P. R. O., CO1-24.

when occasion offered, to defy the law by transporting the Virginia tobacco to foreign markets.[18]   But England was unwilling to leave the colonists even this small loophole.   Parliament decided, in 1672, to place a duty of one penny a pound upon tobacco shipped from one colony to another, and the payment of this duty did not give liberty to the owners to transport it to a foreign country.   This act completely crippled the intercolonial trade.   A few years later, after Bacon's Rebellion, when the Virginia counties were presenting their grievances to the King's commissioners, the people of Lower Norfolk requested that the act of 1672 might be repealed. The only notice taken of their petition was the contemptuous comment of the commissioners that it was wholly mutinous for them "to desire a thing contrary to his Majesty's Royall pleasure & benefitt and also against an Act of Parliament".[19]

It had been suggested, when the price of tobacco began to fall, that the evil might be remedied by governmental restraint upon the annual crop.   The diminution of the demand for the leaf, brought about by the loss of the foreign market, was to be met by a corresponding limitation upon the supply.   Prices would thus be restored and the planter would receive a greater return for a much smaller output.   But for this remedy to be effective, it would be necessary to secure the coöperation of Maryland and perhaps North Carolina, as a cessation in Virginia would accomplish little, if no restraint were put upon the planters of the other colonies.   Moreover, since the proposed step might diminish the revenue from the customs, it would be necessary to obtain the consent of the King.

In 1662 many of the planters and merchants petitioned Charles II to forbid the planting of tobacco in Maryland and Virginia for one year.[20]   At first this appeal was rejected and the colonists were commanded to refrain from presenting similar petitions in the future.   Later, however, the Privy Council secured a reversal of this decision and an order was issued authorizing the Assembly to appoint commissioners to

[18] P. R. O., CO1-30; Bruce, Ec. Hist., Vol. I, p. 357.
[19] P. R. O., CO5-1371-328; Va. Mag., Vol. III, p. 38.
[20] Bruce, Ec. Hist., Vol. I, p. 389.

confer with the Marylanders upon the best means of lessening the excessive crops.[21]   Accordingly a meeting was held at Wiccocomico, May 12, 1664, which recommended that the planting of tobacco after the twentieth of June each year should be prohibited.   The report met with the approval of the Virginians and was promptly ratified by the Assembly, but the Marylanders believed that a partial cessation would be detrimental to their interests and their legislature refused to give its consent.

But as prices sank lower and lower, and poverty became more general, the Virginians once more appealed to Maryland, this time for a total cessation for one year. Numerous letters were exchanged upon the subject, but at first nothing was accomplished.   After many months had been consumed in useless negotiations Governor Berkeley, in the dead of winter, himself journeyed to Maryland and at last succeeded in convincing the leading men of that colony of the necessity of the measure.   As a result, the Maryland Assembly passed an act prohibiting all tobacco planting in their province from February 1666 to February 1667, provided Virginia and North Carolina should do likewise.[22]   The Assembly at Jamestown promptly passed a similar law, but the North Carolinians, owing to Indian troubles, delayed their action so long that the Marylanders repudiated the entire agreement.

Somewhat discouraged the colonists again sent commissioners, this time to Saint Mary's, to resume the broken thread of negotiations.   Here at last success seemed to crown their efforts, for all differences were adjusted, and the cessation was agreed upon by the three colonies.[23]   But the joy of Virginia at this happy outcome was soon turned to grief and indignation, for the Marylanders received a letter from Lord Baltimore, "in absolute and princely terms prohibiting the execution of the . . . articles of cessation".

"This overtook us," wrote Governor Berkeley, "like a storm and enforced us like distressed marriners to throw our dear bought commodities into the sea, when we were in sight of our

[21] Bruce, Ec. Hist., Vol. I, p. 390.   [22] P. R. O., CO1-20.
[23] P. R. O., CO1-20. Ludwell to Arlington.

harbour, & with them so drown'd not only our present reliefs but all future hopes of being able to do ourselves good, whilst we are thus divided and enforced to steere by anothers compasse, whose needle is too often touched with particular interest. This unlimited and independent power . . . of the Lord Baltimore doth like an impetuous wind blow from us all those seasonable showers of your Majesty's Royall cares and favours, and leaves us, and his own province withering and decaying in distress and poverty. . . . This unreasonable and unfortunate prohibition . . . hath not only increased the discontent of many of the inhabitants of his province, but hath raised the grief and anger of allmost all your . . . subjects of this colony to such a height as required great care to prevent those disturbances which were like to arise from their eluded hopes and vain expences."[24]

Can there be any doubt that the Navigation Acts and the futility of all attempts to escape their baleful effects, were largely instrumental in bringing on Bacon's Rebellion? As prosperity and contentment are the greatest safeguards of the public peace, so poverty, nakedness and distress are breeders of sedition. Philip Ludwell spoke of Bacon's army as "a Rabble of the basest sort of People; whose Condicion was such as by a chaunge could not admitt of worse".[25] Had England been less selfish in her treatment of Virginia, there would not have been so many indigent men in the colony eager to join in this wild uprising against the government. Berkeley himself admitted, in 1673, that at least one third of the freemen had been rendered so desperate by poverty and debt that in times of foreign war their loyalty to England could not be relied upon.[26]

But Charles II was indifferent to the welfare of these distant subjects and blind to their growing dissatisfaction. Just when the situation was most critical, he aroused their anger and grief to the highest pitch, by making a gift of the entire colony to Lord Culpeper and the Earl of Arlington. Previously he had granted that portion of Virginia which

[24] P. R. O., CO1-21. Governor and Council to the King.
[25] P. R. O., CO1-37-16.   [26] P. R. O., CO1-80-51.

lies between the Potomac and the Rappahannock rivers, known as the Northern Neck, to Lord Hopton and several other noblemen. These patentees were to receive fees, remainders, reversions and escheats, and were given power to grant patents for all land that had not been taken up. This had caused the people of Virginia, and especially those residing in the Northern Neck, great uneasiness, and had proved a serious hindrance to the settling of that region. The Assembly, dreading the clash of jurisdiction which this grant made almost inevitable, had sent agents to England to persuade the King to annul the patent, or permit the purchase of the tract by the colony. While they were working to this end, there came the unexpected news that Arlington and Culpeper had received a grant of the entire colony. Without consulting in the least the desires of the people, Charles had given them over to two unscrupulous favorites, with the indifference he might have shown in presenting a necklace to his mistress. The colonists, "to their unspeakable griefe and Astonishment", felt now that they were "reduced to a far worse condition than that wherein they had adventured their lives and fortunes for the planting that Country under the Company".[27]

The privileges and powers granted in this patent, had they ever been exercised by Arlington and Culpeper, would have rendered the government at Jamestown almost a nullity. The two lords were to receive all escheats, quit-rents, duties and reservations belonging to the Crown; they were given power to divide the territory into counties, hundreds and parishes; to erect churches and present ministers to them; to make manors, fairs, and markets; to appoint sheriffs, surveyors, and other important officers; to issue patents for land; to appropriate to their own use all arrears of "rents and other profits", accruing since the year 1669.

In great alarm the Virginia Assembly directed the agents in England to use their utmost endeavors to have this grant recalled. At the same time they drew up a statement of their objections to the patent, showing how unjust and ruinous

[27] P. R. O., COI-34-IOI.

were its provisions. It was in direct conflict with numerous royal concessions and patents, given them from time to time under the Great Seal. There was good reason to fear that the lords, by their deputies, might impose upon them new rents and services. They might demand new surveys and new patents for land which had long been occupied. They might, in fact, completely devastate the government of all its "just powers and authorities".

The agents, upon receiving these instructions, went to the Lords Patentees to request them to resign the most obnoxious of their new powers.[28]   In case they refused, the agents threatened to appeal at once to the King. Arlington and Culpeper received them courteously, and, after numerous delays, consented to relinquish the patent, provided Virginia would offer no objection to the passing of a new grant, assuring them the quit-rents and escheated property. The agents were well satisfied with this settlement, for it would relieve the colony of its fear of proprietary government, while the grant of the rents and escheats would impose little additional burden.[29]

In order, however, to prevent the giving away of such disturbing powers in the future, they petitioned the King to grant "Letters Pattents for the incorporacon" of the colony.[30] In this new charter they desired first that permission be given Virginia to purchase the Northern Neck.   They next requested the King to promise that Virginia should have no other dependence than upon the Crown of England, "nor in the future be cantonized into parcells by grants made to particular persons".   "And for the prevention of surreptitious grants" they desired his Majesty to promise in the charter that nothing should again pass concerning Virginia until a hearing had been given to some person impowered by the colony to represent their interests.   Of even greater importance was their desire, "That there shall bee no Taxe or Imposition layd on the people of Virginia, but by their owne

[28] P. R. O., COI-28-20; Burk, Vol. II, Appendix XXXVI.
[29] Hen., Vol. II, pp. 518-543; Burk, Vol. II, Appendix XXXIII-LXII.
[30] P. R. O., COI-34-95.

Consente, and that Express'd by the Representatives in Assembly."[31]

The whole matter came before the King in Council, June 23, 1675, and was referred to the judgment of Attorney-General William Jones and Solicitor-General Francis Winnington.[32] In October these officers reported that in their opinion the patent of incorporation would be beneficial both to the colony and the King's service, and ought to be granted. Charles thereupon gave directions that the papers be drawn up for his signature. But here, for some unknown reason, the matter came to a halt. Several months passed and the patent had not been issued.[33] At last, April 19, 1676, at the urgent request of the agents, his Majesty directed that the Lord Chancellor cause the papers to pass the Great Seal at once. But before this could be done, news came to England of Bacon's Rebellion, and the King immediately reversed his order. Later, other Letters Patent were granted, but they were very different from those sought by the agents, and contained little more than a bare declaration of the colony's direct dependence upon the Crown of England.[34]

This unsatisfactory business caused great irritation among the colonists. The heavy expense of carrying on the negotiations in England "made them desperately uneasie, especially when, after a whole Year's Patience . . . they had no Encouragement from their Agents".[35] A tax of fifty pounds of tobacco per poll, imposed for the purchase of the Northern Neck, aroused widespread dissatisfaction. In April, 1676, Governor Berkeley, fully conscious of the mutterings of revolution, was awaiting with anxiety the arrival of favorable news from the agents. "There are divers," he wrote, "that would fain persuade the people that al their high taxes will bring them no benefit, so that if the most advantageous terms had been proposed to us it would have been impossible to have

[31] P. R. O., CO1-34-96; CO1-34-100; CO1-33-108; CO1-34-95; Hen., Vol. II, p. 529.
[32] P. R. O., CO1-34-100.
[33] P. R. O., CO1-36-48; Hen. Vol. II, p. 534.
[34] P. R. O., CO389.6-133 to 137; Burk, Vol. II, Appendix LXI.
[35] Beverley.

persuaded the people to have parted with more tobacco til a more certain demonstration had been given them of what is already done. I appeased two mutinies this last year raysed by some secret villaines that whispered amongst the people that there was nothing intended by the fifty pounds levy but the enriching of some few people."[36] In 1677, after Bacon's Rebellion, the King's commissioners heard from all sides that the imposition of this tax was one of the main causes of discontent.[37]

The wars of 1664 and 1672 with Holland added much to the distress in Virginia. The bold Dutch mariners, angered at the injury done them by the Navigation Acts, preyed upon the English merchantmen in every sea. Woe to the tobacco ship that encountered a hostile privateer, in its journey across the Atlantic! The English vessels were not safe even in the Virginia rivers, under the guns of their forts. Twice the daring Dutch came through the capes and into the James River itself, where they wrought great damage to the shipping.

It was the custom, during these times of danger, for the merchant vessels of Virginia and Maryland to cross the Atlantic in large fleets, under the protection of English men-of-war. In May 1667, some twenty vessels were anchored in the mouth of James River, near Newport News, awaiting the remainder of their fleet before sailing. Three leagues above them lay the *Elizabeth,* a frigate of forty-six guns, sent by the King for the protection of the colony. She was undergoing repairs, however, having become "soe disabled in her Maste and Leaky in her Hull as that she could not keep at sea", and for the moment afforded little proctection to the merchantmen riding below.[38]

At this juncture, a fleet of five Dutch warships, under the command of Abraham Crimson, appeared off the coast, bent on mischief to the English shipping. The Hollanders, learning of the exposed position of the tobacco fleet from the crew of a shallop which fell into their hands, determined upon a bold attack. On their way to the capes they encountered a

[36] P. R. O., CO1-36-37.   [37] P. R. O., CO5-1371-292, 331.
[38] P. R. O., CO1-21-61.

ship of London bound from Tangier to Virginia. The English master, Captain Conway, "fought them very well for two hours, but at last being wounded himself and over powered with men, was taken by them".[39]

The Dutchmen came into Chesapeake Bay June 4, and anchored there over night. The next morning, taking advantage of a fair easterly breeze, they sailed boldly into the mouth of the James. In order to take their prey entirely by surprise they flew the English colors, and as they passed the merchantmen, hailed them in English and sang out their soundings in English. Proceeding directly up to the unsuspecting frigate, they threw aside their disguise with the roar of three volleys. The captain of the *Elizabeth* had gone ashore, to attend a wedding it was said, and had left but thirty men on board.[40] Without officers, and surprised by superior numbers, the sailors could make no effective resistance. Several rushed to their guns, but they fired only one piece of ordnance before they were forced to surrender. While some of the Dutchmen were securing the *Elizabeth,* the others turned upon the helpless merchantmen and succeeded in capturing the entire fleet. Several of the ships might have saved themselves by running into the Elizabeth River, where the enemy would not have dared to follow them, but they seemed paralyzed with surprise and fell an unresisting prey.[41]

Great was the grief and rage of Sir William Berkeley when news of this disaster reached him. How could he answer to the King for the loss of the royal frigate and twenty English merchantmen? With great promptness and resolution he decided to fit out all available vessels in the colony for a sally upon the enemy. In the upper James were three merchantmen and in the York nine. If these could be supplied quickly with guns and men, there might yet be time to defeat the Dutch and rescue the captured ships. The Governor, who was ever reckless in exposing his person, resolved to direct the attack himself in the good ship *Admirall*. But

[39] P. R. O., CO1-21-61.   [40] P. R. O., CO1-21-63.
[41] P. R. O., CO1-21-61, 62.

some of the masters by no means relished the thought of risking their vessels and their cargoes in a battle with the Dutch. When the Governor impressed them into the King's service by putting the broad arrow upon their masts, they pretended obedience, but used such delays that the fleet could not be prepared in time. Captain Lightfoot, of the *Elizabeth,* grieved by the loss of his ship, "very passionately resolved to hazard himself in the *Admirall",* while several members of the Council and forty other gentlemen volunteered their services. Upon the shore were assembled four regiments of militia, ready to embark should they be needed. Yet the masters continued their procrastination day after day until the Dutch escaped.

Nor had Admiral Crimson shown any haste to be off. Soon after the battle he had burned five or six of the merchantmen, "for want of men to man them". It had also been necessary for him to destroy the frigate, which was still out of repair and far from seaworthy. He had sent parties ashore several times to secure water, which he greatly needed, but they had been driven back with ease. After a stay of five or six days in James River, he sailed away with his prizes, leaving the Governor to dismiss his militia and write home his accusations against the masters.[42]

Warned by this experience, the English government, upon the outbreak of the war of 1672, sent two men-of-war to Virginia. These vessels, in July 1673, were stationed at the mouth of the James guarding a large fleet of merchantmen, when news came that nine Dutch warships were approaching the capes. Instantly preparations were made to fight them. Several of the tobacco ships were forced into service and fitted with guns. Sailors were taken from the smaller vessels to help man the larger. But before all could be put in readiness the enemy came through the capes and anchored at Lynhaven Bay.[48]

The English had as yet little apprehension for the safety of their merchantmen, for they could at any time run under the guns of a fort at Nansemond, or could retreat up the

[42] P. R. O., CO1-21-61, 62, 63.   [48] P. R. O., CO1-30-51, 53, 71.

James while their men-of-war held back the enemy. At this moment, however, there appeared across the waters of the Chesapeake eight sail of the Maryland fleet, unconscious of their danger and bearing down upon the Dutch. The English commanders realized that only instant action could save them. Taking with them six of the tobacco ships they sailed out to give battle.

"But before they came within reach of gun shot 4 of the merchant ships came on ground." One turned back to the James. But the other three ships went on, and unaided fought six of the largest Dutchmen. For three hours the battle continued with great fury. At last Captain Gardner, one of the English commanders, "judging that the enemy (if he checkt them not) would be in with (the) merchant ships riding in James river . . . tacked alone upon them with Extra ordinary courage, and for at least one houre fought them all. . . . But, having all his greate maste and his fore topmast desperately wounded, and most of his rigging shot", he was at last forced to retire. "With as much courage as conduct (and beyond the hopes or expectation of those who saw that brave action) (he) disengaged himselfe . . . and brought off all the Marylanders but one." The Virginia fleet, "which were neere 40 sail", secured "almost a tides way before the enemy, which undoubtedly saved many which otherwise would have bin lost". Some of the merchantmen took refuge at Fort Nansemond, where the enemy dared not attack them, others retreated up the river towards Jamestown. Unfortunately five of them, in the confusion of the flight, ran aground and were afterwards captured. The four ships which had grounded before the battle also fell into the hands of the Dutch. Thus, despite the gallant conduct of the English, the enemy succeeded in capturing a large part of the tobacco fleet.[44]

Great as was the distress caused by the depredations of the Dutch, the planters suffered even more during these wars by the stagnation of trade. The great risk incurred in crossing the ocean necessarily brought an increase both in freight

[44] P. R. O., CO1-30-51, 53.

rates and in the cost of manufactured goods. In 1667 the Governor and Council declared that the planters were "inforced to pay 12 pounds to £17 per ton freight" on their tobacco, "which usually was but at seven pounds".[45] Conditions were even worse during the second war. In 1673 Berkeley complained that the number of vessels that dared come to Virginia was so small, that they had "not brought goods and tools enough for one part of five of the people to go on with their necessary labor". "And those few goods that are brought," he added "have Soe few (and these hard Dealing) Sellers and Soe many Indigent and necessitous buyors that the Poore Planter gets not the fourth part . . . for his tobacco which he usually has had in other times."[46]

In this period, so full of suffering and misfortune, the year 1667 was especially noteworthy for its long series of disasters. In November Secretary Thomas Ludwell wrote Lord Berkeley, "This poore Country . . . is now reduced to a very miserable Condicon by a continuall course of misfortune. In Aprill . . . we had a most prodigeous Storme of haile, many of them as bigg as Turkey Eggs, which destroyed most of our younge Mast and Cattell. On the fifth of June following came the Dutch upon us, and did soe much mischiefe that we shall never recover our reputations. . . . They were not gone before it fell to raineing and continued for 40 dayes together, which Spoiled much of what the haile had left of our English Graine. But on the 27th of August followed the most Dreadful Hurry Cane that ever the colony groaned under. It lasted 24 hours, began at North East and went round northerly till it came to west and soe on till it came to South East where it ceased. It was accompanied with a most violent raine, but no Thunder. The night of it was the most Dismall tyme that ever I knew or heard off, for the wind and rain raised soe Confused a noise, mixt with the continuall Cracks of falling houses. . . . The waves (were) impetuously beaten against the Shoares and by that violence forced and as it were crowded up into all Creeks, Rivers and bayes to that prodigeous height that it hazarded the drownd-

[45] P. R. O., CO1-21-61.   [46] P. R. O., CO1-30-17.

ing many people who lived not in sight of the Rivers, yet were then forced to climbe to the topp of their houses to keep them selves above water. (The waves) carried all the foundation of the fort at point Comfort into the River and most of our Timber which was very chargably brought thither to perfect it. Had it been finished and a garison in it, they had been Stormed by such an enemy as noe power but Gods can restraine. . . . Had the Lightning accompanied it we could have beleeved nothing else from such a confusion but that all the elements were at Strife, which of them should doe most towards the reduction of the creation into a Second Chaos. It was wonderful to consider the contrary effects of that Storme, for it blew some shipps from their Anchors and carryed them safe over shelves of Sand where a wherry could Difficultly passe, and yet knockt out the bottome of a ship . . . in eight foot water more than she drew. But when the morning came and the Sun risen it would have comforted us after such a night, had it not lighted us to ye Ruines of our plantations, of which I thinke not one escaped. The nearest computation is at least 10,000 houses blowne downe, all the Indian Graine laid flatt upon the ground, all the Tobacco in the fields torne to pieces and most of that which was in the houses perished with them. The fences about the Corne fields (were) either blown down or beaten to the ground by trees which fell upon them & before the owners could repair them the hoggs & Cattell gott in and in most places devoured much of what the Storme had left.''[47]

In the midst of the second Dutch war came another scourge no less distressing than the great hurricane. Throughout the 17th century cattle raising was one of the most important industries of the small Virginia proprietors. No planter, however insignificant his holdings, was without his cow and his calf.[48] They constituted a most important portion of his wealth, and an indispensable source of support. In the winter of 1672-3 occurred an epidemic which destroyed more

[47] P. R. O., CO1-21.

[48] This is shown by the wills of this period, many of which have been published in the Virginia Magazine of History and Biography.

than half the cattle of Virginia. The mortality was increased by the cold, which was unusually severe. Many men, in an effort to preserve the poor beasts, gave them all their corn and thus brought hunger upon themselves. Before relief came with the spring, fifty thousand cattle had perished.[49]

Perhaps the people of Virginia might have borne patiently all these misfortunes, had their Governor ruled them with wisdom and justice. Certain it is they would never have turned in wild anger to strike down his government, had that government not done much to make their condition intolerable. Sir William Berkeley was accused of destroying the representative character of the Assembly, of initiating a notorious spoils system, of intimidating Burgesses, of winking at embezzlement of public funds. And, although most of these charges were brought by the Governor's bitter enemies, some of them were undoubtedly true.

In Virginia, during this period, the commons could guard their interests only by means of the House of Burgesses. All other organs of government were controlled by Berkeley and his friends. The people had no voice in the selection of vestrymen, or sheriffs, or justices of the peace, and no control over their actions. The Council was entirely submissive to the Governor's will. Its members not only held their seats at Sir William's pleasure, but were the recipients of numerous other favors that bound them closely to his interest. Thus in the executive, in all branches of the judiciary, and in the upper house of Assembly the Governor was all-powerful.

If then he could control the Burgesses and make them subservient to his desires, he would remove the only obstacle to almost complete despotism. Nor was it a matter of very great difficulty for him to gain a mastery of the House. In every county he could nominate government candidates, and exert tremendous pressure to secure their election. If necessary, they might be seated by fraud at the polls or false returns by the sheriff.[50] "It is true," Bacon declared, "that the people's hopes of redemption did ly in the Assembly, as their Trusts, and Sanctuary to fly to, but I would have all men consider

[49] P. R. O., CO1-30-17; CO1-30-51.   [50] Hen., II, p. 356.

first how poore people are debarred of their fair election, the great men in many places haveing the Country in their debte and consequently in their aw. Secondly how meanly we are provided of men of Learning, ability and courage, nay indeed of honesty, to stand up in the people's behalf and oppose the oppressing party."[51]

And if ever, despite these difficulties, the candidates of the people were elected, the Governor might still win their support in the House, by a judicious use of the patronage. He controlled enough offices of honor and profit to reward richly his friends in the Assembly. If the Burgess was careful never to thwart the wishes of the Governor, or to vote against his measures, he might reasonably expect a collectorship, a sheriff's place, a commission in the militia, or possibly a seat in the Council. A large percentage of the members of the House were office-holders.[52]

If half the charges brought against Berkeley are to be believed, he was guilty of instituting a system of political corruption as effective as that maintained in France by Guizot during the reign of Louis Philippe. He has assumed to himself, it was declared, "the sole nominating, appointing and commissionating of all . . . officers both civil and military amongst us . . . (they) being . . . (the better to increase . . . his party) multiplied to a greate number. . . . All which offices he bestowed on such persons (how unfitt or unskillfull soever) as he conceived would be most for his designs. And that the more firmly to binde and oblige them thereunto and allure others to his party, he . . . permitted or connived at the persons soe commissionated by him . . . unwarrantably . . . to lay and impose what levies and imposicons upon us they should or did please, which they would often extort from us by force and violence, and which for the most part they converted to their owne private lucre and gaine. And . . . Sir William Berkeley, haveing by these wayes and meanes, and by takeing upon him contrary to law the granting collectors places, sherifs, and other offices of profitt to whome he best pleased, he soe gained uppon and obliged all

[51] P. R. O., CO5-1371-241, 246.   [52] Bruce, Inst. Hist., Vol. I, p. 489.

the greatest number of the men of parts and estates in the whole country (out of which it was necessary our representatives and Burgesses should be elected) hath there by soe fortifyed his power over us, as of himselfe without respect to our laws, to doe what soever he best pleased, and from time to time . . . to gaine and procure great quantities of Tobacco and mony from us to his proper use over and besides the Thousand pounds yearly salary . . . and over and besides the fees, profitts and per quisites to the place of Governour belonging."[53]

Bacon himself declared, in justification of his rebellion, that oppression and injustice were rife in the colony, and that it was useless to appeal to the Assembly for redress. "The poverty of the Country is such," he said, "that all the power and sway is got into the hands of the rich, who by extortious advantages, having the common people in their debt, have always curbed and oppressed them in all manner of wayes." The poor, he declared, were kept in such perpetual bondage that it was not possible for labor or industry to extricate them. The great men of the colony had brought misery and ruin upon the common people by perverting all equity and right. The perpetual breach of laws, remiss prosecutions, excuses and evasions, but too plainly attested that things were carried by the men at the helm, "as if it were but to play a booty, game or divide a spoile". "Now consider," he adds, "what hope there is of redress in appealing to the very persons our complaints do accuse."[54]

And when once the Governor had obtained a House that was subservient to his will, he might, by his power of prorogation, continue it indefinitely. During the years from the Restoration to Bacon's Rebellion, there were not more than two general elections, and probably only one—that of 1661.[55]

[53] Va. Mag., Vol. III, pp. 135, 136.   [54] P. R. O., CO5-1371-241.
[55] P. R. O., CO5-1371-316, 319. The Assembly which met in March, 1661, was continued by successive prorogations until October, 1665. This fact is placed beyond question by the copies of the Acts of Assembly now preserved in the British Public Record Office. But there is no statement in these copies that the session of June 5, 1666, had been prorogued from an earlier date. Nor is there any indication given in Hening's

Under these circumstances the Assembly could no longer be said to represent the voters of the colony. The Burgesses might defy or betray the people as they chose, they could not be made to answer at the polls for their misconduct. And their is ample proof that this Long Assembly attended more to the commands of the Governor than to the wishes of electors that could no longer elect. Even Sir William's best friends admitted that his authority in Virginia was almost despotic. Secretary Thomas Ludwell, writing in 1666, declared that the Governor was "the sole author of the most substantial part" of the government, "either for Lawes or other inferior institutions".[56] "Our representatives," complained the Charles City commons eleven years later "(of which for this county in nine yeares time last past there hath been a verry doubtful election as we conceive) have been overswayed by the power and prevalency of . . . Sir Wm. Berkeley and his councell, divers instances of which wee conceive might be given, and have neglected our grievances made knowne to them."[57]

That this overthrow of representative government in the

Statutes that this was not a new Assembly. (Hen., Vol. II, p. 224.) These two omissions, then, might lead us to infer that there was a general election in 1666. But there is other evidence tending to show that the Assembly of 1661 was not dissolved until 1676. Thus William Sherwood wrote during Bacon's Rebellion that the rabble had risen against the Assembly and seemed weary of it, "in that itt was of 14 years continuance". (P. R. O., CO1-37-17; Va. Mag., Vol. I, p. 170.) The account of the Rebellion given in the Collections of the Massachusetts Historical Society also declares that the session had "continued fowerteene yeares". (Mass. S. IV, Vol. IX, p. 169.) The Isle of Wight grievances state that the people of that county had not had an election of Burgesses for twelve years. (Va. Mag., Vol. II, p. 380.) Lists of the members at the sessions of September, 1663, and of October, 1666, have been preserved by Hening. Nineteen Burgesses of the Assembly of 1663 appear also in 1666; eleven have lost their seats and in their places are fifteen new members. But this settles nothing, for it is quite possible that if an election was held in 1666, the Governor's influence might have secured the return of many old Burgesses. There was no election from June 1666 to June 1676. It must remain, then, undetermined whether the Long Assembly continued for ten or for fifteen years.

[56] P. R. O., CO1-20.   [57] Va. Mag., Vol. III, pp. 141, 142.

colony and the substitution of the Governor's despotic sway
contributed greatly to the anger and desperation of the people,
there can be no doubt. The evidence comes not only from the
rebels and from the county grievances, but from disinterested
persons, and even Berkeley's friends. "Whatever palliations,"
wrote Governor Thomas Notley, of Maryland, in 1677, "the
grate men of Virginia may use at the Councell board in England, . . . yett you may be sure . . . much . . . if not every
tittle" of the accusations against them are true. "If the ould
Course be taken and Coll: Jeoffreys build his proceedings upon
the ould ffoundation, its neither him nor all his Majesties
Souldiers in Virginia, will either satisfye or Rule those people.
They have been strangely dealt with by their former Magis-
tracy."[58]   William Sherwood, if we may believe his own
statement, forfeited Sir William's favor by reporting in England that "the general cry of the country was against ye
Governour". And "it is most true", he added, "that the great
oppressions & abuse of ye people by ye Governours arbitrary
will hath been ye cause of the late troubles here".[59]

The illegitimate influence of Berkeley over the Assembly
was the more galling to the people inasmuch as they had no
voice in local government. The justices of the peace, who
exercised the most important powers in the counties, received
their commissions, not by popular election, but by executive
appointment. And the Governor, although often influenced in
his selections by the advice of the Council, gave little heed to
the wishes of the commons. His appointees were invariably
men of means and influence, and could be relied upon to
uphold the interests of the aristocracy and the Governor.

The justices were members of the county courts, and as
such exercised judicial, executive and legislative functions in
local affairs. The courts met every second month, and were
empowered to settle cases involving not more than ten pounds
sterling.[60]   Individual justices could "try and determine any
cause to the value of twenty shillings or two hundred pounds
of tobacco".[61]   Far more important was the power of the

---

[58] P. R. O., CO1-40-88.   [59] P. R. O., CO1-40-43.
[60] Bruce, Inst. Hist., Vol. I, p. 542.   [61] P. R. O., CO1-20.

courts to impose direct taxes. The county levy was usually
very heavy. In fact, during the Restoration period, it often
exceeded the public levy voted by the Assembly. In Lower
Norfolk county, during the years from 1666 to 1683, the local
assessment amounted to 188,809 pounds of tobacco.[62] This
sum seems to us now almost insignificant, but it proved a
very real burden to the indigent freemen of that unhappy
period. Yet perhaps the people would not have complained
had the assessments been voted by a body elected by themselves or representative of their interests. They were bitterly
angered, however, that they should be taxed without their own
consent and against their wishes, by appointees of the Governor; and the sense of wrong was aggravated by the fact that
the taxes were often voted by the courts in secret session,
not without grave suspicions of abuses and fraud.[63] "It has
been the custome," it was declared in the Surry grievances, "of
the County Courts att the laying of the levy to withdraw
into a private Roome by which the poor people not knowing
for what they paid their levy did allways admire how their
taxes could be so high."[64] "Wee desire," declared the people
of the Isle of Wight, "to know for what wee doe pay our
Leavies everie year and that it may noe more be layd in
private."[65] From Charles City came the most startling charges
of fraud and oppression. "The Commisoners or Justices of
peace of this county," it was declared, "heretofore have il-
legally and unwarrantably taken upon them without our
consent from time to time to impose, rayse, assess and levy
what taxes, levies and imposicons upon us they have at any
time thought good or best liked, great part of which they
have converted to theire own use, as in bearing their expense
at the ordinary, allowing themselves wages for severall busi-
nesses which ex officio they ought to do, and other wayes, as
by account of the same on the booke for levies may appeare."[66]

The people were even deprived, during Berkeley's second
administration, of the right of electing the vestries. These

[62] Bruce, Inst. Hist., Vol. II, 566.   [63] Hen., Vol. II, 357.
[64] Va. Mag., Vol. II, p. 172.   [65] Va. Mag., Vol. II, p. 389.
[66] Va. Mag., Vol. III, p. 142.

bodies had always been composed of the foremost men in each parish. At this period they succeeded in shaking off entirely the control of the commons by themselves filling all vacancies in their ranks.[67]   Since they exercised the power of imposing a tax to pay the ministers' salaries and meet other obligations of the parishes, this attempt to make themselves self-perpetuating was a matter of no little importance.[68] The people expressed their disapproval in the most emphatic terms, and after Bacon's Rebellion requests came from many counties that the vestrymen might be chosen, as formerly, by the whole body of parishioners.[69]

The unjust poll-tax, which was then used in the public, county and parish levies, was an unending source of discontent.   There can be no doubt that it bore with too great weight upon the poor people. "They complain," wrote Gyles Bland, on the eve of the Rebellion, "that great Taxes are imposed upon them every yeare, by wayes very unequall, Laying them very heavily, by the Poll, whereby the Poorer sort are in the hardest Condition."[70]   It must be remembered, however, that many of the servants and slaves were listed as tithables, or persons subject to the poll tax. This of course tended to increase the share of the wealthy. Yet the inequality was very real and the burden upon the poor very heavy. The number of tithables assessed of a man was by no means an accurate gage of his wealth. Later in the century, with the great influx of negro slaves, the burden upon the rich planters increased and became more nearly proportionate to their ability to pay.

Bland suggested that all inequality might be eliminated by adopting a land-tax. "Which," he said, "seems to be the most equal imposition and will generally take off the complaint of the people, although perhaps some of the richest sort will not like it, who hold greater proportions of land than they actually plant."[71]   The King's commissioners also thought the land tax just, but considered it "impracticable there".

---

[67] Bruce, Inst. Hist., Vol. I, p. 67.
[68] Bruce, Inst. Hist., Vol. I, p. 77; Hen. Vol. II, p. 356.
[69] Va. Mag., Vol. II, pp. 172, 289, 388.
[70] P. R. O., CO1-36-54.   [71] P. R. O., CO1-36-54.

When the people of Warwick county asked, "That all persons may be rated and taxed according to their Estates", the commissioners reported that this was "a thing to be wish'd but never to be granted them". If the King should command it, they knew not how it would be relished by the landed men, since the common usage had been always taxing by poll.[72]

The universal discontent was still further increased by the wasteful and lax use of public funds. The money which was wrung from the poor people by these unequal taxes, was seldom wisely or economically expended. Much was squandered upon foolish projects, costly in the extreme, and impossible of accomplishment. Such was the attempt to build a city at Jamestown. For many years it had been a matter of regret to the English government that Virginia should remain so entirely a rural country. Not realizing that this was but the result of exceptional economic conditions and not a sign of weakness or decay, they sought more than once to force the building of towns by legislative enactments. Thus, in 1662, in accordance with the King's wishes, the Assembly passed an act providing for the erection of thirty-two brick houses at Jamestown.[73] Each county was required to build one of these houses, a levy of thirty pounds of tobacco per poll being laid for that purpose. This attempt was foredoomed to failure, for if economic conditions could not develop cities in the colony, the mere erection of houses upon the unhealthful Jamestown peninsula could accomplish nothing. We learn from Bacon's Proceedings that the town at the time of the Rebellion consisted of "som 16 or 18 howses, . . . and in them about a dozen families (for all the howses are not inhabited) getting their liveings by keeping ordnaries, at extraordnary rates". That there was corruption or inefficiency in carrying out the orders of the Assembly seems certain. The people of Isle of Wight county complained of "the great Quantities of Tobacco levyed for Building Houses of publick use and reception at Jamestown, which were not habitable, but fell downe before the Finishing of them".[74]

[72] P. R. O., CO5-1371-315.   [73] Hen., Vol. II, p. 172.
[74] P. R. O., CO5-1371-316-19, 304-5.

There were also accusations of laxness and fraud in the erecting and management of the public industrial plants. Very grievous taxes have been laid on the poor people, it was claimed, "for building work houses and stoare houses and other houses for the propogating & encouragem't of handicraft and manufactury, which were by our Burgesses to our great charge and burthen by their long and frequent sitting invented and proposed. Yet for want of due care the said houses were never finished or made useful, and the propagating & manufactury wholy in a short time neglected, and noe good ever effected . . . save the particular profitt of the Undertakers, who (as is usually in such cases) were largely rewarded for thus defrauding us."[75]

Even more frequent and bitter complaints originated with the construction of forts upon the various rivers to protect the colony and the merchant ships from foreign foes. At the outbreak of the war of 1664 it was resolved to build a fortress at Jamestown. The ships' masters were not satisfied with the selection of this site, for obviously it afforded no protection to vessels trading upon the Potomac, York or Rappahannock, and very little to those upon the lower James. After one hundred pounds sterling had been expended at Jamestown, the structure partly completed and fourteen guns brought up, the merchants procured orders from the English government that the fort be transferred to Old Point. The Governor and Council were most reluctant to make this change, but the commands were so positive they dared not disobey. So the guns were conveyed back down the river and the work begun again. But many serious difficulties were encountered. "We have been at 70,000lb tobacco charge," wrote Thomas Ludwell in 1667, "and have lost several men in the worke and many of the materials by storms breaking our rafts whereon we float the timber to that place. . . . After all (we) were forced to quit the work as of impossible manage, for great were the difficulties, and so insupportable would the charge have been."[76] A few months after, when the Dutch

[75] Va. Mag., Vol. III, p. 142; P. R. O., CO1-37-41.
[76] P. R. O., CO1-21.

captured the tobacco fleet in the mouth of the James, this fort seems to have been deserted. It was utterly destroyed by the great hurricane of the following August.

Thereupon it was decided to build five new forts, two on the James and one upon each of the other great rivers. The charges for these structures were to be borne entirely by the counties upon the rivers they were to defend. Whether from mismanagement or dishonesty large sums of money were expended in this undertaking with but little good effect. Berkeley wrote that the colony lacked the skill either to construct or maintain the forts. "We are at continuall charge," he declared, "to repair unskilfull & inartificall buildings." The King's commissioners in 1677, testified that the forts were made of "mudd and dirt", and could be of little service against the enemy.[77] At the beginning of the Dutch war of 1672 the Assembly found them in poor condition and incapable of offering resistance to the enemy. "For as much," it was declared, "as the materials . . . were not substantial or lasting, some have suffered an utter demolition, some very ruinous and some capable of repair." It was thereupon ordered that the forts be at once restored and authority was given for new taxes to cover the cost.[78]

One at least of the reconstructed forts proved of service in the hour of need, for it was under the guns of Nansemond that many of the merchantmen ran in July 1673, from the pursuing Dutch men-of-war. But the people could see in them only a pretext for increasing their taxes. And it was quite impossible to make them believe that such sums could be expended to so little purpose save by fraud or embezzlement. The Charles City commons declared that great quantities of tobacco had been raised for building forts "which were never finished but suffered to goe to ruine, the artillery buried in sand and spoyled with rust for want of care".[79] From James City county came the complaint that although heavy taxes had been paid for fortifications, there was in 1677 "noe Place of defence in ye Country sufficient to secure his Majestys Sub-

[77] P. R. O., CO5-1371-292, 7.   [78] P. R. O., CO1-29-31.
[79] Va. Mag., Vol. III, p. 142.

jects against any Forreign Invasion". The King's commissioners substantiated this statement. "We are well assured," they said, "of the Truth of this Complaint, and doe know that the Forts erected could be of noe use, Endurance or defence. . . . Yet were they of great Expence to the People who paid Excessively for Building them."[80]

The Assembly had from time to time sought to make the merchants trading to Virginia aid in the defense of the colony, by imposing upon them Castle Duties, in the form of a toll of powder and shot. The masters had more than once complained of this duty, but as it was not very burdensome it was allowed to remain. Had all the ammunition thus received been used as intended by law, the people would have been saved great expense, and the forts made more serviceable. But the contributions, if we may believe the complaints of the people, were often stolen by the collectors. "Notwithstanding," said the Isle of Wight commons, "the great quantities of ammunition payd by ships for fort duties for the countries service . . . wee are forced to provide powder and shott at our proper charges."[81] The Nansemond grievances were more explicit in their accusations of fraud. "They Complayne that the Castle duties, accustomed to be paid by the Masters of Shipps in Powder & Shott for the service and security of the Country, is now converted into Shoes and stockings &c as best liketh the Collectors of it and disposed to their own private advantage."[82]

It would not be just to give credence to all the accusations made against Berkeley. The King's commissioners who conducted the investigation into his conduct, were his enemies; while many of the charges were brought by those who had taken part in the Rebellion. Thus the testimony against him is in most cases distinctly partisan. Moreover those that were closely associated with Sir William often expressed extravagant admiration for his ability and energy, and love for his character.[83] "He hath," wrote the Council in 1673, "for

[80] P. R. O., CO5-1371-292, 7; CO1-21.
[81] Va. Mag., Vol. II, p. 387.   [82] P. R. O., CO5-1371-330, 331.
[83] P. R. O., CO1-20, 21.

neare 30 years governed this colony with that prudence and justice which hath gained him both love and reverence from all the Inhabitants here."[84]

Singularly enough Berkeley seems to have prided himself upon his ability as a ruler. He never forgot the compliment paid him by the people in 1660, when they insisted, even against his will, upon making him their Governor. And long after he had forfeited their confidence and esteem he imagined himself as popular as in his first administration. It was a bitter blow to his pride when the commons rose against his government in 1676. His proclamations bear testimony to his pain that the youthful Bacon should have usurped his place in the affections of the people.[85] His letter to the King asking to be recalled from his government was undoubtedly dictated by wounded pride. Upon the eve of his final departure for England he did not scruple to write Colonel Jeffreys, "I will confesse to you that I beleeve that the Inhabitants of this Colony wil quickly find a difference betweene your management and mine."[86]

It would be difficult to reconcile this attitude of mind with Berkeley's oppressive administration, did we not know his views upon governmental matters. He had never been in sympathy with republican institutions. It was the height of folly, he thought, to allow the people to participate either in administrative or legislative affairs. The King alone should rule; the people's duty was to obey. It was but five years before the Rebellion that he wrote to the Lords of Trade and Plantations, "I thanke God there is noe ffree schooles nor printing (in Virginia)[87] and I hope wee shall not have these hundred yeares, for learning has brought disobedience & heresaye and sects into the world and printing has divulged them, and libells against the best Government: God keepe us from both."[88] A man that could utter such sentiments as these

---

[84] P. R. O., CO1-30-71.   [85] P. R. O., CO1-37-1.

[86] P. R. O., CO1-40-54.

[87] Mr. P. A. Bruce, in his Institutional History of Virginia in the Seventeenth Century, has shown that this statement is incorrect.

[88] P. R. O., CO1-26-77.

would not scruple to throttle, if he could, all representative institutions in his government. If he intimidated voters and corrupted the Burgesses, it was perhaps because he thought himself justified in any measures that would render the Governor, the King's substitute, supreme in the government.

But whatever is the verdict of posterity upon the conduct and motives of Sir William Berkeley, the causes of the Rebellion stand out with great clearness:—England's selfish commercial policy, the Culpeper-Arlington grant, the Dutch wars, storms and pestilence, inefficient if not corrupt government, excessive taxes. The only wonder is that the insurrection did not occur earlier. In fact two mutinies did break out in 1674, when the excessively heavy taxes of that year were announced, but the rebels lacked leaders and were suppressed without great difficulty.[89] As early as 1673 the defection of the planters was so great that it was feared many might attempt to deliver the colony into the hands of the Dutch. Berkeley wrote that a large part of the people were so desperately poor that they might reasonably be expected upon any small advantage of the enemy to "revolt to them in hopes of bettering their Condition by Shareing the Plunder of the Country with them".[90] A certain John Knight reported "that the planters there doe generally desire a trade with the Dutch and all other nations and would not be singly bound to the trade of England, and speake openly there that they are in the nature of slaves, soe that the hearts of the greatest part of them are taken away from his Majesty".[91] Thus the downtrodden planters, alienated from England, angered at the Governor, even distrusting their own Assembly, waited but an occasion and a leader to rise in open rebellion. A new Indian war offered the occasion, and they found their leader in young Nathaniel Bacon.

[89] P. R. O., CO1-36-37; CO1-36-54.   [90] P. R. O., CO1-30-51.
[91] P. R. O., CO1-30-78.

CHAPTER VI

Bacon's Rebellion

For many years Virginia had been at peace with the neighboring Indians.[1] The long series of wars which had filled most of the first half of the seventeenth century had broken the spirit and power of the Pamunkeys, the Nansemonds and the Nottoways.[2] The remnants of these nations had become dependent upon the English, paying them tribute and looking to them for protection from their enemies.[3] In 1675, however, these friendly relations were disturbed by a southward movement of some of the northern Indians. Large bodies of the warlike Senecas, pressing upon the Susquehannocks at the head of the Chesapeake Bay, were driving them down into Maryland and Virginia. Here their indigence and their restlessness became a menace to the whites and an element of disturbance to their relations with the other tribes.[4]

In the summer of 1675 a party of savages rowed across the Potomac river, committed several murders and made good their escape into Maryland.[5] In anger and alarm the planters of Stafford county seized their arms to protect their homes and to avenge their neighbors. A band of thirty or more, led by Colonel Mason and Captain Brent, pursued the savages up the Potomac into the Maryland woods.[6] Coming in the early dawn upon two diverging trails, "each leader with his party took a separate path". "In less than a furlong either found a cabin", one crowded with Doeg Indians, the other with Susquehannocks. The king of the Doegs, when he saw his hut surrounded by Brent's men, "came trembling forth,

[1] Mass. S. IV, Vol. IX, p. 165; P. R. O., CO1-30-71.
[2] Hen., Vol. I, pp. 323, 380.   [3] Hen., Vol. II, p. 141.
[4] T. M., p. 9; Mass. S. IV, Vol. IX, pp. 165, 167.
[5] T. M., p. 9; P. R. O., CO5-1371-370; CO1-36-36; CO1-36-37.
[6] T. M., p. 8; Mass. S. IV, Vol. IX, p. 165.

and wou'd have fled". But Captain Brent, "catching hold of his twisted lock, which was all the hair he wore", commanded him to deliver up the men guilty of the recent murders. "The king pleaded ignorance and slipt loos", whereupon Brent shot him dead. At this the savages in the cabin opened fire, and the Virginians answered with a deadly volley. "Th' Indians throng'd out at the door and fled." "The English shot as many as they cou'd, so that they killed ten . . . and brought away the kings son." "The noise of this shooting awaken'd th' Indians in the cabin which Coll. Mason had encompassed, who likewise rush'd out and fled, of whom his company shot ffourteen."[7]

This unfortunate affair was the beginning of a deadly war between the English and the Indians, which brought untold suffering upon the people of Maryland and Virginia. The Susquehannocks, enraged at the slaughter of their warriors, became the most implacable enemies of the white men. Joining with the other tribes in a league against the English, they began a series of outrages and murders which continued many months, and cost the lives of hundreds of men, women and children. During the year 1676 alone, more people were butchered in Virginia by the savages than fell in the massacre of 1644.[8] This fearful mortality was due to the fact that the Indians were now supplied with firearms. Governor Berkeley and his friends, in their greed to secure the valuable beaver and otter skins, had not hesitated to purchase them with powder, shot and guns.[9] The savages had now almost entirely discarded the bow and arrow, and were so skilful with their new weapons that the English often hired them "to kill Deare".[10] So that when the war cry was once more heard upon the frontier, the savages, although less numerous than in the days of Powhatan or Opechancanough, were far more to be feared.

It was Maryland that first felt the resentment of the savages.

[7] T. M., pp. 8-9; P. R. O., CO5-1371-370; Mass. S. IV, Vol. IX, p. 165.
[8] P. R. O., CO1-39-10; CO1-36-78; W. & M. Q., Vol. IX, p. 10.
[9] W. & M. Q., Vol. IX, p. 6; T. M., p. 11.
[10] W. & M. Q., Vol. IX, p. 6.

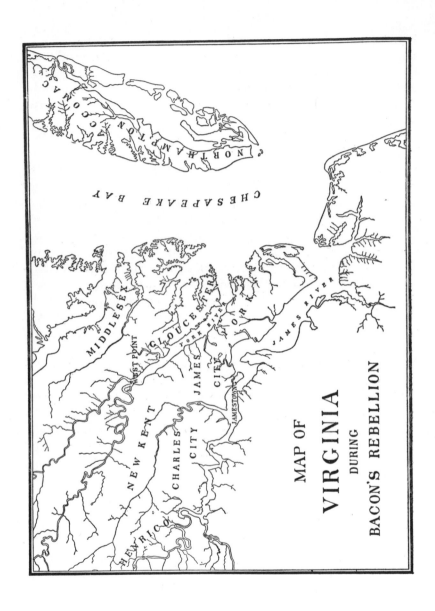

MAP OF

VIRGINIA

DURING

BACON'S REBELLION

The people of this province had taken no part in the attack of Mason and Brent, but the Susquehannocks were not in the humor to make nice distinctions. In seeking revenge for the murder of their braves they held all whites equally guilty, and fell immediately upon the nearest plantations. Thus were the Marylanders made to suffer for the rashness of the Virginia frontiersmen.

Feeling that it was his duty to aid the neighboring province in this war brought on by the hasty action of two of his own officers, and fearing that depredations upon the Virginia frontiers could not long be prevented, Sir William Berkeley decided to join Governor Calvert in a vigorous attack upon the savages. Colonel John Washington, great-grandfather of George Washington, at the head of several hundred men, was despatched across the Potomac to effect a junction with the Maryland troops.[11] The combined forces of the two colonies are said to have numbered "neer a thousand men".[12]

Unable to withstand this army in the open field, the Indians fell back upon a fort which they had erected upon the north bank of the Potomac, and here awaited the approach of the English. Their fortress had been constructed with such care and skill that the white men were unable to carry it by storm. The outer works consisted of lines of tree trunks, from five to eight inches in diameter, "watled 6 inches apart to shoot through", their tops firmly twisted together. Behind this was a ditch, and within all a square citadel, with high walls and "fflankers having many loop-holes". The fire of the red-skins from behind these works proved so deadly that hopes of a successful assault had to be abandoned. Nor could breaches be effected, for the allies were not provided with heavy guns. The moist and swampy ground surrounding the fort made it impossible to approach by means of trenches.[13]

So the English cast their camp before the fort hoping to starve out the enemy. Lines were drawn about the place, as closely as the nature of the ground would permit, while boats

[11] Mass. S. IV, Vol. IX, p. 165; P. R. O., CO1-36-78.
[12] P. R. O., CO5-1371-369; T. M., p. 9.
[13] T. M., p. 10.

patrolled the river to cut off escape to the Virginia shore. Fearing, no doubt, that lack of provisions would soon make it necessary for them to come to terms with the besiegers, the Indians sent out several of their leaders to treat for peace. But so deep was the animosity aroused by the recent murders, that the white men violated the flag of truce by detaining these envoys, and finally beating out their brains.[14] This flagrant act aroused the Indians to a desperate defense. In numerous sallies they inflicted severe loss upon the besiegers, and captured enough horses to supply themselves with food. At last, after six or seven weeks of fighting, they resolved to effect their escape. On a dark night, when the English were least expecting it, they sallied forth, bringing with them their women and children. Awakening the white men with their savage yells, they burst in among them, killing and wounding many, and before resistance could be made, were through the lines and gone.[15]

And now the Virginians were made to pay dearly for their part in this ill-managed affair. Early in January, 1676, the Susquehannocks crossed the Potomac and came plundering and murdering through the frontier counties.[16] Separating into small bands, the Indians fell upon the more isolated plantations, and in a few days had killed no less than thirty-six persons. Those whose wretched fate it was to be captured, were put to death with all the tortures that devilish ingenuity could devise. Some were roasted, others flayed alive. The sufferings of the victims were long and protracted, while the savages knocked out their teeth or tore off their nails or stuck feathers and lighted wood into their flesh.[17]

In terror the people of the frontier began to desert their homes, seeking shelter in the more populous settlements.[18]

[14] T. M., p. 9; P. R. O., CO392.1-173, 178; Cotton, p. 3; Inds' Pros. p. 5; P. R. O., CO5-1371-370.

[15] P. R. O., CO1-36-78; CO5-1371-369; T. M., pp. 9-10; Inds' Pros., pp. 7-8; Mass. S. IV, Vol. IX, p. 165.

[16] P. R. O., CO5-1371-370.

[17] Inds' Pros., p. 7; P. R. O., CO5-1371-370; CO1-36-66; Mass. S. IV, Vol. IX, p. 176.

[18] W. & M. Q., Vol. IX, p. 7.

In a few weeks one parish, upon the upper waters of the Rappahannock, was reduced from seventy-one plantations to eleven.[19] Those that remained were concentrated upon the largest farms, which they fortified with palisades and redoubts.[20]

When the news of these atrocities reached Sir William Berkeley, hasty preparations were made for an expedition against the invaders. Sir Henry Chicheley was put at the head of forces of horse and foot, with orders to give immediate pursuit to the savages. But just as all was in readiness and the command to march hourly expected, the Governor decided that the expedition should be abandoned. Chicheley's commission was annulled, his forces disbanded and the soldiers sent to their homes.[21]

What induced Berkeley to take this strange step none could tell. The murders of the savages were continuing. The frontier was defenseless. Messages were coming from the exposed plantations imploring aid. Why should he desert the people and expose them to the fury of the Indians? It is possible that he detected symptoms of mutiny among the troops and thought it better to abandon the expedition than to run the risk of a rebellion. He was well aware of the discontent of the people, and his letters to England show that he dreaded an insurrection.[22] The unhappy planters ascribed the Governor's strange conduct to avarice. He and his friends had a monopoly of the Indian trade, and it was hinted that he preferred to allow the atrocities to continue rather than destroy his source of revenue. He was determined, was the cry, "that no bullits would pierce beaver skins".[23] More probable seems the explanation that Berkeley hoped to prevent further depredations by the help of the Pamunkeys and other friendly tribes, and feared that an invasion of the Indian lands might defeat this purpose.[24]

But an Assembly was summoned in March and instructed

[19] P. R. O., CO5-1371-372; Va. Mag., Vol. III, p. 35.
[20] T. M., p. 10.   [21] P. R. O., CO5-1371-373, 411.
[22] P. R. O., CO1-30-51; CO1-36-37.
[23] T. M., p. 11; W. & M. Q., Vol. IX, p. 7; P. R. O., CO5-1371-375.
[24] P. R. O., CO1-36-36.

by the Governor to take immediate measures to secure the frontier.[25]   Acting, no doubt, under Berkeley's influence, the Assembly resolved not to carry the conflict into the enemy's territory, but to wage a defensive war.   Forts were to be erected upon the upper waters of the great rivers, and manned with regular troops as a protection to the outer plantations. To defray the cost, new and heavy taxes were put upon the people.[26]

This last act of the Long Assembly caused bitter dissatisfaction.   The border counties had hoped that provision would be made for an expedition against the Indians.   No headway could be made unless the whites took the offensive and hunted down the savages in their own villages.   The erection of forts was useless.[27]   The Indians would experience no difficulty in avoiding them in their murderous raids.   They could approach the remote plantations, or even those far within the frontiers, without fear of detection by the soldiers, for the numerous swamps and dense woods afforded them ample covert.   It was not intended that the forts should be used as bases for expeditions into the enemy's country; nor could the soldiers leave them to pursue and punish the plundering savages.   What then, it was asked, could be the value of fortresses, if they were to defend only the ground upon which they stood?[28]

The event proved the people right.   The forts, when built, were but slight obstacles to the invasions of the Indians. The murders became more frequent than before.   The impotency of the defenses of the colony seems to have inspired them to more terrible and vigorous attacks.   The cry against the forts became more bitter.   "It was a design," the people thought, "of the grandees to engross all their tobacco into their own hands".[29]   As the cries of their women and children grew more piteous and distressing, the men of the frontier spoke openly of disobedience.   Rather than pay the taxes for the

[25] Mass. S. IV, Vol. IX, p 165; Hen., Vol. II, p. 326.
[26] P. R. O., CO5-1371-373; Hen., Vol. II, pp. 327-329.
[27] Inds' Pros., pp. 8, 9.
[28] P. R. O., CO5-1371-378.   [29] P. R. O., CO5-1371-374.

accursed forts they would plant no more tobacco. If the Governor would not send an expedition against the Indians, they themselves would march out to avenge their wrongs. The forts must be dismantled, the garrisons dismissed.[30]

From all parts of the colony came the insistent demand that the Assembly, which had so long been but a mockery of representative government, should be dissolved and the people given a free election.[31] But Berkeley was not the man to yield readily to this clamor. Never, in all the long years that he had ruled over Virginia, had he allowed the rabble to dictate his policies. He would not do so now. When petitions came from the frontiersmen, asking leave to go out against the Indians, he returned a brusk and angry refusal.[32] A delegation from Charles City county met with a typical reception from the irritable old man. As they stood humbly before him, presenting their request for a commission, they spoke of themselves as the Governor's subjects. Upon this Berkeley blurted out that they were all "fools and loggerheads". They were subjects of the King, and so was he. He would grant them no commission, and bade them be gone, and a pox take them.[33] Later he issued a proclamation forbidding under heavy penalties all such petitions.[34]

Unfortunately, at this juncture came news that large bodies of Indians were descending upon the upper waters of the James, and that another bloody assault might soon be expected.[35] In terror and anger the people of Charles City county seized their arms, determined to repel this threatened storm, with or without the Governor's permission. Parties went about from place to place beating up volunteers with the drum. The magistrates were either in sympathy with the movement, or were unable to prevent it.[36] Soon a considerable body of rough, determined men were assembled, awaiting only a leader to march out against the enemy.

This leader they found in one of the most interesting and

[30] P. R. O., CO5-1371-378; Inds' Pros., p. 8.
[31] P. R. O., CO5-1371-379; CO1-37-17.
[32] P. R. O., CO5-1371-375.   [33] P. R. O., CO1-40-106.
[34] P. R. O., CO5-1371-375.   [35] Ibid.
[36] Ibid.

picturesque characters in Virginia history. Nathaniel Bacon
is depicted as twenty-nine years of age, black-haired, of
medium height and slender, melancholy, pensive, and taciturn.
In conversation he was logical and convincing; in oratory
magnetic and masterful.[37] His successful expeditions against
the Indians and the swift blows he directed against the loyal
forces mark him as a military commander of no mean
ability.[38]

Bacon was almost a stranger in Virginia, for he had left
England less than two years before.[39] He was fortunate,
however, in having a cousin, also named Nathaniel Bacon,
high in the favor of Sir William Berkeley.[40] It was doubtless
through the influence of this relative that the young man attained a position of great influence, and was appointed to the
Council itself.[41] But submission to the will of the imperious
Governor was the price paid by all that wished to remain long
in favor in Virginia. Bacon did not approve of Berkeley's
arbitrary government; he disliked the long continuation of
the Assembly, the unjust discriminations, the unusual taxes,
the incapacity of officials; and it was not in his fiery temper
to conceal his opinions. Soon, it would seem, the frowns of
the Governor began to fall upon him, and he grew weary of
coming to Council.[42]

Bacon had made his home in Henrico, at that time one of
the extreme frontier counties. His marked ability, his liberal
education, his place in the Council soon gave him a position
of great influence among his rough but hardy neighbors.
None could be better suited to assume command over the
desperate volunteers that had gathered in Charles City
county.

But it was a very serious step to accept the leadership of
this band which had taken arms in defiance of the Governor's
commands. It would expose him to the charge not only of
disobedience, but of open rebellion. Bacon, however, like all

[37] Bac's Pros., p. 9.   [38] P. R. O., CO5-1371-376.
[39] Cotton, p. 4; Mass. S. IV, Vol. IX, p. 180; P. R. O., CO1-37-1.
[40] Va. Mag., Vol. II, pp. 125-129.   [41] P. R. O., CO5-1371-375.
[42] Va. Mag., Vol. III, pp. 134-135.

that dwelt upon the frontiers, was angered at the inadequate protection given by the government. When news came to him that depredations had been committed upon one of his own plantations, and that his overseer had been killed, he was eager to take revenge.[43]

Now some of Bacon's friends, as anxious as he for an Indian expedition, and thinking him most proper to conduct it, suggested his name to the volunteers. The men were quite willing to accept so influential a commander, but it was not so easy to persuade Bacon to take the dangerous place. He consented, however, to row across the river, and visit the soldiers in their camp. Here the men gathered around him, and with joyous shouts of, "A Bacon! A Bacon!" proclaimed him their leader. His friends pressed him to accept. They would, they said, accompany him on his expedition. If the Governor ordered them to disband, they would defy him. "They drank damnation to their souls", if they should prove untrue to him. Touched by these proofs of confidence, and fired perhaps with ambition, the young man yielded, and Bacon's Rebellion had begun.[44]

From the very first the movement assumed the character of an insurrection.[45] Amid the hearty applause of his rough followers, Bacon spoke of the negligence, the incapacity and wickedness of the government. Their betrayal into the hands of the savages was but one of many grievances. The laws were unjust, the taxes oppressive. Something must be done to redress these wrongs and to end misgovernment.[46] And as the poor people flocked in to him, he listed their names in a huge round-robin and bound them to him by an oath of fidelity.[47]

A message was dispatched to the Governor to request a commission authorizing the expedition against the Indians.[48]

[43] P. R. O., CO5-1371-376; W. & M. Q., Vol. IX, pp. 4, 7.
[44] P. R. O., CO5-1371-376.
[45] P. R. O., CO1-36-54; CO1-36-37; CO1-37-1.
[46] P. R. O., CO5-1371-376, 7; CO1-36-54; CO1-37-1; Mass. S. IV, Vol. IX, p. 166.
[47] P. R. O., CO5-1371-376, 7.
[48] W. & M. Q., Vol. IX, p. 7; Mass. S. IV, Vol. IX, p. 166.

But Bacon promised his men that if Sir William withheld his assent, he would lead them forth without it; and in the meanwhile, without waiting for the Governor's reply, he crossed over into New Kent, "a county ripe for rebellion", where he expected to strengthen his position and perhaps attack the Pamunkeys.[49] This nation had for many years been friendly to the English, and had more than once given them invaluable assistance against other Indian tribes. Their present queen was the widow of Tottopottomoi, who had been killed while fighting as the ally of the white men against the Richahecrians.[50] They now occupied land allotted them by the Assembly, upon the frontier of New Kent, where, it was supposed, they would act as a protection to the colony against the raids of hostile tribes.[51] When the Susquehannocks began their depredations Governor Berkeley expected valuable assistance from these allies, whom he termed his "spyes and intelligence" to search out "the bloody enimies".[52] But the Pamunkeys not only failed to check the invasion of the Susquehannocks, but seem to have joined with them in the work of bloodshed and pillage. The people of the frontier believed that almost all the Indians were leagued together for their ruin. The Pamunkeys, they were sure, had taken part in the recent atrocities. And as they were their close neighbors, knowing all their customs and all their habitations, they were especially fitted for the work of destruction. The New Kent planters were now impatient to march out against them to take revenge for the recent horrible murders. But the Pamunkeys, upon hearing of Bacon's approach, deserted their reservation and took refuge in the wilderness.[53]

It is not hard to imagine the Governor's anger when he heard of these proceedings. Despite the testimony of the frontiersmen, he had refused to believe the Pamunkeys guilty, and he still relied upon them for assistance against the Susquehannocks. Bacon's proceedings, in frightening them

[49] P. R. O., CO5-1371-377; W. & M. Q., Vol. IX, p. 4.

[50] Hen., Vol. I, p 422; Burk, Vol. II, pp. 104-106; Force, Vol. I, Tract VIII, p. 14.

[51] Hen., Vol. I, p. 380.   [52] Mass. S. IV, Vol. IX, pp. 166, 180.

[53] Mass. S. IV, p. 166.

from their lands, upset all his plans of defense. Yet had the volunteers contented themselves with attacking the Indians, it is conceivable that Berkeley would have yielded. But when they took up arms without his permission, put themselves under the command of a discontented Councillor, and demanded redress of grievances from the government, it was necessary for him to resort to repression. The commission was refused and a proclamation issued denouncing Bacon's conduct as illegal and rebellious. He and his men were offered pardon, but only on condition that they lay down their arms, and return immediately to their obedience.[54]

But the mutineers would not obey. Are we, they complained, to return passively to our homes, there to be slaughtered by the savage foe? The Governor has given us no protection. The Indians are coming. Already the blood of our butchered relatives cries aloud to Heaven. We hope we have still enough English blood in our veins to think it more honorable to die in fair battle with the enemy, than to be sneakingly murdered in our beds. If we lie still, we are destroyed by the heathen; if we defend ourselves, we are accounted rebels and traitors. But we will fight. And if we must be hanged for killing those that will destroy us, let them hang us, we will venture that rather than lie at the mercy of our barbarous enemies. So, turning their backs upon the plantations, they struck out into the dense woods.[55]

When Berkeley heard that his authority was still defied, and his pardon rejected, he was resolved at all hazards to compel obedience. Gathering around him a party of three hundred gentlemen, "well armed and mounted", he set out, on the third of May, to intercept the rebels.[56] But learning, upon his arrival at the falls of the James, that Bacon had crossed the river and was already far away, he decided to encamp in the frontier counties and await his return.[57]

But he sent out a party under Colonel Claiborne to pursue the Pamunkeys, and induce them, if possible, to return to their

[54] P. R. O., CO5-1371-377; CO1-36-55; CO1-37-1.
[55] P. R. O., CO5-1371-377; CO1-36-66; CO1-37-14.
[56] Mass. S. IV, Vol. IX, p. 167.   [57] P. R. O., CO5-1371-377.

reservation. The savages were found entrenched in a strong
position, "encompassed with trees which they had fallen in the
branch of an Impassable swamp".[58] Their queen refused to
abandon this retreat, declaring that since the Governor had
not been able to command the obedience of Bacon, he could not
save her people from his violence. But she promised that the
Pamunkeys should remain peaceable and should take no part
in the raids of the Susquehannocks. "Of this the Governor
was informed, who resolved not to be soe answered but to
reduce her and the other Indians, soe soone as Bacon could
be brought to submit."[59]

On May the tenth Berkeley issued a new proclamation.
The taking of arms by Bacon, he said, against his wishes and
commands, was an act of disloyalty and rebellion. If permitted to go unpunished, it would tend to the ruin and overthrow of all government in the colony. It was his duty to use
all the forces at his command to suppress so dangerous a
mutiny. Should the misguided people desert their leader, and
return to their allegiance, he would grant a free and full pardon. And as Nathaniel Bacon had shown himself by his
rash proceedings utterly unworthy of public trust, he suspended him from the Council and from all other offices held
by him. It was amazing, he said, that after he had been Governor of Virginia so many years, and had done always equal
justice to all men, the people should be seduced and carried
away by so young and turbulent a person as Bacon.[60]

But although Berkeley was determined to suppress the rebels
by force of arms, the attitude of the commons in other parts
of the colony became so threatening that he was forced to
make some concessions. To the great joy of the people he
dissolved the unpopular Long Assembly, and ordered a new
election. It was with sorrow, he declared, that he departed
with the present Burgesses, who had given frequent proof of
ability and wisdom. But the complaints of many inhabitants
of the long continuance of the old Assembly had induced him
to grant a free election. And if any man had grievances against

[58] Mass. S. IV, Vol. IX, p. 168.   [59] Ibid.
[60] P. R. O., CO1-37-1.

his government, or could accuse him of injustice or bribery, he was to present his complaint by his Burgesses to the Assembly, where it would be examined.[61]

It was indeed time for the Governor to act, for the rebellion was spreading to the older and more populous counties.[62] The people there too were denouncing the forts, and demanding redress of grievances. Some began to arm, and it seemed not improbable that the entire colony might soon be ablaze. Hastening back to his residence at Green Spring, he sought to appease the people by dismantling the obnoxious forts and dismissing their garrisons.[63]

In the meanwhile Bacon was making his way through the woods southward from the falls of the James in pursuit of the Susquehannocks that had committed the recent murders upon the frontier.[64] These savages had not attempted to return to their homes north of the Potomac, but had retired to the country of the Occaneechees, where they had entrenched themselves in two forts.[65] The Occaneechees dwelt in the southernmost part of Virginia, near the site of Clarksville.[66] They are described as a stout people, and the most enterprising of traders. Their chief town, situated upon an island in the Roanoke River and defended by three strong forts, was "the Mart for all the Indians for att least 500 miles" around.[67] The beaver skins stored in this place at the time of Bacon's expedition are said to have valued no less than £1,000.[68] Persicles, their king, was reported to be an enlightened ruler, "a very brave man & ever true to ye English".[69]

It was toward this island that Bacon led his men. But a quest for Indian allies took him far out of his route. Every-

[61] P. R. O., CO1-36-64. Berkeley's proclamation, addressed to the sheriff of Rappahannock county, dissolving the Assembly, and the proclamation denouncing Bacon as a traitor were both issued in Henrico, on May 10, 1676.
[62] P. R. O., CO5-1371-379.   [63] P. R. O., CO5-1371-379, 411.
[64] W. & M. Q., Vol. IX, p. 1; Va. Mag., Vol. I, p. 180; P. R. O., CO1-36-77; CO1-37-16.
[65] Va. Mag., Vol. I, p. 180.   [66] W. & M. Q., Vol. XI, p. 121.
[67] Mass. S. IV, Vol. IX, p. 167.   [68] Ibid.
[69] P. R. O., CO1-37-16; Va. Mag., Vol. I, p. 182.

where he found the savages reluctant to aid him, even those nations that had formerly been most friendly to the English now holding aloof from them. This embarrassed him greatly for he had relied upon receiving aid from several tribes, and his food was not sufficient for a long march. As the little army went further and further into the wilderness, they began to face the possibility of starvation. When at last they approached the Occaneechee country and received promises of aid from Persicles, their provisions were nearly exhausted.[70]

Upon reaching the Roanoke the English crossed the north branch of the river and encamped upon the Occaneechee island.[71] To his deep satisfaction, Bacon found Persicles embroiled with the Susquehannocks, and already preparing for their destruction. When these wanderers from the north first came to him, Persicles had received them with kindness and had relieved their needs. But they, "being exercised in warr for many years with the Senecaes, and living on rapin, endeavoured to beat the Ockinagees of their own Island".[72] Persicles had defeated them, however, and forced them to take refuge in their two forts.[73]

Now the Susquehannocks, in their southward march, had subdued and brought with them some members of the Mannakin and Annelecton tribes.[74] These savages, although they lived with their conquerors, had no love for them, and were quite willing to join in any plan for their destruction. Persicles, it would seem, was plotting with them to surprise and cut off the Susquehannocks, when Bacon appeared with his men. Fearing, no doubt, that the participation of the English in the attack would render secrecy impossible, Persicles left them on the island, and went out alone against the enemy.[75] The Mannakins and Annelectons proved true to their allies and the Susquehannocks were easily defeated. Persicles returned in triumph, bringing with him several prisoners. These he

[70] P. R. O., CO1-36-77.   [71] Va. Mag., Vol. I, p. 181.
[72] Mass. S. IV, Vol. I, p. 167.   [73] Ibid.
[74] Va. Mag., Vol. I, p. 181; P. R. O., CO1-37-16; W. & M. Q., Vol. IX, p. 2.
[75] P. R. O., CO1-37-16.

wished the English to execute, but they "refused to take that office".[76] Thereupon he himself put them to death with all the usual Indian tortures, "running fyer brands up their bodys & the like".[77]

But now the friendship of Persicles and the English came abruptly to an end. The Berkeley party afterwards claimed that Bacon deliberately picked a quarrel with his allies, and attacked them without provocation.[78] It would be unjust, however, to place too much confidence in these charges. Bacon's men found themselves in a most critical situation. They were many miles from the plantations, surrounded by the savages, their provisions exhausted. Persicles, they asserted, had failed to keep his promise to supply them with food. He was assuming a threatening posture, manning his forts, and lining the river bank with his warriors. For Bacon to retreat from the island under these circumstances, would have exposed his company to destruction. To remain passive was to starve.[79]

As the English became more insistent in their demands for food, Persicles retired to one of his forts, and refused further conference. Many of the savages, seeing hostilities imminent, deserted their cabins and began to rush in through the entrances of their fortresses. But Bacon interposed his men, and succeeded in shutting out many of them.[80] Now from the Indians across the river came a shot, and one of the English fell dead.[81] Instantly Bacon ordered a general attack. The defenseless men, women and children left in the cabins were mercilessly butchered. At the same time fire was opened upon the forts. The soldiers rushed up to the portholes, and poured their volleys directly in upon the wretched savages.[82] A hideous din arose. The singing and howling of the warriors was mingled with the moans of the dying. Fire was set to one of the forts, in which were the king's wife and children. As the flames arose, three or four braves made a dash for

[76] P. R. O., CO1-36-77.
[77] Mass. S. IV, Vol. IX, p. 167; P. R. O., CO1-37-16; CO1-36-77.
[78] Mass. S. IV, Vol. IX, p. 167.   [79] P. R. O., CO1-36-77.
[80] Mass. S. IV, Vol. IX, p. 168.   [81] P. R. O., CO1-37-16.
[82] W. & M. Q., Vol. IX, p. 7.

safety through the line of the English. All others in this fort, including the king's family, perished amid the burning timbers.[83]

The next day the fight was continued from morn till night. Several times the savages sallied forth from their remaining forts, and placing themselves behind trees, opened fire upon the English. But Bacon's frontiersmen were accustomed to this method of warfare. So well were they posted and so cleverly concealed, that most of the enemy were picked off as they stood. At last Persicles himself led forth a party of about twenty men in a desperate attack upon his enemy. With great bravery they rushed around the English in a wide circle, howling and firing. But they too were unsuccessful. Persicles was killed. Several of his men were shot on the bank of the river, and fell into the water. Of all this party seven only were seen to escape.[84]

It now seemed hopeless for the Indians to fight further. With their king and many of their warriors dead, and with one of their forts in ruins, their ultimate destruction was certain if they remained upon the island. So, with their women and children, they deserted the remaining forts and escaped. How they managed to slip past the victorious white men and make their way across the river is not explained. Thinking it best not to follow, Bacon secured his plunder, and turned his face back towards the plantations.[85]

The news of the victory over the savages was received with enthusiasm in the frontier counties. Bacon had been popular with the people before; he now became their idol.[86] He and his men, upon their return, found the entire colony deeply interested in the election of a new House of Burgesses. In various places popular candidates, men in sympathy with Bacon, were being nominated.[87] In Henrico county the people showed their contempt for the Governor's proclamations by electing Bacon himself.[88]

---

[83] P. R. O., CO1-36-77.   [84] W. & M. Q., Vol. IX, p. 7.

[85] P. R. O., CO1-36-77; CO1-36-16; T. M., p. 11.

[86] W. & M. Q., Vol. IX, p. 5.   [87] P. R. O., CO5-1371-379.

[88] Bac's Pros., p. 11; T. M., p. 12.

But it would be a matter of no little risk for him to go to Jamestown to take his seat in the Assembly. While surrounded by his loyal frontiersmen in his own county he might well ignore the proclamations against him, but if he put himself in the Governor's power, that fiery old man might not hesitate to hang him as a rebel. His friends would not allow him to go unprotected, and insisted upon sending with him a guard of forty or fifty armed men.[89] Embarking with this company in a sloop, Bacon wended his way down the crooked James to the capital. He cast anchor a short distance above the town and sent to the Governor to know whether he would be allowed to take his seat in the Assembly without molestation.[90] For reply Sir William opened fire upon the sloop with the guns of the fort.[91] Whereupon Bacon sailed further up the river out of danger.[92] But that night he landed with twenty of his men, and unobserved by any, slipped silently into town.[93]

In the place resided Richard Lawrence and William Drummond, both deeply impressed with the need of reform in Virginia, and both in sympathy with Bacon's movement. Repairing to Lawrence's house, Bacon conferred with these two friends for several hours.[94] Upon reëmbarking he was discovered. Alarm was immediately given in the town and several boats filled with armed men pursued him up the river. At the same time Captain Gardner, commanding the ship *Adam and Eve,* was ordered to follow the fugitives, and capture or sink the sloop. For some hours Bacon eluded them all. Finally, however, about three the next afternoon, he was driven by the small boats under the guns of the *Adam and Eve,* and forced to surrender.[95] Coming on board he was entrusted to Captain Gardner and Captain Hubert Farrill, and by them conducted to the Governor.[96]

As the prisoner was led before him, the old man lifted his

[89] P. R. O., CO5-1371-369; CO1-37-16, 17; Bac's Pros., p. 11; Mass. S. IV, Vol. IX, p. 170.
[90] P. R. O., CO5-1371-379.   [91] Ibid.
[92] Ibid.   [93] Ibid.
[94] P. R. O., CO5-1371-380; CO1-37-16; Mass. S. IV, Vol. IX, p. 170.
[95] Ibid.   [96] Ibid.

eyes and arms to Heaven, exclaiming, "Now I behold the greatest Rebell that ever was in Virginia!"[97] After some moments he added, "Mr. Bacon, doe you continue to be a gentleman? And may I take your word? If so you are at liberty upon your parol."[98] Later, when the rebel expressed gratitude at this mild treatment and repentance for his disobedience, Berkeley promised to grant him a free pardon. And should he offer a humble submission, he was to be restored to his seat in the Council, and even receive the long desired commission.[99]

In this unexpected leniency the Governor was probably actuated not by magnanimity, but by policy, or perhaps necessity. When the rebel was out upon his Indian expedition, Sir William had not scrupled to tell Mrs. Bacon that he would most certainly hang her husband, if ever he got him in his power.[100] But now he dared not do so. Bacon was regarded by a large part of the people as their leader in a struggle for justice and liberty; to treat him too harshly might set the entire colony ablaze. In fact, many frontiersmen, when they heard of the capture of their hero, did hasten down to Jamestown with dreadful threats of revenge should a hair of his head be touched.[101] And throughout the colony the mutterings of impending insurrection were too loud to be mistaken or ignored.[102]

A few days after the capture, at a meeting of Council and Assembly, the Governor arose from his chair, saying, "If there be joy in the presence of the angels over one sinner that repenteth, there is joy now, for we have a penitent sinner come before us. Call Mr. Bacon." Whereupon the rebel entered, and dropping upon his knee, presented his submission. "God forgive you," said the Governor, "I forgive you." "And all that were with him?" asked one of the Council. "Yea," said Sir William, "all that were with him."[103] That very day Bacon was restored to his seat in the Council.[104] The soldiers

[97] CO5-1371-380. [98] Ibid.
[99] Va. Mag., Vol. I, p. 171; Hen., Vol. II, p. 543.
[100] W. & M. Q., Vol. IX, p. 5. [101] T. M., p. 15.
[102] W. & M. Q., Vol. IX, p. 8. [103] T. M., pp. 12-13.
[104] P. R. O., CO1-37-16.

that had been captured with him were freed from their chains and permitted to return to their homes.[105] And, to the great joy of the people, it was publicly announced by one of the Burgesses, that Bacon had been granted a commission as general in the Indian war.[106] Feeling that all was now well, and that their presence in Jamestown was no longer necessary, the sturdy frontiersmen shouldered their fusils, and returned to their plantations.[107]

But the reconciliation could be but temporary. Bacon's repentance and submission had been forced from him while helpless in the Governor's power. He did not consider it morally binding. And so long as the people's grievances were not righted, and the Indian war was neglected, he could not be content to remain inactive and submissive. On the other hand, Sir William probably felt that his promise of a commission had been exacted by the unlawful threats of Bacon's friends, and might be broken without dishonor.[108]

After waiting several days for his papers, Bacon became suspicious of the Governor's intentions, and set out for his home in Henrico.[109] Berkeley consented to his departure, and he took "civill leave", but immediately afterwards he repented bitterly that he had let his enemy thus slip through his fingers. It is probable that information came to him just too late, that Bacon was again meditating resistance. Parties of men were sent out upon the roads and up the river to intercept his flight. The very beds of his lodging house were searched in desperate haste, in the hope that he had not yet left Jamestown. But all in vain. Bacon had ridden quietly out of town, without servants or friends, and was now far on his way towards the frontier.[110]

On his arrival at Henrico, his old comrades flocked around him, eager to be led out against the Indians, and confident in the belief that Bacon was authorized to command them. And when they learned that he had not secured a commission, and was once more a fugitive, they "sett their throats in one com-

[105] Mass. S. IV, Vol. IX, p. 170; P. R. O., COI-37-16.
[106] W. & M. Q., Vol. IX, p. 8.
[107] Ibid.
[108] Ibid.
[109] W. & M. Q., Vol. IX, p. 9.
[110] Va. Mag., Vol. I, p. 171.

mon key of Oathes and curses, and cried out aloud, that they would either have a Commission . . . or else they would pull downe the Towne".[111] And as the news spread from place to place, rough, angry men came flocking in to Bacon, promising that if he would but lead them to the Governor, they would soon get him what he pleased. "Thus the raging tumult came downe to Towne."[112]

Vague rumors began to reach the Assembly that Bacon was marching on Jamestown at the head of five hundred men.[113] By June the twenty-second, it became definitely known that the rebels were approaching.[114] Berkeley sent out several messengers to demand their intentions, but could get no satisfactory reply. Hasty preparations were made to defend the town.[115] The neighboring militia was summoned. Four guns were dragged to Sandy Bay to command the narrow neck of land that connected the peninsula with the left bank of the river.[116] It was proposed to construct palisades across the isthmus. Early on the morning of the 23d, Berkeley went out himself to direct the mounting of the guns.[117] But it was too late. On all sides the people were crying, "To arms! To arms! Bacon is within two miles of the town." The rebels were threatening, it was reported, that if a gun was fired against them, they would kill and destroy all.[118] Seeing that resistance would be useless, and might be fatal, the Governor ordered the guns to be dismounted, withdrew his soldiers, and retired to the state house.[119]

And so the rebels streamed unresisted into the town, a motley crew of many sorts and conditions: Rough, weatherbeaten, determined frontiersmen, bent on having the commission for their leader; poor planters, sunk deep in debt, denouncing the government and demanding relief from their taxes; freedmen whose release from bondage had brought them little but hunger and nakedness. Moderation and reason were not to be expected of such a band, and it is not strange

[111] P. R. O., CO5-1371-381.
[113] Mass. S. IV, Vol. IX, p. 171.
[115] P. R. O., CO1-37-16.
[117] Ibid.
[119] Ibid.

[112] P. R. O., CO5-1371-382.
[114] P. R. O., CO1-37-17.
[116] P. R. O., CO1-37-17.
[118] Ibid.

that many of them talked openly of overthrowing the government and sharing the property of the rich among themselves. Sixteen years of oppression and injustice were bearing their natural fruit—rebellion.[120]

"Now tagg, ragg & bobtayle carry a high hand."[121] Bacon leaves a force to guard Sandy Bay, stations parties at the ferry and the fort, and draws up his little army before the state-house.[122] Two Councillors come out from Berkeley to demand what he wants. Bacon replies that he has come for a commission as general of volunteers enrolled against the Indians. And he protests that if the Assembly intends a levy for new forces, his men will refuse to pay it. The ragged troops shout their approval with cries of "Noe Levies! Noe Levies!"[123]

It is easy to imagine with what anger the Governor drew up and signed the commission. But he dared not refuse it. He was in the power of the rebels, who were already muttering threats of bloodshed and pillage. To defy them might bring instant ruin.[124] When the commission was brought out, and Bacon had read it to his soldiers, he refused to accept it, declaring the powers granted insufficient. Thereupon he drew up the heads of a new paper, in which his loyalty to the king and the legality of his past actions were attested, and an appointment given him as general of all the forces in Virginia used in the Indian war.[125]

These new demands throw the old Governor into an uncontrollable rage. He rushes out to Bacon, gesticulating wildly, and declaring that rather than sign such a paper he will have his hands cut off.[126] In his excitement he opens his bosom, crying out, "Here, shoot me, fore God fair mark."[127] Then he offers to measure swords with the rebel before all his men, shouting, "Let us settle this difference singly between ourselves."[128] But Bacon ignores these ravings. "Sir," he says, "I come not nor intend to hurt a haire of your Honors head.

[120] P. R. O., CO1-37-16.   [121] P. R. O., CO1-37-17.
[122] P. R. O., CO1-37-16, 17; T. M., p. 16.
[123] P. R. O., CO1-37-17.   [124] P. R. O., CO1-37-16.
[125] Ibid.   [126] P. R. O., CO1-37-16.
[127] P. R. O., CO5-1371-382.   [128] P. R. O., CO1-37-16.

And for your sword, your Honor may please to put it up, it will rust in the scabbard before ever I shall desire you to draw it. I come for a commission against the Heathen who daily inhumanly murder us and spill our bretherens blood."[129]

In the general distraction somebody takes the proposals to the Burgesses, now sitting in an upper chamber of the state house. Bacon struts impatiently below, muttering threats and "new coyned oathes".[130] At a window of the Assembly room are a number of faces, looking out on the exciting scenes below. Bacon calls up to them, "You Burgesses, I expect your speedy result." His soldiers shout, "We will have it, we will have it." At a command from Bacon the rebels cock their fusils, and take aim at the crowded window. "For God's sake hold your hands," cry the Burgesses, "forbear a little and you shall have what you please."[131] And now there is wild excitement, confusion and hurrying to and fro. From all sides the Governor is pressed to grant the commission in Bacon's own terms. At last he yields, and the paper is signed.

But new humiliation awaited him. The next morning Bacon entered the House of Burgesses with an armed guard, demanding that certain persons active in obeying the Governor's orders should be deprived of all offices, and that recent letters to the King denouncing him as a rebel should be publicly contradicted. When Berkeley heard of these demands, he swore he would rather suffer death than submit to them. But the Burgesses, who thought it not unlikely that they might soon have their throats cut, advised him to grant whatever was demanded.[132] So a letter was written to the King, and signed by the Governor, the Council and the Burgesses, expressing confidence in Bacon's loyalty and justifying his past actions.[133] Several of Berkeley's friends were committed to

---

[129] P. R. O., CO5-1371-382.   [130] P. R. O., CO1-37-16.

[131] P. R. O., CO5-1371-382. In the various accounts left us of these scenes there is usually agreement upon the essential points. But in details and the sequence of events there is much discrepancy. The author has endeavored to present the facts in accordance with the greatest weight of evidence.

[132] P. R. O., CO1-37-16, 17.

[133] P. R. O., CO5-1371-383; CO1-37-15.1.

prison. Blank commissions for officers to command under Bacon in the Indian war were presented for signature. The Governor granted all, "as long as they concerned not life and limb", being "willing to be ridd of him". The Assembly finished its session, and thinking to appease the rebels, sent their laws out to be read before them. But they rose up like a swarm of bees, and swore they would have no laws.[134] Yet the legislation of this session was exceedingly liberal. The elections had been held at a time when the people were bitterly angry with the Governor and disgusted with the old régime. In several counties popular candidates, men bent upon reform, had been elected over Berkeley's friends.[135] These men, aided by the menacing attitude of the people, had initiated a series of bills designed to restrict the Governor's power and to restore to the commons their rightful share in local government. But it was probably the presence of Bacon with his ragged troops at Jamestown that brought about the final passage of the bills. The Governor and the Council would hardly have given their consent, had they not been forced to do so at the sword's point.

Indeed these laws aimed a telling blow at the aristocratic cliques that had so long controlled all local government. It was to be illegal in the future, for any man to serve as sheriff for two consecutive terms.[136] Surveyors, escheators, clerks of the court and sheriffs should hold only one office at a time.[137] The self-perpetuating vestries which had long controlled the parishes and levied church taxes, were to give place to bodies elected tri-annually by the freemen.[138] An act was passed restricting the power of the county courts. For the future the people were to elect representatives, equal in number with the justices, to sit with them, and have a voice "in laying the countie assessments, and of making wholesome lawes".[139] Councillors were no longer to be exempt from taxation. The act of 1670, restricting the right to vote for Burgesses to freeholders was abolished, and the franchise

[134] P. R. O., CO1-37-16.
[135] P. R. O., CO5-1371-379.
[136] Hen., Vol. II, p. 353.
[137] Hen., Vol. II, p. 354.
[138] Hen., Vol. II, p. 359.
[139] Hen., Vol. II, p. 357.

extended to all freemen.[140]   And since "the frequent false returns" of elections had "caused great disturbances", it was enacted that any sheriff found guilty of this crime should be fined twenty thousand pounds of tobacco.[141]

Hardly had the Assembly closed its session when the news was received that the Indians were again on the war-path, having killed eight persons in the upper counties.   This caused great alarm in the rebel army, and Bacon found it necessary the next day to lead them back to the frontier that they might guard their homes and families.[142]

Here active preparations were made for a new expedition against the savages.   Now that Bacon had a commission signed by the Governor and confirmed with the public seal, men were quite eager to follow him.   On all sides volunteers flocked in to offer their services against the brutal enemy.   Even Councillors and Burgesses encouraged their neighbors to enlist, declaring that no exception could be taken to the legality of the commission.[143]   Thus hundreds swallowed "down so fair a Bait, not seeing Rebellion at the end of it".[144]

In the meanwhile, the Governor, angered at the great indignities put upon him, was planning to regain his lost authority. A petition was drawn up in Gloucester county by Sir William's friends, denouncing Bacon, and asking that forces be raised to suppress him.[145]   Although most of the Gloucestermen, it would seem, had no part in this request, Berkeley crossed over the York River to their county and began to enlist volunteers.[146]   But he met with little success.   Even in this part of the colony Bacon was the popular hero, and men refused to serve against him.   It seemed outrageous to many that while he was out to fight the common enemy, the Governor should attack him in the rear.   All his desperate efforts were in vain.   Sick at heart and exhausted from exertions too great for his age, he is said to have fainted away in the saddle.[147]

The news that Berkeley was raising forces reached Bacon

[140] Hen., Vol. II, p. 356.
[141] Ibid.
[142] P. R. O., CO1-37-16.
[143] CO5-1371-384, 385.
[144] P. R. O., CO5-1371-383.
[145] Mass. S. IV, Vol. IX, p. 181.
[146] P. R. O., CO5-1371-385.
[147] P. R. O., CO5-1371-387; T. M., p. 20.

at the falls of James River, just as he was going to strike out into the woods. "Immediately he causes the Drums to Beat and Trumpets to sound for calling his men to-gether."[148]. "Gentlemen and Fellow Soldiers," he says, when they are assembled, "the news just now brought me, may not a little startle you as well as myselfe. But seeing it is not altogether unexpected, wee may the better beare it and provide our remedies. The Governour is now in Gloster County endeavouring to raise forces against us, having declared us Rebells and Traytors. . . . It is Revenge that hurries them on without regard to the Peoples safety. (They) had rather wee should be Murder'd and our Ghosts sent to our slaughter'd Countrymen by their actings, then wee live to hinder them of their Interest with the Heathen. . . . Now then wee must be forced to turne our Swords to our own Defence, or expose ourselves to their Mercyes. . . . Let us descend to know the reasons why such a proceedings are used against us . . . (why) those whome they have raised for their Defence, to preserve them against the Fury of the Heathen, they should thus seek to Destroy. (Was there) ever such a Theachery . . . heard of, such Wickednesse and inhumanity? But they are damned Cowards, and you shall see they will not dare to meet us in the field to try the Justnesse of our Cause."[149]

Whereupon the soldiers all cried, "Amen. Amen." They were ready to follow him. They would rather die fighting than be hanged like rogues. It would be better to attack the Governor at once than have him come upon their rear while they were engaged in the woods with the savages.[150] And so, with universal acclaim, they gathered up their arms, and set out to give battle to the Governor.

But Berkeley had fled. Upon finding that the militia of Gloucester and Middlesex would not support him, he had taken ship for the Eastern Shore. Here, for the time being, he was safe from the angry rebels. It would be difficult for Bacon to secure vessels enough to transport his men over to Accomac; to march them hundreds of miles around the head of Chesapeake Bay was out of the question.

[148] P. R. O., CO5-1371-385. [149] P. R. O., CO5-1371-385.
[150] P. R. O., CO5-1371-386.

The flight of the Governor left Bacon undisputed master of all the mainland of Virginia. Everywhere he was hailed by the people as their hero and deliverer. Those that still remained loyal to Sir William either fled with him or rendered their submission to the rebel. For a while, at least, he could prosecute the Indian war and redress the public grievances without fear of interruption.[151]

But now Bacon was confronted with the question of what attitude he should assume to the English government. Berkeley had written home denouncing him as a rebel and traitor. The King assuredly would not tolerate his conduct. No doubt preparations were already being made to send British troops to the colony. Should he defy the King and resist his soldiers in the field of battle?

Bacon made up his mind to fight. The dense woods, the many swamps and creeks, the vast distances of the colony would all be favorable to him. He would resort to the Indian method of fighting. His men were as brave as the British; were better marksmen. Five hundred Virginians, he was sure, would be a match for two thousand red coats. If England sought to bring him to his knees, by blockading the coast and cutting off all foreign trade, he would appeal to the Dutch or even to the French for assistance. Assuredly these nations would not neglect so favorable an opportunity of injuring their old rival and enemy. He even cherished a wild dream of leading his rebels back into the woods, to establish a colony upon an island in the Roanoke river.[152]

But Bacon knew that the people would hesitate to follow him into open resistance to England. Ties of blood, of religion, of interest were too strong. All the injustice done them by the King, all the oppression of the Navigation Acts, could not make them forget that they were Englishmen. So he found it necessary to deceive them with a pretence of loyalty. He himself took the oath of allegiance and supremacy, and he imposed it upon all his followers. His commands were issued in the King's name. He even went to the absurd extremity of

[151] P. R. O., CO5-1371-387.
[152] P. R. O., CO5-1371-232-240; CO1-39-38.

declaring it for the service of the Crown to disobey the King's commands, to arrest the King's Governor, to fight the King's troops.[153]

Realizing that resistance to his plans would come almost entirely from the upper classes, Bacon made especial efforts to seduce the wealthy planters. On August the third, a number of influential gentlemen assembled upon his summons at Middle Plantation, to discuss the means of protecting the people from the Indians, and preventing civil war. After delivering a long harangue, justifying his own actions and denouncing the Governor, Bacon requested the entire company to take three oaths which he had prepared. First, they were to promise to assist him in prosecuting the Indian war. Secondly, they must combat all attempts of the Governor and his friends to raise troops against him. Thirdly, they were asked to declare it consistent with their allegiance to the King to resist the royal troops until his Majesty could be informed by letter from Bacon of the justice of his cause.[154] This last article caused prolonged and bitter controversy. But Bacon locked the doors, it is said, and by persuasion and threats induced them all to sign. The three oaths were taken by no less than sixty-nine prominent men, among them Thomas Swann, Thomas Milner, Philip Lightfoot and Thomas Ballard.[155]

Bacon now felt himself strong enough to take active control of the administration of the government. He did not assume, however, the title of Governor, but styled himself "General by the consent of the people".[156] Nor did he venture to proceed in the alteration of laws or the redress of grievances without the advice and support of the representatives of the people. In conjunction with four members of the Council, he issued orders for an immediate election of a new Assembly, to meet on the fourth of September, at Jamestown.[157]

Having settled these matters, Bacon turned his attention to two military expeditions—one against the Indians, the other

[153] P. R. O., CO1-37-41.
[155] Ibid.
[157] P. R. O., CO1-37-43.

[154] P. R. O., CO1-37-42.
[156] P. R. O., CO1-37-41.

against the Governor. The continued activity of the savages and the exposed condition of the frontier demanded his personal attention, but he was resolved not to leave the lower counties exposed during his absence to attack from the Eastern Shore. Seizing an English ship, commanded by a Captain Larrimore, which was lying in James River, he impressed her, with all her crew, into his service against the Governor. In this vessel, with a sloop and a bark of four guns, he embarked a force of two hundred or more men.[158] The expedition was placed under the command of Captain William Carver, "a valiant, stout Seaman", and Gyles Bland, both devoted to Bacon's cause and high in his favor. They were ordered to patrol the coast to prevent raids upon the Western Shore, and, if possible, to attack and capture the Governor.

Bacon himself hastens to Henrico, "where he bestirs himself lustily in order to a Speedy March against the Indians". It was his intention to renew his attack upon the Occaneechees and the Susquehannocks, but for some reason he gave up this design to turn against the Pamunkeys. Hastening across from the James to the York, Bacon met Colonel Gyles Brent, who brought with him reinforcements from the plantations upon the upper waters of the Rappahannock and Potomac. Their united forces marched to the extreme frontier and plunged into the wilderness. Discovering a narrow path running through the forest, the English followed it to a small Pamunkey village situated upon a neck of land between two swamps. As Bacon's Indian scouts advanced upon the place they were fired upon by the enemy. Whereupon the English came running up to assault the village. But the Pamunkeys deserted their cabins and fled into the adjacent swamps, where the white men found it impossible to pursue them. All made good their escape except one woman and one little child.[159]

Continuing his march, Bacon stumbled upon an old squaw, the nurse of the Pamunkey queen, whom he ordered to act as his guide. But the woman, unwilling to betray her people, led him far astray, many miles from the Indian settlements. The

[158] P. R. O., CO5-1371-388; Burk, Vol. II, p. 271.
[159] P. R. O., CO5-1371-390.

English followed her "the remainder of that day & almost another day" before they discovered that they were being deceived. When sure of her treachery, "Bacon gave command to his soldiers to knock her on the head, which they did, and left her dead on the way".[160] The army now wandered around at random in the woods, following first one path and then another, but could not discover the enemy. The appointed time for the new Assembly was approaching, and it was imperative for Bacon to be at Jamestown to open the session. He was resolved, however, not to return to the colony until he had struck a decisive blow at the Indians. Sending a message to the people "that he would be with them with all possible speed", he resumed his discouraging quest.[161]

But the Indians still eluded him. It seemed a hopeless task to discover their villages amid the dense woods and treacherous swamps. His men became discouraged. "Tyred, murmuring, impatient, hunger-starv'd", many begged him to lead them back to the plantations. But Bacon would not abandon the expedition. He would rather die in the woods, he said, than disappoint the confidence reposed in him by the people. Those that felt it necessary to return home, he would permit to depart unmolested. But for himself, he was resolved to continue the march even though it became necessary to exist upon chincapins and horse flesh.[162] Whereupon the army was divided, one part setting out for the colony, the other resuming the search for the savages.

That very day Bacon runs upon the main camp of the Pamunkeys and immediately attacks them. The savages are encamped upon a "piece of Champion land", protected on three sides by swamps, and covered with a dense growth of "small oke, saplings, Chinkapin-Bushes and grape vines". As the English charge in among them they offer little resistance, but desert their habitations and flee. Some are shot down, many are captured. Bacon takes possession of all their goods—"Indian matts, Basketts, Match cotes, parcells of Wampameag and Roanoke, Baggs, Skins, ffurs", etc.

[160] P. R. O., CO5-1371-391.   [161] P. R. O., CO5-1371-392.
[162] P. R. O., CO5-1371-392.

The poor queen fled for her life with one little boy, and wandered fourteen days in the woods, separated from her people. "She was once coming back with designe to throw herself upon the mercy of the English", but "happened to meet with a deade Indian woman lying in the way, . . . which struck such terror in the Queen that fearing their cruelty by that ghastly example, shee went on . . . into the wild woodes". Here she was preserved from starvation by eating part of a terrapin, found by the little boy.[163] After this victory, Bacon secured his plunder and his captives, and hastened back to the plantations.

In the meanwhile the expedition against Accomac had ended in disastrous failure.[164] Carver and Bland had been given instructions to capture the Governor, and Bacon proposed, if ever he got him in his power, to send him to England, there to stand trial for his misgovernment and his betrayal of the people to the barbarous Indians.[165] Even though it was quite probable that the King would send him back, the colony would for a time be rid of his troublesome presence.

Upon the arrival of the little fleet off the coast of Accomac, it was decided to send Carver ashore under a flag of truce, to treat with the Governor.[166] Leaving Bland to guard the fleet with a force not superior in number to the English sailors, Carver set out in the sloop "with the most trusty of his men".[167] In the meanwhile Captain Larrimore and his sailors, who resented their enforced service with the rebels, were plotting to betray them to the enemy. In some way Larrimore contrived to get a message to Berkeley, requesting him to send out a party of loyal gentlemen in boats, and promising to deliver his ship into their hands.[168] The Governor at first was loath to venture upon such a hazardous undertaking.[169] The whole thing might be a snare to entrap his men. Yet his situation was desperate; he must take desperate chances.

[163] P. R. O., CO5-1371-393.   [164] P. R. O., CO5-1371-393.
[165] P. R. O., CO5-1371-394.   [166] Ibid.
[167] T. M., p. 22.
[168] P. R. O., CO5-1371-394; Burk, Vol. II, p. 271.
[169] Burk, Vol. II, p. 271.

Placing a party of twenty-six men in two small boats, he sent them out under the command of Colonel Philip Ludwell, to surprise the ship.[170]   Fearing that Carver might return before the capture could be effected, Berkeley "caressed him with wine", and detained him with prolonged negotiations. Upon reaching the ship, Ludwell and his men rowed up close under her side, and clambered in at "the gun room ports". "One courageous gentleman ran up to the deck, and clapt a pistoll to Bland's breast, saying you are my prisoner."[171]   The rest of the company followed upon his heels, brandishing their pistols and swords.   Captain Larrimore and his crew caught up spikes, which they had ready at hand, and rushed to Ludwell's assistance.   The rebels, taken utterly by surprise, many no doubt without arms, "were amazed and yielded".[172]

A short while after, Carver was seen returning in the sloop from his interview with the Governor.   "They permit the boat to come soe neere as they might ffire directly downe upon her, and soe they alsoe commanded Carver on Board & secured him.   When hee saw this surprize he stormed, tore his haire off, and curst, and exclaimed at the Cowardize of Bland that had betrayed and lost all their designe."[173]   Not long after he was tried for treason by court martial, condemned, and hanged.[174]

Elated by this unexpected success, the Governor determined to make one more effort to regain his lost authority.   The rebels were now without a navy; they could not oppose him upon the water, or prevent his landing upon the Western Shore.   With the gentlemen that had remained loyal to him, the troops of Accomac, many runaway servants and English sailors he was able to raise a force of several hundred men.[175] Embarking them in Captain Larrimore's ship, in the *Adam and Eve,* and sixteen or seventeen sloops, he set sail for Jamestown.[176]

[170] Ibid.   [171] T. M., p. 22.
[172] T. M., p. 22.   [173] P. R. O., CO5-1371-394.
[174] T. M., p. 23; P. R. O., CO5-1371-52, 54.
[175] The account of the King's commissioners places the number at six hundred; in Bacon's Proceedings it is given as one thousand.
[176] P. R. O., CO5-1371-394; Bac's Pros., p. 21.

In the meanwhile the appointed date for the convening of the Assembly had come. It is probable that the members were arriving to take their seats when the news of the Governor's approach reached the town.[177] Bacon was still absent upon the Pamunkey expedition. There seems to have been no one present capable of inspiring the rebels with confidence, or of leading them in a vigorous defense. When the sails of the Governor's fleet were seen, on the seventh of September, wending their way up the river, the place was thrown into the wildest confusion. Sir William sent a message ashore, offering a pardon to all, with the exception of Lawrence and Drummond, that would lay down their arms and return to their allegiance.[178] But few seem to have trusted him, "feareing to meet with some afterclaps of revenge".[179] That night, before the place could be fully invested, the rebels fled, "every one shifting for himselfe with no ordnary feare".[180] "Collonell Larence . . . forsooke his owne howse with all his wealth and a faire cupbord of plate entire standing, which fell into the Governour's hands the next morning."[181]

This was the unwelcome news which greeted Bacon upon his return from the Indian expedition. So many of his soldiers had left for their homes before the final defeat of the Pamunkeys, that he now had with him less than one hundred and fifty men.[182] Yet he resolved to march at once upon Jamestown to attack the Governor. His little band gave him enthusiastic assurance of loyal support. He knew that he had the well wishes and prayers of the people, while his opponents were "loaded with their curses". Berkeley's men, although so much more numerous than his own, he believed to be cowards that would not dare appear against him in the field. Victory would be easy and decisive.[183]

So, after delaying a short while to gather reinforcements from New Kent and Henrico, he marched with extraordinary swiftness down upon the enemy.[184] Everywhere along the

[177] Bac's Pros., p. 22.
[179] Bac's Pros., p. 22.
[181] Bac's Pros., p. 22.
[183] P. R. O., CO5-1371-395.

[178] Bac's Pros., p. 22.
[180] Bac's Pros., p. 22.
[182] P. R. O., CO5-1371-394.
[184] P. R. O., CO5-1371-395.

route he was hailed by the people as their deliverer. The sight of the sullen Indian captives that he led along with him "as in a Shew of Triumph", caused enthusiastic rejoicing. Many brought forth fruit and other food to refresh his weary soldiers. The women swore that if he had not men enough to defeat the Governor, they themselves would take arms and follow him. All prayed for his success and happiness, and exclaimed against the injustice of his enemies.[185]

Before Berkeley had been in possession of Jamestown one week, Bacon was upon him. On the evening of September the thirteenth, the little rebel band arrived at Sandy Bay, driving before them a party of the Governor's horse.[186] With singular bravado, Bacon himself rode up to the enemy, fired his carbine at them, and commanded his trumpets to sound their defiance.[187] Few thought, however, he would attempt to capture the town, for the Governor's position was very strong. The narrow isthmus, by which alone the place could be approached, was defended by three heavy guns planted behind strong palisades.[188] Upon the left, "almost close aborde the shore, lay the ships, with their broadesides to thunder" upon any that dared to assault the works. The loyal forces had recently been augmented to a thousand men, and now outnumbered the rebels three to one. Yet Bacon seems to have meditated from the first an attack upon the place, and was confident of success.[189]

Although his men had marched many miles that day he set them immediately to work within gun-shot of the enemy, building an entrenched camp.[190] All night long, by the light of the moon, the soldiers toiled, cutting bushes, felling trees and throwing up earthworks. But it soon became apparent that their utmost efforts would not suffice to complete the trenches before dawn, when the enemy's guns would be sure to open upon them. In this dilemma, Bacon hit upon a most unmanly expedient to protect his men at their work. Sending out several small parties of horse, he captured a number of ladies, the

[185] P. R. O., CO5-1371-395.
[187] P. R. O., CO5-1371-397, 400.
[189] Bac's Pros., p. 24.

[186] P. R. O., CO5-1371-396.
[188] Bac's Pros., p. 24.
[190] P. R. O., CO5-1371-396.

wives of some of Berkeley's most prominent supporters. "Which the next morning he presents to the view of there husbands and ffriends in towne, upon the top of the smalle worke hee had cast up in the night, where he caused them to tarey till hee had finished his defence."[191]   The husbands were enraged that the rebels should thus hide behind the "white aprons" of their innocent wives, but they dared not make an assault.

When, however, the ladies were removed, "upon a Signall given from ye Towne the Shipps fire their Great Guns and at the same tyme they let fly their small-Shott from the Palaisadoes.   But that small Sconse that Bacon had caused to be made in the night, of Trees, Bruch, and Earth soe defended them that the Shott did them noe damage at all, and was returned back as fast from the little Fortresse."[192]

Fearing that this cannonade will be followed by an assault upon his works, Bacon places a lookout on the top of a near-by brick chimney, which commands a view of the peninsula.   On the sixteenth, the watchman announces that the enemy are preparing for an assault, and the rebels make ready to give them a warm reception.   The Governor's forces, six or seven hundred strong, dash across the Sandy Bay, in an attempt to storm Bacon's redoubts.[193]   Horse and foot "come up with a narrow front, pressing very close upon one another's shoulders".   But many of them fight only from compulsion, and have no heart for their task.   At the first volleys of shot that pour in upon them from the rebel army, they throw down their arms and flee.   They marched out, as one chronicler says, "like scholars going to school . . . with heavy hearts, but returned hom with light heels".[194]   Their officers were powerless to stem the rout, until they were safe under the protection of the palisades.[195]

---

[191] Cotton, p. 8; Bac's Pros., p. 24. The report of the commissioners places this incident some days later, after the assault of the 15th.   The author has followed the account given in Bacon's Proceedings, which seems to him probably more correct.   Bacon could have no object in exposing the ladies after his trenches were completed, his heavy guns mounted and the enemy defeated.

[192] P. R. O., CO5-1371-397.   [193] Bac's Pros., p. 25.

[194] Bac's Pros., p. 25.   [195] P. R. O., CO5-1371-398, 400.

The Governor's losses in dead and wounded were very small, but the moral effect of his defeat was great. The rebels were so elated at their easy victory, and so scornful of their cowardly opponents, "that Bacon could scarce keep them from immediately falling to storm and enter the Towne".[196] On the other hand, the loyal troops were utterly discouraged. Many of them, that had been "compelled or hired into the Service", and "were intent only on plunder", clamored for the desertion of the place, fearing that the victorious rebels would soon burst in upon them.[197]

"The next day Bacon orders 3 grate guns to be brought into the camp, two whereof he plants upon his trench. The one he sets to worke against the Ships, the other against the entrance into the towne, for to open a pasage to his intended storm."[198] Had the rebels delayed no longer to make an assault it seems certain they could have carried the palisades with ease, taken many of the enemy, and perhaps captured the Governor himself. The loyal soldiers were thinking only of flight. "Soe great was the Cowardize and Basenesse of the generality of Sir William Berkeley's party that of all at last there were only some 20 Gentlemen willing to stand by him." So that the Governor, "who undoubtedly would rather have dyed on the Place than thus deserted it, what with (the) importunate and resistless solicitations of all was at last over persuaded, nay hurried away against his will".[199] "Takeing along with him all the towne people, and their goods, leaveing all the grate guns naled up, and the howses emty", he left the place a prey to the rebels.[200] "So fearful of discovery they are, that for Secrecy they imbarque and weigh anchor in the Night and silently fall down the river."[201]

Early the next morning Bacon marched across the Sandy Bay and took possession of the deserted town.[202] Here he learned that the Governor had not continued his flight, but had cast anchor twenty miles below, where he was awaiting

[196] P. R. O., CO5-1371-400.   [197] Ibid.
[198] Bac's Pros., p. 25.   [199] P. R. O., CO5-1371-400.
[200] Bac's Pros., p. 26.   [201] P. R. O., CO5-1371-400.
[202] P. R. O., CO5-1371-401; Bac's Pros., p. 26.

a favorable opportunity to recapture the place.[203]   At the same time, news came from the north that Colonel Brent, Bacon's former ally, was collecting troops in the counties bordering upon the Potomac River, and would soon be on the march to the Governor's assistance, with no less than a thousand men.[204] Should this new army, by acting in concert with the fleet, succeed in blocking Bacon up at Jamestown, the rebels would be caught in a fatal trap.   The peninsula could hardly be defended successfully against superior forces by land and water, and they would be crushed between the upper and nether millstones.   On the other hand, should they desert the town, in order to go out against Brent, Berkeley would undoubtedly return to take possession of it, and all the fruits of their victory would be lost.

After long consultation with his chief advisors, Bacon decided to destroy the town.[205]   That very night he set fire to the place, which in a few hours was reduced to ashes.   Not even the state-house, or the old church were spared.   Drummond and Lawrence, it is said, showed their unselfish zeal for the cause by applying the torch to their homes with their own hands.[206]   As the Governor, from his ships, saw in the distance the glare of the burning buildings, he cursed the cowardice of his soldiers that had forced him to yield the place to the rebels. But as it could now serve him no longer as a base, he weighed anchor, and set sail for Accomac.[207]

Deserting the ruined town, Bacon led his men north to Green Spring, and thence across York River into Gloucester county.   Here there came to him a messenger riding "post haste from Rapahanock, with news that Coll: Brent was advancing fast upon him".[208]   At once he summons his soldiers around him, tells them the alarming news, and asks if they are ready to fight.   The soldiers answer "with showtes and acclamations while the drums thunder a march to meet the promised conflict".[209]

[203] Bac's Pros., p. 26.   [204] Bac's Pros., p. 26.
[205] P. R. O., CO5-1371-401.   [206] P. R. O., CO5-1371-405.
[207] P. R. O., CO5-1371-401; CO1-39-22; Bac's Pros., p. 26.
[208] Bac's Pros., p. 26.   [209] Bac's Pros., p. 26.

Bacon had advanced not "above 2 or 3 days jurney, but he meets newes . . . that Brents men were all run away, and left him to shift for himselfe".[210] Like the troops that had so signally failed of their duty in the battle of Sandy Bay, these northern forces had no desire to meet Bacon. Many of them were undoubtedly pressed into service; many were in sympathy with the rebellion. At all events they deserted their leaders before the hostile army came in sight, and fled back to their homes.

Thus Bacon once more found himself master of all the mainland of Virginia. But his situation was more critical than it had been in July and August. Many of the prominent gentlemen that had then given him their support, and had taken his three oaths, were now fighting on the side of the Governor. It was quite certain that royal forces were being equipped for an expedition to Virginia, and might make their appearance within the capes before many more weeks. Moreover, the disastrous failure of Carver and Bland had left him without a navy and exposed all the Western Shore to attack from the loyal forces in Accomac.

Realizing his danger, Bacon felt it necessary to bind the people to him more closely. Summoning the militia of Gloucester to meet him at their county court-house, he delivered a long harangue before them and tendered them an oath of fidelity. They were asked to swear that if the King's troops attempted to land by force, they would "fly to-gether as in a common calamity, and jointly with the present Army . . . stand or fall in the defense of . . . the Country". And "in Case of utmost Extremity rather then submitt to so miserable a Slavery (when none can longer defend ourselves, our Lives and Liberty's) to acquit the Colony.[211]

The Gloucestermen were most reluctant to take this oath. A Mr. Cole, speaking for them all, told Bacon that it was their desire to remain neutral in this unhappy civil war. But the rebel replied that if they would not be his friends, they must be his enemies. They should not be idle and reap the benefit of liberty earned by the blood of others. A minister, named

---

[210] Bac's Pros., p. 26. [211] P. R. O., CO5-1371-402.

Wading, who was active in persuading the men to refuse the oath, was committed to prison by Bacon, with the warning that the church was the proper place for him to preach, not the camp. Later, it seems, fearing the consequences of further refusal, the Gloucester troops yielded and took the binding engagement.[212]

Bacon now turned his thoughts, it is said, to an expedition against Accomac. But his preparations were never completed. For some time he had been ill of dysentery and now was "not able to hould out any longer".[213] He was cared for at the house of a Mr. Pate, in Gloucester county, but his condition soon became worse.[214] His mind, probably wandering in delirium, dwelt upon the perils of his situation. Often he would enquire if the guard around the house was strong, or whether the King's troops had arrived. Death came before the end of October.[215] Bacon's place of burial has never been discovered. It is supposed that Lawrence, to save the body of his friend from mutilation by the vindictive old Governor, weighted the coffin with stones and sunk it in the deep waters of the York.[216]

The death of Bacon proved an irreparable loss to the rebels. It was impossible for them to find another leader of his undaunted resolution, his executive ability, his power of command. No one could replace him in the affections of the common people. It would not be correct to attribute the failure of the rebellion entirely to the death of this one man, yet it undoubtedly hastened the end. Had he continued at the head of his faithful army, he might have kept the Governor indefinitely in exile upon the Eastern Shore, or even have driven him to take refuge upon the water. In the end Bacon would have been conquered, for he could not have held out against the English fleet and the English troops. But he would have made a desperate and heroic resistance.

The chief command fell to Lieutenant-General Ingram.

[212] P. R. O., CO5-1371-401; Bac's Pros., p. 27.

[213] Bac's Pros., p. 28.   [214] P. R. O., CO5-1371-404.

[215] Bacon's Proceedings places the death of Bacon on Oct. 18; the Commissioners give the date as Oct. 26.

[216] T. M., p. 24.

The selection seems to have been popular with the soldiers, for when it was announced, they "threw up their caps, crying out as loud as they could bellow, God save our new Generall".[217] Ingram is depicted by some of the chroniclers as a man of low birth, a dandy and a fool, but there is reason to believe their impeachment too harsh. Although he lacked Bacon's force of character and had no executive ability, as a general he showed considerable talent, and more than held his own against the Governor.

The mastery of the water was an advantage to Berkeley of the very greatest importance. The numerous deep rivers running far up into the country made it easy for him to deliver swift, telling blows at any point in the enemy's position. In order to guard the James, the York and the Rappahannock it became necessary for the rebels to divide their forces into several small bands. On the other hand, the entire strength of the loyalists could be concentrated at any time for an unexpected attack.

Ingram made his chief base at West Point, where the Mattapony and the Pamunkey unite to form the broad and stately York.[218] Here he could watch both banks of the river, and could concentrate his men quickly either upon the Peninsula, or in Gloucester or Middlesex. At this place were gathered several hundred rebels under Ingram himself. But it was deemed wise to leave other detachments at various places lower down in the country, to prevent the enemy from landing, and to suppress any rising of the people in favor of the Governor. At the house of Colonel Bacon, in York county, a force of thirty or forty men were posted under the command of Major Whaly.[219] "The next Parcell, considerable, was at Green Spring, the Governours howse, into which was put about 100 men and boys." Their leader, a Colonel Drew, fortified the place strongly, barricading all approaches, and planting three large guns "to beate of the Assailants". Another small detachment, under Colonel Hansford, was posted "at the Howse where Coll: Reade did once live", the site of famous old Yorktown.[220]

[217] Ing's Pros., p. 32.   [218] Ing's Pros., p. 39.
[219] Ing's Pros., p. 40.   [220] Ing's Pros., p. 39.

This last post, situated near the mouth of the river, was especially exposed to attack from the Eastern Shore. A few days after the death of Bacon, Major Robert Beverley, with a small force, sailed across the bay to effect its capture.[221] The rebels "kep a negligent Gard", and were caught completely by surprise. Hansford was taken prisoner, with twenty of his men, and brought in triumph to Accomac.

Here he was at once charged with treason, tried by court martial, and condemned to die. He pleaded passionately to "be shot like a soldier and not to be hanged like a Dog. But it was tould him . . . that he was not condemned as he was merely a soldier, but as a Rebell, taken in Arms."[222] To the last he refused to admit that he was guilty of treason. To the crowd that gathered around the scaffold to witness his execution he protested "that he dyed a loyal subject and a lover of his country".

"This business being so well accomplish'd by those who had taken Hansford, . . . they had no sooner deliver'd there Fraight at Accomack, but they hoyse up there sayles, and back againe to Yorke River, where with a Marvellous celerity they surprise one Major Cheise-Man, and som others, amongst whom one Capt. Wilford, who (it is saide) in the bickering lost one of his eyes, which he seemed little concern'd at, as knowing that when he came to Accomack, that though he had bin starke blinde, yet the Governour would take care for to afford him a guide, that should show him the way to the Gallows."[223]

The Governor was resolved to make the rebel leaders pay dearly for the indignities they had put upon him. Those that were so luckless as to fall into his hands, were hastened away to their execution with but the mockery of a trial. Doubtless Berkeley felt himself justified in this severity. To him rebellion against the King was not merely a crime, it was a hideous sacrilege. Those guilty of such an enormity should receive no mercy. But this cannot explain or excuse the coarse

---

[221] The news of Hansford's capture reached Captain Morris near Nansemond Nov. 12th.

[222] Ing's Pros., p. 33.   [223] Ing's Pros., p. 35.

brutality and savage joy with which he sent his victims to the scaffold. It is impossible not to feel that many of these executions were dictated, not by motives of policy or loyalty, but by vindictiveness.

Nothing can make this more evident that the pathetic story of Madam Cheesman. "When . . . the Major was brought in to the Governor's presence, and by him demanded, what made him to ingage in Bacon's designes? Before that the Major could frame an Answer . . . his Wife steps in and tould his honr: that it was her provocations that made her Husband joyne in the Cause that Bacon contended for; ading, that if he had not bin influenced by her instigations, he had never don that which he had don. Therefore (upon her bended knees) she desires of his honr . . . that shee might be hang'd, and he pardon'd. Though the Governour did know, that that what she had saide, was neare to the truth," he refused her request and spurned her with a vile insult. It is with a sense of relief that we learn that her husband died in prison and was thus saved the ignominy of the gallows.[224]

Encouraged by his successes, Berkeley now planned a more formidable invasion of the Western Shore. Public sentiment, he hoped, was beginning to turn in his favor. The death of Bacon had deprived the rebellion of all coherency and definiteness of purpose. The country was getting weary of the struggle, and was anxious for the reëstablishment of law and order. In Gloucester and Middlesex especially there were many prominent planters that awaited an opportunity to take up arms against the rebels. And although the common people were indifferent to the Governor's cause, they would be forced to enlist under him could he but get a firm foothold in those counties.[225]

So he sailed into York River with a fleet of four ships and several sloops, and a force of one hundred soldiers.[226] Landing a party, under command of Major Robert Beverley, upon the north bank, he surprised and captured a number of the enemy at the residence of a Mr. Howard.[227] He then set up

---

[224] Ing's Pros., p. 36.
[226] Ing's Pros., p. 38.
[225] Ing's Pros., p. 38.
[227] Ing's Pros., p. 38.

his standard at the very house in which Bacon had died, and sent out summons to all loyal citizens to come to his support. Here there soon "appeared men enough to have beaten all the Rebells in the countrey, onely with their Axes and Hoes".[228] They were quickly organized into an army and placed under the command of Major Lawrence Smith.[229] Almost simultaneously the people of Middlesex began to take up arms in support of the Governor, and for a while it seemed that the rebels would be overwhelmed and driven back upon the frontiers.

But Ingram acted with vigor and promptness. He dispatched a body of horse, under Lientenant-General Walkelett, to attack and disperse the Middlesex troops before their numbers become formidable. With the main body of the rebels he himself remained at West Point, to watch the movements of the enemy in Gloucester. When Major Smith heard of Walkelett's advance, he at once hastened north to intercept him, leaving a garrison at Mr. Pate's house, to guard that post and maintain intact his communication with the fleet in York River. But he was not quick enough. Before he could complete his march, news came to him that Walkelett had dispersed the Middlesex troops and was preparing to give battle to him.[230]

In the meanwhile, Ingram, hearing that Smith had marched north, "by the advice of his officers strikes in betweene him and his new made Garrisson at M. Pates. He very nimbly invests the Howse", and forces its defenders to surrender. Hardly had he accomplished this task, "but M. L. Smith, having retracted his march out of Middlesex . . . was upon the back of Ingram before he was aware". This new move placed the rebels in no little peril, for the Gloucester forces were between them and their base at West Point. Defeat at this juncture would have meant utter destruction for Ingram's army.

As the two bands faced each other, "one Major Bristow (on Smith's side) made a Motion to try the equity, and justness of the quarrill, by single combett . . . proffering him-

---

[228] Ing's Pros., p. 40.   [229] Ing's Pros., p. 40.
[230] Ing's Pros., p. 40.

selfe against any one (being a Gent.) on the other side. . . .
This motion was as redely accepted by Ingram, as proffered
by Bristow; Ingram swaring, the newest oath in fashion, that
he would be the Man; and so advanceth on foot, with sword
and Pistell, against Bristow; but was fetched back by his owne
men", who had no desire to risk their leader in this duel.[231]

But the Gloucester troops were not inspired to deeds of
courage by the intrepidity of their champion. They had no
desire to encounter the veterans that had defeated the Governor before Jamestown and twice hunted the savages out of
their hidden lairs. Despite all the efforts of their officers they
opened negotiations with Ingram and agreed to lay down
their arms. No less than six hundred men, it is said, thus
tamely surrendered to the rebels. Major Smith and some of
his officers, when they found themselves betrayed by their
men, fled and made good their escape. Other "chiefe men"
fell into the enemy's hands and were held as prisoners of war.
Ingram "dismist the rest to their own abodes".[232]

It was a part of the Governor's plan to secure a foothold
also upon the right bank of the river and to drive the rebels
out of York county. With this in view, he sent out one hundred and twenty men, under Captain Hubert Farrill, to surprise
and capture the rebels commanded by Major Whaly, at
Colonel Bacon's house. To advise and assist Farrill, Colonel
Ludwell and Colonel Bacon himself accompanied the expedition. They decided to steal silently up to the place in the
early hours of the morning before dawn, drive in the sentries
and "enter pell mell with them into the howse". But their
plans miscarried woefully. "The Centrey had no sooner made
the challenge . . . who comes there? . . . but the other
answer with their Musquits (which seldom speakes the language of friends) and that in so loud a maner, that it alarmed
those in the howse to a defence, and then to a posture to
salley out." The attacking party took refuge "behinde som
out buildings, . . . giving the Bullits leave to grope their
owne way in the dark". Here they stood their ground for a
short while and then fled back to their boats. Several were

[231] Ing's Pros., p. 42.   [232] Ing's Pros., p. 42.

taken prisoners, but none were killed save Farrill himself, "whose commission was found droping-wett with blood, in his pockett".[233]

The failure of these operations in the York were partly offset by successes in the southern counties. Late in December a loyal force, consisting in part of English sailors, landed on the right bank of the James and defeated a party of the rebels, killing their leader and taking thirteen prisoners. Four days later, they captured one of the enemy's forts. Soon large parts of Isle of Wight and Surry had been overrun and the people reduced to their allegiance. During the first week of January several hundred rebels gathered upon the upper James to retrieve their waning cause, but they seem to have melted away without accomplishing anything, and at once all the south bank of the river submitted.[234]

Almost simultaneously in all other parts of the colony the rebellion collapsed. The defeats of the Governor in Gloucester, Middlesex and York had not long postponed the end. The failure of the movement was due, not to military successes by Berkeley, but to hopeless internal weakness. Since the death of Bacon the insurgent leaders had been unable to maintain law and order in the colony. Ingram, although he showed some ability as a general, proved utterly unfitted to assume control of civil affairs. Bacon, when Sir William fled to Accomac, had grasped firmly the reins of government, calling a part of the Council to his assistance, summoning a new Assembly, and retaining sheriffs and justices in their offices. Like Cromwell, he had shown himself not only a soldier, but a civil ruler of force and ability. But Ingram could not command the respect and obedience of the people. Under him the machinery of government seems to have broken down. The unhappy colony was given over to disorder and anarchy. We are inclined to wonder why Drummond or Lawrence did not assume the chief command in the government after Bacon's death. Both were men of intelligence and ability, both esteemed by the people, and both devoted heart and soul to the

[233] Ing's Pros., p. 43.
[234] P. R. O., CO5-1371-416; CO1-37-52; CO1-39-10.

rebellion. For some reason, neither could take the leadership, and affairs fell into hopeless confusion.

Without a government to supply their needs, or to direct their movements, the rebel bands found it necessary to maintain themselves by plundering the estates of the Governor's friends. Many wealthy planters paid for their loyalty with the loss of their cattle, their sheep, their corn and wheat, and often the very furniture of their houses. At times the rebel officers could not restrain their rough soldiers from wanton waste and destruction. Crops were ruined, fences thrown down, houses burned.[235] Disgusted with this anarchy, and seeing that Ingram could not preserve order, many of the people began to long for the end of the rebellion. Even the misgovernment of Berkeley was better than lawlessness and confusion.

Ingram himself seems to have perceived that the end was at hand. Intelligence came to him that some of his own party, dissatisfied with his conduct, were awaiting an opportunity to deprive him of the chief command. The long expected arrival of the English troops would bring swift and complete ruin, for under the present conditions, he could not hope for success against them. So he soon became quite willing "to dismount from the back of that horse which he wanted skill, and strength to Manidge". Could he but secure a pardon from the Governor, he would gladly desert the failing cause of the people, and return to his allegiance.[236]

Nor was Sir William less anxious to come to terms with Ingram. It had been a bitter humiliation to him to be thrust headlong out of his government by the rebellious people. It would add to his shame to be restored by English troops. Could he but reduce the colony before the arrival of the red coats, his position would appear in a much better light, both in Virginia and in England. So he sent a Captain Grantham to negotiate with Ingram and to offer him immunity and pardon in return for prompt submission. The rebel leader willingly accepted these terms and returned to his allegiance.[237]

[235] P. R. O., CO1-40-45.   [236] Ing's Pros., p. 45.
[237] Ing's Pros., p. 45; P. R. O., CO5-1371-416.

More delicate was the task of inducing the troops at West Point to follow the example of their general. It was a question whether Ingram, "or any in the countrye could command them to lay down their arms". An attempt to betray them, or to wring the sword out their hands by violence would probably end in failure. It was thought more prudent to subdue "these mad fellows" with "smoothe words", rather than by "rough deeds". So Grantham presented himself to them, told of Ingram's submission and offered them very liberal terms of surrender. They were to be paid for the full time of their service since the granting of Bacon's commission; those that so desired were to be retained in arms to fight the Indians; all servants among them were to secure immediate release from their indentures. Deserted by their leader and tempted by these fair promises, the men were at last persuaded to yield. Grantham embarked them on the fleet and took them down to Tindall's Point, there to make their submission and "kiss the Governour's hand".[238]

Almost at the same time overtures were made by the Governor to General Walkelett. Could this man be induced to surrender himself and his troops, the last great obstacle to peace would be removed. So anxious was Sir William to seduce him from the cause of the rebels, that he offered him not only his pardon, but part of the plunder taken by Bacon from the Indians.[239] Walkelett assented, and agreed to lead his troops to Tindall's Point, and "declare for ye King's Majesty, the Governour & Country". He was to find there "a considerable Company of resolved men", to assist him in case his own party offered resistance.[240] This arrangement seems to have been carried out successfully and Walkelett's entire command was taken.[241]

The collapse of the rebellion sounded the death knell of those "chiefe Incendiaries" Drummond and Lawrence. These men had long protested against Berkeley's arbitrary government, and had been largely instrumental in bringing on the insurrection. Bacon had considered them his chief advisors

[238] Ing's Pros., p. 46; P. R. O., CO5-1371-416.
[239] P. R. O., CO1-39-13.   [240] P. R. O., CO5-1371-501.
[241] P. R. O., CO5-1371-416.

and friends. So deep was the Governor's hatred of them that in his recent proclamations he had excepted them from the general pardon.[242]

When Ingram and Walkelett surrendered, these "arch rebels" were stationed on the south side of the York River, at a place called Brick House. When they heard of Ingram's intended desertion, they made desperate but futile efforts to prevent his designs. Failing in this, they determined to gather around them the remnants of the rebel forces and march towards the frontier, in hopes of kindling anew the waning spirit of resistance. "They sent downe to Coll: Bacons to fetch of the Gard there, under . . . Whaly, to reinforce their own strength." Whaly, whose position was more exposed than their own, promptly obeyed, and succeeded in bringing off his force with "the last remains of Coll: Bacon's Estate". The rebel leaders now mustered about three hundred men, and with these they retreated through New Kent, "thinking (like the snow ball) to increase by their rouleing". "But finding that in stead of increasing there number decreast; and that the Moone of there fortune was now past the full, they broke up howse-keeping, every one shifting for him selfe."[243]

And now the chief rebels were hunted down like wild beasts by the Governor's troops. Thomas Hall, formerly clerk of the New Kent county court, Thomas Young, Major Henry Page, and a man named Harris were captured and led before Sir William. They were all tried by court martial, on shipboard off Tindall's Point, convicted of treason, and at once sent to their execution.[244]

A few days later Drummond was found, exhausted and half starved, hiding in Chickahominy swamp.[245] When he was brought before the Governor, that resentful old man could not restrain his joy. He is said to have "complimented him with the ironicall sarcasm of a low bend", declaring that he was more welcome than any other man in Virginia, or even his own brother.[246] The next day Berkeley went to Colonel Bray's house and here Drummond was conducted on foot to

[242] P. R. O., CO1-39-10; Ing's Pros., p. 47.

[243] Ing's Pros., p. 48.   [244] Ing's Pros., p. 49.

[245] Drummond was captured Jan. 14, 1677.

[246] T. M., p. 23; Ing's Pros., p. 49.

stand his trial. "In his way thither he complained very much that his Irons hurt him, and . . . expressed abundance of thankes for being permitted to rest himselfe upon the Roade, while he tooke a pipe of Tobacco."[247]   But he refused the offer of a horse, saying he would come soon enough to his death on foot.

At his trial he was treated with brutal harshness, his clothes stripped from his back and his ring torn from his finger. Although the rebellion was now over, he was denied jury trial, and was condemned by court martial after a hearing of but half an hour.   Some months later, when this matter came to the attention of the English Privy Council, the Lord Chancellor exclaimed that "he knew not whether it were lawful to wish a person alive, otherwise he could wish Sir William Berkeley so, to see what could be answered to such barbarity".[248]

Thus ended the rebellion.   Apparently it had accomplished nothing for the cause of liberty or the relief of the oppressed commons.   Few of the abuses that had caused the people to take arms had been rectified.   The taxes were heavier than ever, the Governor was more severe and arbitrary.   English troops were on their way to the colony to enforce submission and obedience.   Charles II, irritated at the independent spirit of the Virginians, was meditating the curtailment of their privileges and the suppression of their representative institutions.   Yet this attack of an outraged people upon an arbitrary and corrupt government, was not without its benefits. It gave to future Governors a wholesome dread of the commons, and made them careful not to drive the people again into the fury of rebellion.   It created a feeling of fellowship among the poor planters, a consciousness of like interests that tended to mould them into a compact class, ready for concerted action in defense of their rights.   It gave birth in the breasts of many brave men to the desire to resist by all means possible the oppression of the Stuart kings.   It stirred the people to win, in their legislative halls, victories for the cause of liberty, as real as those which Bacon and his followers had failed to secure on the field of battle.

[247] Ing's Pros., p. 50.

[248] Burk, Vol. II, p. 266; P. R. O., CO1-41-74, 75; CO389.6. Lawrence and Whaly made good their escape into the forest. They probably perished, however, from exposure, or at the hands of the Indians.

CHAPTER VII

The Period of Confusion

When the news reached England that the common people of Virginia were in open revolt against their Governor, and had driven him from his capital, the King was not a little surprised and alarmed. The recollection of the civil war in England was still fresh enough in his memory to make him tremble at the mutterings of rebellion, even though they came from across the Atlantic. Moreover, since the customs from the Virginia tobacco yielded many thousand pounds annually, he could but be concerned for the royal revenue. If the tumults in the colony resulted in an appreciable diminution in the tobacco crop, the Exchequer would be the chief loser. Nor did the King relish the expense of fitting out an army and a fleet for the reduction of the insurgents.

His anxiety was increased by lack of intelligence from the colonial government. Several letters telling of Bacon's coercion of the June Assembly had reached him, but after that months passed without word from the Governor or the Council. From private sources, however, came reports of "uproars so stupendous" that they could hardly find belief.[1] It was rumored in England that Sir William had been defeated, driven out of the colony, and "forced to lie at sea".[2]

Charles seems to have perceived at once that Berkeley must have been responsible for the Rebellion. He probably cared very little whether the old Governor oppressed the people or not, so long as he kept them quiet, but it was an inexcusable blunder for him to drive them into insurrection. Charles himself, it is said, had resolved long before, never to resume his travels; he now wondered why Sir William had brought upon himself this forced journey to Accomac. He decided to institute an investigation to find out what the Governor had

[1] P. R. O., CO 389.6-177.   [2] Ibid.

been doing so to infuriate the people. A commission, consisting of Colonel Herbert Jeffreys, Sir John Berry and Colonel Francis Moryson, was appointed to go to Virginia to enquire into and report all grievances and pressures.[3]

Early in June, 1676, Berkeley had written the King, complaining that his age and infirmities were such that he could no longer perform properly his office in Virginia, and requesting that he be allowed to retire from active service.[4] The Council had protested against this resignation, but Charles thought it best to take Sir William at his word and to recall him from the government he had not been able to preserve in peace and quiet. In honor of his long service, and his well known loyalty, he was, however, to retain "the title and dignity of Governor".[5] He was ordered to return to England "with all possible speed", to report upon his administration and to give an account of the extraordinary tumults in the colony.[6] During his absence the duties of his office were to be entrusted to Colonel Herbert Jeffreys, who was to bear the title of Lieutenant-Governor.[7] He was not, however, to be the deputy or assistant of Sir William, and "to all intents and purposes" was made Governor-in-chief. Berkeley was to be "no wayes accountable" for his actions good or bad.[8]

The King instructed Colonel Jeffreys, before attempting to subdue the rebels by force of arms, to exhaust all peaceable means of securing their submission. In order to make this task more easy, he drew up and had printed a proclamation of pardon, which he directed him to publish throughout the colony. All, it declared, with the sole exception of Bacon, that should surrender themselves, and take the oath of allegiance and supremacy, were to receive free and full forgiveness. Charles felt that most of the colonists were at heart still loyal, and would, if their grievances were redressed, be glad to accept his royal offer of grace.

[3] The commission had consisted at first of Sir John Berry, Colonel Francis Moryson and Thomas Fairfax. P. R. O., CO1-37-53.
[4] P. R. O., CO389.6-113, 174.   [5] P. R. O., CO389.6-113.
[6] P. R. O., CO389.6-121, 174, 175.   [7] P. R. O., CO389.6-113.
[8] P. R. O., CO389.6-137, 139, 140, 144; CO1-38-7.

But he did not rely entirely upon gentle measures, for, after all, the stubborn Virginians might distrust his promises and reject the pardon. So he resolved to send to the colony a strong body of troops to bring them to their senses, if necessary, at the point of the bayonet. A thousand men, thoroughly equipped for active service, were put under the command of Colonel Jeffreys and embarked for the colony.[9]

In the meanwhile, Governor Berkeley, having regained his authority, was busily engaged in reimbursing himself and his friends for their losses in the Rebellion. There can be no doubt that many of the loyalists had suffered severely by the depredations of the insurgents.[10] Those that followed the Governor into exile upon the Eastern Shore, had been compelled to leave their estates to the mercy of the enemy. And the desperate rebels, especially after death had removed the strong arm of Bacon, had subjected many plantations to thorough and ruthless pillage. Crops had been destroyed, cattle driven off, farm houses burned, servants liberated. Almost every member of the Council had suffered, while Berkeley himself claimed to have lost no less than £10,000.[11]

Thus, it was with a spirit of bitterness and hatred that the loyalists, in January and February, returned to their ruined homes. Quite naturally, they set up a clamor for compensation from the estates of those that had plundered them. Now that the King's authority had been restored, and the cause they had contended for had triumphed, they demanded that the vanquished should be made to disgorge their plunder and pay for their wanton destruction. Surely the Governor's followers could not be expected to accept readily all these great losses as a reward for their loyalty.

But restoration upon a large scale would almost certainly entail injustice, and would fan again the flames of bitterness and hatred. It might be possible to restore many articles yet remaining in the hands of the rebels, but most of the plundered goods had long since been consumed. It was often impossible to determine what persons had been guilty of specific acts of

[9] P. R. O., CO389.6-116.   [10] P. R. O., CO5-1371-149, 154.
[11] P. R. O., CO1-40-110; CO5-1371-27, 33, 62, 63, 64.

pillage, while many of the most active rebels were very poor men, from whom no adequate compensation could be obtained.

There ensued an undignified and pernicious scramble by the loyalists to seize for their own use the property of the few well-to-do insurgents. On all sides confiscation, unauthorized seizures, and violence marked the collapse of the Rebellion. In these proceedings Sir William took the lead. His servants went out, under pretence of searching for his stolen property, to take for his use the sheep, the cattle, and other goods of the neighboring rebels.[12] He showed, it was declared, "a greedy determination thoroughly to heale himselfe before hee car'd to staunch the bleeding gashes of the woefully lacerated country. . . . Making and treating men as delinquents, before any due conviction or attainder, by seizing their estates, cattle, servants and carrying off their tobacco, marking hogsheads and calling this securing it to the King's service."[13]

Even more unjustifiable was the conduct of Sir William in resorting to arbitrary compositions with his prisoners to fill his exhausted purse.[14] Men were arrested, thrown into jail, terrified with threats of hanging, and released only upon resigning to the Governor most or all of their estates.[15] One James Barrow was locked up at Green Spring and refused permission to plead his case before the Governor. He was told that his release could be secured only upon the payment of a ruinous composition. "By reason," he said, "of the extremity of Cold, hunger, lothsomnesse of Vermin, and other sad occasions, I was forct to comply."[16] Edward Loyd was held for twenty-one days, while his plantation was invaded, and his wife so frightened that she fell into labor and died.

It was proposed by the loyalists to share among themselves the estates of all that had been executed for treason, had died in arms against the King, or had fled from the colony to escape the Governor's vengeance.[17] It did not matter to them that the wretched widows and orphans of these men would be

---

[12] P. R. O., CO1-39-11, 17; CO5-1371-68, 69, 62, 63, 64, 78, 79, 81, 82, 132.
[13] P. R. O., CO5-1371-152. [14] P. R. O., CO5-1371-132.
[15] CO1-40-1 to 37; CO1-40-43; CO5-1371-81, 82.
[16] P. R. O., CO1-40-23. [17] P. R. O., CO5-1371-27, 33.

left destitute. Nor did they stop to consider that these estates, if forfeited at all, could not be seized legally for private use, but should revert to the Crown. They thought only of repairing their own ruined fortunes.[18]

In the midst of this confusion and lawlessness Berry and Moryson, with a part of the fleet and seventy of the English soldiers, arrived in the James River.[19] They had left Portsmouth November the nineteenth, but it was January the twenty-ninth before they reached Virginia.[20] Without waiting for Jeffreys and the main body of the fleet, they notified the Governor of their arrival and requested an immediate conference. Berkeley came aboard their flag-ship, the *Bristol,* February the first, where he was notified of their mission and intrusted with official letters.[21] He poured into the ears of the commissioners the recital of the exciting events of the past months—the destruction of Jamestown, Bacon's death, the surrender of Ingram and Walkelett, the execution of the leading rebels, the return of "the poore Scattered Loyal party to their ruined homes".[22] Although peace had been restored not three weeks before, he pretended astonishment that the King had thought it necessary to send soldiers to his aid.

Nor could he conceal his irritation at the mission of Berry and Moryson. That Charles should think it necessary to make an investigation of affairs in Virginia betokened a lack of confidence in the Governor. Berkeley's friends claimed, no doubt truly, that he was the author of every measure of importance adopted by the government of Virginia. An inquiry into conditions in the colony could but be an inquiry into his conduct. And the Governor, perhaps, knew himself to be guilty of much that he did not wish to have exposed before his royal master.

Moreover, Berkeley was not in the humor to brook interference at this juncture. He was inexorably resolved that the chief rebels should be brought to the gallows and that his own followers should be rewarded for their faithfulness. If

---

[18] P. R. O., CO1-39-38.
[20] Ibid.
[22] Ibid.

[19] P. R. O., CO5-1371-17, 20.
[21] P. R. O., CO5-1371-27, 33.

the commissioners intended to block these measures, or protest against his actions when in violation of law, they might expect his bitter hostility.

Before the commissioners had been in Virginia two weeks their relations with the Governor became strained. The disposing of the "delinquents Estates", they announced, must be referred to the King. Loyal sufferers should not secure restitution except by due process of law. Seizures of tobacco and other goods must stop. Soon the meetings in the cabin of the *Bristol* became so stormy that the commissioners decided to hold all future communication with Sir William in writing. This they thought necessary because his "defect of hearing" not only made privacy impossible, but looked "angrily, by loud and fierce speaking".[23]

A few days later Colonel Jeffreys arrived with the remainder of the fleet. He and his fellow commissioners found the whole country so ruined and desolate that they experienced considerable difficulty in securing a place of residence.[24] As the Governor disobeyed flatly the King's commands to entertain them at Green Spring,[25] they were compelled to accept the hospitality of Colonel Thomas Swann and make their home at his seat on the James River.[26] On the twelfth of February, Jeffreys, Berry and Moryson went to Green Spring, where they held a long conference with Berkeley and the Council.[27] Jeffreys produced his commission, and read the clauses which instructed Berkeley to return immediately to England, and to resign the government into his hands.[28]

It is easy to imagine with what anger Berkeley and his Council received this command. If Sir William must embark for England and give up his government to this stranger, they would be foiled in their revenge in the very moment of triumph. Jeffreys would probably put an end to the wholesale plundering of the rebels: the illegal distribution of confiscated estates, the seizure of goods, the unjust compositions. It was true that Sir William had written the King in June asking

[23] P. R. O., CO5-1371-55, 60.　　　[24] P. R. O., CO5-1371-90, 94.
[25] P. R. O., CO391.2-173, 178.　　　[26] P. R. O., CO5-1371-90, 94.
[27] P. R. O., CO5-1371-83, 85, 90, 94.　　[28] P. R. O., CO289.6-121.

his recall, but many things had happened in Virginia since he penned that letter. He was passionately opposed to leaving his government at this juncture.

And the old man's quick wit found an excuse for remaining in Virginia. The word "conveniency" in his orders gave him a loophole.[29] It was evident to all that the King wished him to return without delay, but Berkeley pretended to believe that this word had been inserted in order to permit him to use his own convenience in selecting the date of departure. The question was put to the Council and this body gave a ready and joyous support to the Governor's interpretation. Jeffreys and the commissioners begged them to consider that the word referred not to Sir William's "conveniency", but to that of the King's service, yet they would not heed them.[30] So Jeffreys went back to Swann's Point in discomfiture and the old Governor remained in Virginia for three months more to carry to completion his plans of restitution and revenge.[31] That he should have dared thus to trifle with his royal master's commands, which all his life he had considered sacred, reveals to us vividly his furious temper at this juncture. The humiliation and indignities he had experienced during the Rebellion had deprived him of all prudence.

Had Colonel Jeffreys been a man of force he would not have submitted to this juggling with the King's commands. With a thousand British troops at his back, he could easily have arrested Sir William and forced him to take ship for England. Although this would have been harsh treatment for one that had so long served the King, it was fully justified by the Governor's flagrant disobedience. And it would have relieved the colony of the presence of a man whose inhuman cruelty had rendered him odious to the people. But Jeffreys knew that the Governor's brother, Lord John Berkeley, was high in the King's favor, and might take revenge should he resort to violent measures. So he contented himself with writing home his complaints, and sat quietly by, while Berkeley carried to completion his principal designs.

[29] P. R. O., CO5-1371-50, 83.   [30] P. R. O., CO5-1371-93, 94.
[31] P. R. O., CO1-40-88.

The Governor was deeply displeased with the King's proclamation of pardon. Should he publish it at once, as he was ordered to do, it would greatly hinder him in his work of revenge and render more difficult his illegal seizures and confiscations. Since the pardon excepted only Bacon, under its terms such notorious rebels as Robert Jones, or Whaly, or even Lawrence, might come in out of the wilderness and demand immunity. This Berkeley was determined should not be. He thought at first of suppressing the pardon entirely, and of setting out one of his own based upon it, excepting the most notorious rebels.[32] The commissioners urged him to publish the papers unchanged, as the King would undoubtedly resent any attempt to frustrate his intentions.[33] And they insisted that there should be no delay. "Observing the generality of the people to look very amazedly one upon another", at the arrival of the English soldiers, as though dreading a terrible revenge by the King, they thought it highly desirable to "put them out of their paine".[34] It was, they declared, by no means unlikely that a new rebellion would break out, for the people were still deeply dissatisfied and "murmured extremely".

After several days of hesitation, Berkeley decided to issue the King's proclamation unchanged. Accordingly, on the tenth of February, to the great relief of "the trembling people", the printed copies brought over by the commissioners were made public.[35] But with them the Governor published a proclamation of his own, which limited and modified that of his Majesty.[36] Gyles Bland, Thomas Goodrich, Anthony Arnold, and all other rebels then in prison were to be denied the benefit of the pardon. The King's mercy was not to extend to Lawrence and Whaly; or to John Sturdivant, Thomas Blayton, Robert Jones, John Jennings, Robert Holden, John Phelps, Thomas Mathews,[37] Robert Spring, Stephen Earleton and Peter Adams; or "to John West and John Turner, who being legally condemned for rebellion made their escapes by

[32] P. R. O., CO1-39-24.   [33] P. R. O., CO5-1371-32.
[34] P. R. O., CO5-1371-55, 60.   [35] P. R. O., CO5-1371-32, 38.
[36] P. R. O., CO5-1371-276, 286.
[37] This Thomas Mathews was probably the author of the T. M. account of Bacon's Rebellion.

breaking prison"; or to Sara Grindon, "who by her lying and scandalous Reports was the first great encourager and Setter on of the ignorant" people; or even to Colonel Thomas Swann, Colonel Thomas Beale or Thomas Bowler, former members of the Council.[38] The commissioners thought it highly presumptuous in Berkeley thus to frustrate the King's wishes, and they were careful to let his Majesty know the Governor's disobedience, but the Council of Virginia endorsed all his actions and the people dared not disobey.

And so the trials and executions of the wretched rebels continued. As a result, no doubt, of the protests of the commissioners, the proceedings of the court martial were closed, and the accused were now examined before the court of oyer and terminer.[39] Gyles Bland, who for some months had been a prisoner aboard the *Adam and Eve,* was now made to answer for his participation in the Rebellion.[40] He possessed many powerful friends in England, but their influence could not save him. It was rumored that the Duke of York had blocked all efforts in his behalf, vowing "by God Bacon and Bland shoud dye".[41] Accordingly, on the eighth of March, he was condemned, and seven days later was executed.[42] Other trials followed. In quick succession Robert Stoakes, John Isles, Richard Pomfoy, John Whitson and William Scarburgh were sent to the scaffold.[43] Some of the Governor's friends expressed fear that the rabble might attempt to rescue these men, and "Counsell'd the not sending them to dye without a strong Guard", but the people dared not rise in their behalf.[44]

Robert Jones was condemned, but was saved from the gallows by the intercession of Colonel Moryson. Jones had fought with Charles I in the English civil wars, and now exhibited the wounds received in the service of the father as a plea for pardon for his rebellion against the son. Moryson was moved

[38] P. R. O., CO2-39-31; CO5-1371-276, 286.
[39] P. R. O., CO5-1371-125, 127.   [40] P. R. O., CO1-39-38; CO1-41-79.
[41] T. M., p. 24.
[42] P. R. O., CO1-39-35; Hen., Vol. II, p. 550.
[43] P. R. O., CO1-39-35; Hen., Vol. II, p. 553.
[44] P. R. O., CO5-1371-152.

to pity at the plight of the old veteran and wrote to Madam Berkeley requesting her to intercede for him with the Governor.[45] "If I am at all acquainted with my heart," wrote the Lady in reply, "I should with more easinesse of mind have worne the Canvas Lynnen the Rebells said they would make me be glad off, than have had this fatal occasion of interceding for mercy."[46] None the less Berkeley consented to reprieve Jones, and many months later the King pardoned him.[47]

Anthony Arnold, who had been one of the most active of the rebel leaders, boldly defended the right of peoples to resist the oppressions of their rulers. He declared that kings "had no rights but what they gott by Conquest and the Sword, and he that could by force of the Sword deprive them thereof, had as good and just a Title to it as the King himselfe. . . . If the King should deny to doe him right he would make noe more to sheathe his sword in his heart or Bowells then of his own mortall Enemyes."[48] For these and other treasonable words this "horrible resolved Rebell and Traytor" was condemned to be "hang'd in Chaines in his own County, to bee a more remarkable Example than the rest".[49]

The Governor, even now, showed no inclination to put an end to the trials and executions. No sooner would the courts empty the jails of prisoners than he would fill them up again. The unhappy rebels, finding that the King's pardon gave them little protection, and that Berkeley excepted from it whom he wished, could not know where next the axe would fall.[50] None can say how far Sir William would have carried his revenge had not the Assembly requested him "to hold his hand from all other Sanguinary punishment".[51] This brought him to his senses and he consented, though with extreme reluctance, to dismiss his witnesses and juries, and put an end to the executions. And even then "he found out a new way" to punish his victims, "ffyning some of their Treasons and Rebellions and condemning others to banishment to England".[52]

[45] P. R. O., CO5-1371-178, 179. [46] P. R. O., CO5-1371-180, 181.
[47] P. R. O., CO1-45-3. [48] P. R. O., CO5-1371-152.
[49] P. R. O., CO5-1371-152; Hen., Vol. II, p. 550.
[50] P. R. O., CO5-1371-32, 152. [51] P. R. O., CO5-1371-152.
[52] P. R. O., CO5-1371-152.

The Governor's extreme severity and the insatiable greed of the loyal party brought the colony to the verge of another rebellion. The people were deeply angered. Had there appeared any person to lead them, "bould and courageous . . . that durst venture his neck", the commons were ready "to Emmire themselves as deepe in Rebellion as ever they did in Bacon's time".[53]   For many months it was feared that Lawrence, "that Stubborn desperate and resolved Rebell", would emerge from seclusion to put himself at the head of a new swarm of mutineers.[54]   Were he to appear at this juncture, not even the presence of the English troops could prevent Bacon's veterans from flocking to his standard. "Soe sullen and obstinate" were the people that it was feared they would "abandon their Plantacons, putt off their Servants & dispose of their Stock and away to other parts". Had England at this juncture become involved in a foreign war, the Virginians would undoubtedly have sought aid from the enemies of the mother country.[55]

Nor could the people expect relief or justice from the General Assembly which met at Green Spring, February the twentieth, 1677.[56]   The elections had been held soon after the final collapse of the Rebellion, amid the general terror inspired by the numerous executions, and had resulted in an overwhelming victory for the loyalists. In many counties, staunch friends of the Governor had been put in nomination, and the commons given an opportunity of showing the sincerity of their repentance by electing them to the Assembly. William Sherwood declared that most of the Burgesses were Berkeley's "owne Creatures & choase by his appointments before the arrivall of the Commissioners".[57]   In several places fraud as well as intimidation seems to have been used to secure the election of loyalists. The commons of Charles City complained that there had been illegal voting in their county and seventy of them signed a petition, demanding a new election, which they posted upon the court house door.[58]   That the

[53] P. R. O., CO1-40-88.
[54] P. R. O., CO5-1371-132.
[55] P. R. O., CO5-1371-32.
[56] P. R. O., CO1-39-35.
[57] P. R. O., CO1-40-43.
[58] P. R. O., CO1-40-73, 106.

Assembly was in no sense representative of the people seems to have been recognized even in England, for some of the King's ministers declared that it had been "called when ye Country was yet remaining under great distractions, and uncapable of making their Elections after ye usual manner".[59]

Certain it is, that the House of Burgesses as well as the Council, was filled with ardent loyalists and friends of the Governor. They passed several acts confirming all Berkeley's recent measures, and inflicting further punishment upon the luckless rebels.[60] Some that had escaped the gallows were forced to pay heavy fines, others were banished.[61] Many were compelled to make humble submission, with ropes around their necks, upon their knees before the Governor or the county magistrates. Large sums of money were voted to reward the most active of Berkeley's supporters. All that had held command among the rebels, even Ingram and Walkelett, were made forever "incapable of any office civil or military in Virginia". To speak ill of the Governor and Council or of the justices of the peace, was declared a high crime, punishable by whipping. If the people, to the number of six, assembled in arms, they were to be considered mutineers and rebels. And the Burgesses showed great reluctance to reduce their own salaries, which the people considered so excessive. The Governor feared to insist upon it, "least perhaps he might thereby disoblige and thwart his own ends and interest in the Assembly", and only the positive commands of the King, delivered to them by the commissioners, could induce them to make any reduction at all.[62]

They passed resolutions praising the wisdom, the bravery, the justice and integrity of the Governor, and exonerating him for all blame for the outbreak of the Rebellion.[63] "The distempered humor predominant in the Common people", which had occasioned the insurrection, they declared the result of false rumors "inspired by ill affected persons, provoking an itching desire in them to pry into the secrets of the grand

[59] P. R. O., CO1-40-114.　　[60] P. R. O., CO1-39-35.
[61] P. R. O., CO1-39-35.
[62] P. R. O., CO5-1371-168 to 175; CO1-39-35.
[63] P. R. O., CO1-39-38.

assembly".[64] They snubbed the King's commissioners, replying to their request for assistance in discovering the common grievances that the Assembly alone was the proper body to correct the people's wrongs.[65] Yet when the commons did come to the Burgesses with their complaints they were repulsed with harsh reproofs and even severe punishment. Certain grievances from Isle of Wight county were denounced as "libellous, Scandalous and rebellious" and "the chiefe persons in the Subscriptions" were to be punished "to the merits of their Crymes".[66] A petition from Gloucester county was declared to savor so strongly of the "old leaven of rebellion" that it must be expunged from the records. When the people of Nansemond appealed for a more just method of taxation, they were answered briefly, "It is conceived the pole is the equallest way."[67]

One is inclined to wonder why the people, thus finding the Assembly but an instrument of oppression in the Governor's hands, did not turn eagerly for support and relief to the King's commissioners. These men had invited them to bring in all their pressures, without restraint or fear of punishment. His Majesty, they announced, was anxious to know what had caused them to rise against his authority. All just complaints would be carefully considered and all grievances redressed.[68] But dread of Sir William's anger held the people back. Their chief grievance was the old Governor himself, but there were few that dared say so, even with the promise of the King's protection. The commissioners wrote Secretary Coventry that until "the awe of his stay" was removed, they could "never thoroughly search and penetrate into the bottome of the Businesse".[69] Berkeley, they said, continually impeded their investigations and prevented the people from testifying. It might be necessary for Colonel Jeffreys to send him home, before the mists he cast before them could be dispelled.[70] When he was gone, a short time would show boldly those things that as yet only cautiously peeped forth.[71]

[64] P. R. O., CO1-39-38.
[65] P. R. O., CO1-39-39.
[66] P. R. O., CO1-39-38.
[67] P. R. O., CO1-39-38.
[68] P. R. O., CO5-1371-39 to 44.
[69] P. R. O., CO5-1371-132.
[70] P. R. O., CO5-1371-182, 187.
[71] P. R. O., CO5-1371-193 to 198.

The violent opposition which the commissioners encountered from the Governor and the loyalists soon forced them to become the leaders of the defeated party. The poor people looked forward with hope to the day when Sir William would leave and Colonel Jeffreys assume control of the executive. Then, they were sure, the persecutions would end and justice be done them.

The hatred and contempt of the Governor's friends for Colonel Jeffreys and his colleagues is shown by an interesting and unique incident. Having heard that Sir William was at last preparing to sail for England, they went to Green Spring, on the twenty-second of April, to bid him farewell.[72] This they thought due his dignity and rank, even though their relations with him had been far from cordial.[73] As they left the house, after paying their respects to the Governor and his lady, they found Sir William's coach waiting at the door to convey them to their landing.[74] But before they rode away a strange man came forward, boldly putting aside the "Postillion that used to Ryde" and got up himself in his place. The Governor, several Councillors, and others saw what occurred, but did not offer to interfere. Lady Berkeley went "into her Chamber, and peep'd through a broken quarrell of the Glass, to observe how the Show look'd".[75] After reaching their boat, the commissioners found to their horror that the strange postilion was none other than the "Common Hangman that . . . put the Halters about the Prisoner's Necks in Court when they were to make their submission". This seemed to them so gross an insult, not only to the "Great Seal", but to their "persons as Gentlemen", that they were resolved to make his Majesty himself acquainted with it.[76] "The whole country rings of . . . the public Odium and disgrace cast upon us," they said, "as the Exchange itselfe shortly may."[77]

It is probable that Lady Berkeley alone was responsible for this incident, which, as the commissioners themselves said, looked "more like a woman's than a man's malice".[78] The

[72] P. R. O., CO5-1371-208 to 211   [73] P. R. O., CO5-1371-212, 213.
[74] P. R. O., CO5-1371-220, 231.   [75] P. R. O., CO5-1371-220, 231.
[76] P. R. O., CO5-1371-212, 213.   [77] P. R. O., CO5-1371-220, 231.
[78] P. R. O., CO5-1371-220, 231.

Governor denied with passionate vehemence that he was in any way guilty. "I have sent the Negro[79] to be Rebuked, Tortur'd or whipt, till he confesse how this dire misfortune happen'd," he wrote the commissioners, "but I am soe distracted that I scarce know what I doe."[80]

Even before Berkeley left the colony Colonel Jeffreys issued a proclamation, formally taking possession of the government.[81] For some time it had been apparent that the Lieutenant-Governor's long delay in entering upon his duties was greatly weakening him in the estimation of the people. Since he had been forced to sit idly by for several months while Sir William carried to completion matters of the utmost importance, and had not dared to take his office so long as it pleased the old man to linger in the colony, many thought, quite naturally, that he could not have been entrusted with full authority to act as Governor. And this opinion had been industriously furthered by the loyal party. The departure of Sir William, they declared, did not mean a permanent change of administration. Jeffreys was to act only as his deputy during his absence and would retire upon his return.[82] Feeling that these views, if universally accepted, would undermine his influence and authority, Jeffreys entered a vigorous denial in his proclamation. He had been appointed, he declared, to exercise the power of Governor, as fully as Berkeley or any of his predecessors had done. No man should dare to belittle his office or authority. Berkeley was going home at his own request because his great age and infirmities rendered him unfit to sustain further the burdens of his position. The new executive had refrained from assuming his duties earlier, "because an Assembly being . . . ready to convene, the issueing forth a new Summons . . . must needs have greatly retarded the publique Weale".[83] Nor did he scruple to claim the full title of "Governour and Captain Generall of Virginia".

This proclamation aroused Berkeley's deepest ire. "Your ejecting me," he wrote Jeffreys, "from having any share in

---

[79] Probably the real postilion. [80] P. R. O., CO5-1371-214 to 217.
[81] This proclamation was issued April 27, 1677. P. R. O., CO1-40-53.
[82] P. R. O., CO1-41-121; CO1-42-23. [83] P. R. O., CO1-40-53.

the Government whilst yet I am in the Countrey . . . I beleeve can neither be justified by your Comision nor mine."
"You say that his Majesty out of the knowledge of my inability
to govern did surrogate so able a man as Coll: Jeffreys to
supply my defects. I wish from my heart Coll: Jeffreys were
as well known to the King and Counsel as Sir William Berkeley
is, for then the difference would be quickly decided." The
letter was addressed to the "Right honorable Coll: Herbert
Jeffreys, his Majesty's Lieutenant Governor of Virginia", and
was signed "William Berkeley, Governor of Virginia till his
most Sacred Majesty shall please to determine otherwise".[84]

In the meanwhile the letters of the commissioners, reporting
Berkeley's disobedience to the King's commands, had arrived
in England. Charles was angered, not only at his delay in
surrendering the government, but also at his presumption in
disregarding the royal proclamation of pardon. "You may
well think," he wrote Berkeley, "we are not a little surprised
to understand that you make difficulty to yield obedience to our
commands, being so clear and plain that we thought no man
could have raised any dispute about them. Therefore . . . we
do . . . command you forthwith . . . without further delay
or excuse (to) repair unto our Presence as We formerly
required you."[85]

Secretary Coventry wrote even more severely. We understand, he said, that to the King's clear and positive orders for
you to resign the government to Colonel Jeffreys, "upon certain
pretences which are no wayes understood here, you have delayed at least if not refused obedience. . . . His Majesty . . .
seemeth not a little surprised as well as troubled to find a
person that had for so many years served his Royal Father
and himself through ye worst of times with so unshaken a
loyalty, and so absolute obedience and resignation, should now
at one time fall into two such great errors as to affront his
Proclamation by putting out one of his owne at ye same time
with his, and in that to exempt several persons from pardon,
which were by the King's owne Proclamation made capable

[84] P. R. O., CO1-40-54.
[85] This letter was written May 13, 1677.

of Pardon; then after positive orders given for your immediate return . . . you yet stay there . . . and continually dispute with his Majesty's commissioners. I will assure you, Sir, his Majesty is very sensible of these miscarriages, and hath very little hopes that ye people of Virginia shall be brought to a right sense of their duty to obey their Governours when the Governours themselves will not obey the King. I pray you, Sir, . . . take not councell from your owne nor any other body's passion or resentment, to take upon you to judge either conveniency or not conveniency of the King's orders, but obey them, and come over; and whatever you have to say . . . you will be heard at large."[86]

Even before these letters were written Sir William had left the colony. He had embarked for England, May the fifth, in Captain Larrimore's sturdy ship which had stood him in such good stead in the hour of need.[87] But the old man, worn out by his violent passions and unusual exertions, was physically unfit for the long voyage across the Atlantic. He became very ill on shipboard, and reached England a dying man. "He came here alive," wrote Secretary Coventry, "but so unlike to live that it had been very inhumane to have troubled him with any interrogacons."[88] The news of the King's displeasure at his conduct added much to his suffering. He pleaded for an opportunity "to clear his Innocency" even though the "tedious passage & griefe of mind" had reduced him "to extreame weaknesse".[89] That Charles did not refuse him this privilege is attested by a letter written to Berkeley by Secretary Coventry. "I am commanded by his Majesty," he said, "to let you know that his Majesty would speake with you as soone as you can, because there are some ships now going to Virginia, and his Majesty would see what further Instructions may be necessary to be sent by them."[90] But Berkeley could not attend the King, either to give information or to plead his own cause. His condition rapidly became critical, and a few days later he died.[91]

---

[86] P. R. O., CO389.6-195 to 198.
[87] P. R. O., CO1-40-88.
[88] P. R. O., CO389.6.
[89] P. R. O., CO1-40-110.
[90] P. R. O., CO389.6-207.
[91] P. R. O., CO389.6-210.

Hardly had Sir William breathed his last than Thomas Lord Culpeper "kissed the King's hand as Governour".[92] This nobleman had received a commission, July 8, 1675, which was to take effect immediately upon the death, surrender or forfeiture of the office by Berkeley.[93]   It had never been Charles' intention that Colonel Jeffreys should remain permanently at the head of the government of Virginia, and he now notified him to prepare to surrender his office to the new Governor.[94]   The King, who felt that the unsettled condition of Virginia required Culpeper's immediate presence, ordered him to depart "with all speed", and told the colonists they might expect him by Christmas "without fayle".[95]   But this pampered lord, accustomed to the luxury of the court, had no desire to be exiled in the wilderness of the New World.   By various excuses he succeeded in postponing his departure for over two years, and it was not until the spring of 1680 that he landed in Virginia.[96]   Thus, for a while, Colonel Jeffreys was left as the chief executive of the colony.

In the meanwhile the commissioners, freed from the baleful presence of the old Governor, were continuing their investigation into the causes of the Rebellion.   Berkeley had advised them, when they first announced their mission, to carry out their work through the county courts.[97]   But they had refused to accept this plan.   The justices were almost all henchmen of Sir William, many were hated by the people and some were the objects of their chief accusations.   Had the investigation been intrusted to their hands, they would most certainly have suppressed the principal complaints.[98] The commissioners, therefore, appointed especial officers in the counties to hear the people's grievances, draw them up in writing and bring them in for presentation to the King.[99]   Even

[92] P. R. O., CO389.6-212.

[93] P. R. O., CO5-1355-299; CO389.6-271 to 273.

[94] P. R. O., CO389.6-210, 215.   [95] P. R. O., CO389.6-210.

[96] P. R. O., CO5-1355-377.   [97] P. R. O., CO5-1371-45.

[98] Nothing can show this more clearly than the reception in the Assembly, which was largely composed of justices of the peace, of the county grievances.

[99] P. R. O., CO391.2-180.

then the loyal party attempted, by intimidation, to prevent the commons from explaining without reserve what had caused them to take up arms against the government. Sir William, they were careful to report, would most certainly return, and any that dared charge him or his friends with corruption might expect the severest punishment.[100]   But the announcement by the commissioners that his Majesty himself had promised his protection to all informants relieved the fears of the people and many came forward with the story of their wrongs.[101] These seem to have been faithfully drawn up by the officers and in time presented to the King.

The loyal party complained loudly that the commissioners used in this matter none but the enemies of the Governor.[102] Lord John Berkeley declared that they had sought information from such only as were known "to be notorious actors in the rebellion".[103]   But the commissioners were undoubtedly right in insisting that all grievances should come from those that had been aggrieved. They themselves, they declared, were not responsible for the truth of the charges; their function was only to receive and report them. The King had sent them to Virginia to make the royal ear accessible to the humblest citizen. This could be done only by brushing aside the usual channels of information and going directly to the commons themselves. That some of the accusations were exaggerated or even entirely false seems not improbable; many were undoubtedly true. Posterity must accept them, not as the relation of established truth, but as the charges of a defeated and exasperated party.

In their work of investigation the commissioners found that they had need of the records of the House of Burgesses. In April, 1677, after the adjournment of the session at Green Spring, they came to Major Robert Beverley, the clerk of the Assembly, and demanded "all the Originall Journals, Orders, Acts", etc., then in his custody.[104]   Beverley required them to show their authority, and this they did, by giving him a sight

[100] P. R. O., CO5-1371-132.   [101] P. R. O., CO5-1371-132.
[102] P. R. O., CO391.2-180; Burk, Vol. II, pp. 259, 260.
[103] P. R. O., CO391.2-173 to 178; Burk, Vol. II, p. 260.
[104] P. R. O., CO1-41-87.

of that part of their commission which concerned his delivery of the records.[105] He then offered to allow them to examine any of the papers necessary to the investigation, but he refused absolutely to relinquish their custody.[106] The commissioners, who distrusted Beverley and perhaps feared that he might conceal the records, "took them from him by violence".[107]

When the Assembly met in October, 1677, the House of Burgesses sent a vigorous protest to Colonel Jeffreys against these proceedings of the commissioners. Their action, they declared, "we take to be a great violation of our privileges". The power to command the records which the commissioners claim to have received from the King, "this House humbly suppose His Majesty would not grant or Comand, for that they find not the same to have been practiced by any of the Kings of England in the likewise. . . . The House do humbly pray your Honour . . . will please to give the House such satisfaction, that they may be assured no such violation of their privileges shall be offered for the future."[108]

When Charles II heard of this bold protest he was surprised and angered. It seemed to him a "great presumption of ye said Assembly . . . to call in Question" his authority.[109] Referring their representation to the Lords of Trade and Plantations, he directed them "to examine ye same, & to Report" what they thought "fitt to be done in Vindication of . . . (the) Royall Authority, & for bringing the said Assembly to a due sence & acknowledgement of their Duty & Submission".[110] The Lords gave it as their opinion that the declaration was so "Seditious, even tending to Rebellion", that the new Governor should be directed to rebuke the Assembly and punish the "authors and abettors of this presumption".[111] The King commanded Lord Culpeper to carry these recommendations into effect. On the third of July, 1680, Culpeper brought the matter before the Virginia Council, preparatory to delivering the rebuke. But the Councillors made a vigorous defense of the action of the Assembly, and unanimously ad-

[105] P. R. O., CO1-42-138.
[106] P. R. O., CO5-1376-273.
[107] P. R. O., CO5-1376-273.
[108] P. R. O., CO1-41-87.
[109] P. R. O., CO1-42-141.
[110] P. R. O., CO1-42-141.
[111] P. R. O., CO391.2-300, 301.

vised the Governor to suspend the execution of the King's command.[112] After some hesitation, Culpeper yielded, and the matter was referred back to the Privy Council. Charles was finally induced to rescind the order, but he insisted that all reference to the declaration "be taken off the file and razed out of the books of Virginia".[113]

The work of the commission being completed, Berry and Moryson, in July, 1677, sailed with the royal squadron for England.[114] Their report, which was so damaging to the Virginia loyalists, was not allowed to go unchallenged. Sir William Berkeley, upon his death bed, had told his brother, Lord John Berkeley, of the hostility of the commissioners, and charged him to defend his conduct and character. And Lord Berkeley, who was a member of the Privy Council and a man of great influence, did his best to refute their evidence and to discredit them before the King.[115] Their entire report, he declared, was "a scandalous lible and invective of Sir William . . . and the royal party in Virginia".[116] His brother's conduct had been always prudent and just, and it was noticeable that not one private grievance had ever been brought against him before this rebellion.[117] The meetings of Lord Berkeley with the commissioners in the Council chamber were sometimes stormy. On one occasion he told Berry, "with an angry voice and a Berklean look, . . . that he and Morryson had murdered his brother". "Sir John as sharply returned again" that they had done nothing but what they "durst justify".[118]

As the other members of the Privy Council protected the commissioners, and upheld their report, the attacks of the angry nobleman availed nothing. Secretary Coventry averred that Berry and Moryson had been most faithful in carrying out the King's directions, and he showed his confidence in their honesty and their judgment by consulting them upon all important matters relating to the colony.[119] And for a while, their

[112] P. R. O., CO5-1355-354.
[113] Sains., Vol. XVIII, p. 129.
[114] P. R. O., CO1-41-17.
[115] Burk, Vol. II, p. 263.
[116] Burk, Vol. II, p. 259; P. R. O., CO391.2-180.
[117] Burk, Vol. II, p. 264.
[118] Burk, Vol. II, p. 266.
[119] P. R. O., CO391.2-180.

influence in shaping the policy of the Privy Council in regard to Virginia was almost unlimited.

Nor did they scruple to use this great power to avenge themselves upon those men that had so antagonized them and hindered their investigation. Robert Beverley they represented to the Privy Council as a man of low education and mean parts, bred a vulgar seaman and utterly unfit for high office.[120] Colonel Edward Hill was the most hated man in Charles City county.[121] Ballard, Bray and some of the other Councillors were rash and fiery, active in opposing the King's orders and unjust to the poor people.[122] The Privy Council was so greatly influenced by these representations that they determined to reconstruct the Virginia Council, upon lines suggested by Berry and Moryson. Colonel Philip Ludwell, Colonel Ballard and Colonel Bray were expressly excluded from the Council, while Colonel Hill and Major Beverley as "men of evil fame and behavior" were deprived of all governmental employment whatsoever, and "declared unfit to serve His Majesty".[123] On the other hand, Colonel Thomas Swann, who had been excluded from the Council by Governor Berkeley, was now, for his kindness to the commissioners, restored to his seat.[124]

The departure of Sir William Berkeley by no means ended the opposition to Colonel Jeffreys. A part of the Council, realizing that continued hostility could result only in harm to themselves, made their peace with the new administration, and were received into favor, but the more violent of the loyal party remained defiant and abusive. Philip Ludwell, Beverley, Hill, Ballard and others openly denounced Jeffreys as a weakling, entirely unsuited for the important office he now occupied, and did their best to render him unpopular with the people.[125] The Lieutenant-Governor retaliated with considerable spirit, depriving some of their lucrative offices, and suspending others

---

[120] P. R. O., CO1-41-121. Major Beverley was of good family. His military leadership in Bacon's Rebellion, and his services as clerk of the Assembly, testify to his ability. Va. Mag., Vol. II, p. 405.

[121] P. R. O., CO1-41-121.   [123] P. R. O., CO391.2-173 to 178.

[122] P. R. O., CO391.2-305.   [124] P. R. O., CO391.2-173 to 178.

[125] P. R. O., CO1-41-138; CO1-42-117.

from the Council. Ludwell, whose conduct had been especially obnoxious, was ousted from the collectorship of York
River.[126] Ballard was expelled from a similar office.[127] And
many months before the changes in the Council ordered by the
English government became known in Virginia, no less than
six of the most active loyalists had been suspended by the
Lieutenant-Governor.[128]

But events soon took a more favorable turn for the Berkeley party. The departure of Berry and Moryson deprived
Jeffreys of his staunchest friends and advisors. And, before
the end of the summer, he was prostrated by the Virginia
sickness, which was still deadly to those unaccustomed to the
climate of the colony. For several months he was too ill to
attend properly to his duties or to resist the machinations of
his enemies, and the government fell into the hands of the
Council.[129] And since this body, despite its pretended support
of the Lieutenant-Governor, was at heart in full sympathy with
Beverley and Ludwell and the other loyalists, the policy of the
administration was once more changed. The work of extor-
tion was actively resumed and the courts again busied themselves with suits against the former rebels.[130]

But consternation seized the Green Spring faction, as the
loyalists were now called, upon the arrival of the King's
order, annulling Berkeley's proclamation of February 10, 1677,
and reaffirming the general pardon.[131] If this command were
put into effect, most of the confiscations secured since the
Rebellion, would become illegal, and restitution would have
to be made. So desperately opposed to this were the loyalists
that they resolved to suppress the King's letter. They believed that it had been obtained by the influence of the commissioners, and this, they hoped, would soon be rendered
nugatory by the presence at court of Sir William Berkeley.
If they could keep the order secret for a few weeks, new instructions, dictated by the Governor, might arrive to render

[126] Va. Mag., Vol. XVIII, p. 18; P. R. O., CO1-42-55.
[127] Sains., Vol. XVII, p. 19. [128] P. R. O., CO1-41-121.
[129] P. R. O., CO1-42-17.1, 23. [130] P. R. O., CO1-42-23.
[131] P. R. O., CO1-42-17.1, 23.

its execution unnecessary. Colonel Jeffreys protested against their disobedience, but he was too weak to oppose the will of the Council.[132] So, for six weeks, his Majesty's grace "was unknown to ye poore Inhabitants", while the innumerable suits and prosecutions were pushed vigorously. Not until October the twenty-sixth, when all hope of its revocation had been dispelled by fresh information from England, did the Council consent to the publication of the letter.[133]

In September, 1677, writs were issued for an election of Burgesses.[134] Had Jeffreys not been ill, he would perhaps have refused to allow a new session of the Assembly. The contest at the polls could but result in a victory for the Green Spring faction, as the electoral machinery was in their hands. The Lieutenant-Governor, although he had removed some of the higher colonial officials, had made few changes in the personnel of the county courts.[135] The sheriffs, by resorting to the old methods, made sure of the election of most of the nominees of the loyal party. Complaints came from James City county, New Kent county and other places that intimidation and fraud had been used to deprive the people of a fair election.[136] If we may believe the testimony of William Sherwood, the Berkeley faction carried things with a high hand. "The Inhabitants of James City County," he wrote, "did unanimously elect me a Burgess . . . but several of my professed enemies . . . procured another writt for a new election, with a positive command not to choose me. The people then being under amazement consented to whome soever the Sheriffe would returne, & so my enemies to make their party the stronger in ye house . . . causd three Burgesses to serve for James City County."[137]

"By this means," wrote Colonel Daniel Parke, "and by persuading the burgesses that Sir William Berkeley was coming in Governour again, (the loyal party) got all confirmed that was done at the Assembly before held at Greene Spring."[138] In order to compensate themselves for their great losses and to fulfil the promises made by Berkeley to his followers during

[132] P. R. O., CO1-42-17.1, 23. [133] P. R. O., CO1-42-17.1.
[134] P. R. O., CO1-42-23. [135] P. R. O., CO1-42-23.
[136] P. R. O., CO1-42-17.1. [137] P. R. O., CO1-42-23.
[138] P. R. O., CO1-42-17.1.

the Rebellion, they levied a tax upon the people of one hundred and ten pounds of tobacco per poll. "This with the county tax and parish tax," said Parke, "is in some counties 250lbs, in some 300, and in some 400lbs, which falls very heavie upon the poorer people." The county grievances were again rejected by the Burgesses as false and scandalous, and the persons presenting them were severely punished.[139] But the Assembly expressed an earnest desire to bring about a reconciliation between the hostile factions in the colony, and prescribed a heavy penalty for the use of such opprobrious epithets as "traytor, Rebell Rougue, Rebell", etc.[140]

The news of Berkeley's death was a severe blow to the Green Spring party. All the hope they had entertained that he would accomplish the overthrow of the work of the commissioners, at once fell to the ground. But they were somewhat consoled by the appointment of Lord Culpeper. This nobleman was related to Lady Berkeley, and they had good reason to believe he would reverse the policy of the present administration and ally himself with the loyalists.[141]

In the meanwhile the Lieutenant-Governor was regaining his health and spirits, and was taking a more active part in public affairs. He had been deeply angered with Colonel Philip Ludwell for his many insults, and he now determined to prosecute him "for scandalizing the Governor, and abusing the Authority of his Majesty".[142] Ludwell's unpardonable crime, it would seem, consisted in calling Jeffreys "a pitiful little Fellow with a perriwig".[143] He had also been heard to say that the Lieutenant-Governor was "a worse Rebel than Bacon", that he had broken the laws of Virginia, that he had perjured himself, that he "was not worth a Groat in England". Nor was it considered a sufficient excuse that Ludwell had made those remarks immediately after consuming "part of a Flaggon of Syder".[144] The jury found him guilty of "scandalizing the Governor", but acquitted him of any intention of abusing his Majesty's authority. The General Court, upon the

[139] P. R. O., CO5-1376. [140] P. R. O., CO5-1376.
[141] P. R. O., CO1-42-55; Va. Mag., Vol. II, p. 408.
[142] Va. Mag., Vol. XVIII, p. 20. [143] Va. Mag., Vol. XVIII, p. 12.
[144] Va. Mag., Vol. XVIII, p. 11.

motion of Colonel Jeffreys, referred the case to the King and
Privy Council, that they might "advise a punishment propor-
tionable to the offence".[145]   Against this decision the defen-
dant, as he had an undoubted right to do, appealed to the
General Assembly.   Ludwell felt, no doubt, that should the
appeal be allowed, his great influence in the House of Burgesses would secure him a light sentence.   But the court
declared the case so unprecedented that the whole matter,
including the question of appeal, must be decided by the King.

With the return of hot weather, Colonel Jeffreys, not yet
being acclimated, or "seasoned", as the Virginians expressed
it, again became seriously ill.[146]   The Council elected a president to act in his place and once more assumed control of the
administration.[147]   The Green Spring faction, whom only the
Lieutenant-Governor could restrain, again lifted its head and
endeavored "to continue their old exactions & abuses".[148]   Feeling, perhaps, a sense of security in their remoteness from the
King, which made it impossible for him to watch their actions
closely, or to mete out to them prompt punishment, they still
disregarded his pardon and his reiterated commands.[149]   "The
colony would be as peaceful as could be wished," wrote William
Sherwood in August, 1678, "except for the malice of some discontented persons of the late Governor's party, who endeavour
by all ye cunning contrivances that by their artifice can be
brought about, to bring a Contempt of Colonel Jeffreys, our
present good Governor. . . . Those persons who are the
troublers of the peace . . . are . . . Lady Berkeley, Colonel
Philip Ludwell, Colonel Thomas Ballard, Colonel Edward
Hill, Major Robert Beverley, all of which are cherished by
Mr. Secretary Ludwell (who acts severely.)   It is to be feared,
unless these fiery Spiritts are allayed or removed home, there
will not be that settled, happy peace and unity which otherwise
might be, for they are entered into a faction, which is upheld
by the expectation of my Lord Culpeper's doing mighty things
for them & their interest."[150]

[145] Va. Mag., Vol. XVIII, p. 23.   [146] P. R. O., CO1-42-103.
[147] Va. Mag., Vol. IX, p. 307.   [148] P. R. O., CO1-42-103.
[149] P. R. O., CO1-42-107.   [150] P. R. O., CO1-42-117.

Colonel Jeffreys died in November, 1678.[151]   It was the fortune of this Governor to come to the colony in one of the greatest crises of its history. Had he been a man of ability and firmness he could have rendered the people services of great value. He might have put an end to the reign of terror inaugurated by Berkeley, prevented the unending law suits, confiscations and compositions, reorganized the county courts and assured to the people a fair election of Burgesses. He seems to have wished to rule justly and well, but he was too weak to quell the strife between the rival factions and bring quiet to the distracted colony.

So bitter was the loyal party against Colonel Jeffreys, that after his death they sought to revenge themselves upon his widow. The Lieutenant-Governor had received no part of his salary from March, 1678, to the day of his death, and had, as a result, incurred considerable debt. As Mrs. Jeffreys was unable to meet all her husband's obligations, she was detained in Virginia, and, according to one account, thrown into prison.[152]   "T'is plain," she wrote Secretary Coventry, "they seek my Life in malice to my husband, though none of them can tax him with any injustice. . . . I cannot hope to outlive this persecution, but I most humbly beseech you to intercede for me to his Majesty, that my child may not be ruined."[153]   Mrs. Jeffreys later received the arrears due her husband, and was thus enabled to free herself from the power of her enemies.[154]

Upon the death of Colonel Jeffreys, Sir Henry Chicheley, by virtue of a commission granted in 1674, assumed control of the government.[155]   The new Governor had long served with distinction in the Council, and seems to have been a "most loyal, worthy person and deservedly beloved by the whole country".[156]   But he was now too "old, sickly and crazy" to govern the colony with the vigor and firmness that were so greatly needed.[157]   During the eighteen months of his administration the people were "not reconciled to one another", and "ill blood" only too often was manifested by both factions.[158]

[151] Va. Mag., Vol. IX, p. 307.
[153] P. R. O., CO5-1355-305.
[155] Va. Mag., Vol. IX, p. 307.
[157] Sains., Vol. XVII, p. 230.
[152] P. R. O., CO5-1355-304, 305, 309.
[154] P. R. O., CO5-1355-370.
[156] P. R. O., CO1-41-121.
[158] Sains., Vol. XVII, p. 230.

Sir Henry had himself been a severe sufferer by the Rebellion. He had fallen into Bacon's hands and had even, it would seem, been threatened with death, in retaliation for Berkeley's execution of Captain Carver. Yet he attempted to rule impartially and well. Writs were issued in the spring of 1679 for an election of Burgesses, and the people were protected from intimidation at the polls. The Assembly, as a result, showed itself more sane, more sensitive to the wishes of the commons, than had been either of the sessions of 1677.[159] Several laws were enacted redressing some of the most flagrant evils of the old governmental system of Berkeley. The voters of each parish were empowered to elect two men "to sit in the severall county courts and have their equall votes with the severall justices for the makeing of by lawes".[160] An act was passed putting a limit upon the excessive fees charged by the collectors of the customs.[161] And the clamor of the loyalists for the payment of their claims upon the treasury were unheeded, and all public debts were referred for settlement to the next session.[162]

Chicheley's administration came temporarily to an end with the arrival of Lord Culpeper. The period from the close of the Rebellion to May, 1680, when the new Governor-General took the oath of office, seems, at first sight, characterized only by confusion and disaster. The violent animosities, the uncertainty of property rights, the lack of a firm and settled government kept the people in constant uneasiness and discontent. The numerous banishments and executions had deprived the colony of some of its most intelligent and useful citizens, while the plundering of both parties during the Rebellion, and the numberless forfeitures that followed the establishment of peace, had reduced many men to poverty. Nor had the most pressing of the grievances that had caused the people to rise against the government been redressed. The Navigation Acts were still in force, the commons were yet excluded from their rightful share in the government, the taxes were more oppressive than ever.

[159] Hen., Vol. II, p. 433.
[161] Hen., Vol. II, p. 443.
[160] Hen., Vol. II, p. 441.
[162] Hen., Vol. II, p. 456.

Yet amid the melancholy confusion of the times, important changes for the better were taking place. Never again was an English Governor to exercise the despotic power that had been Sir William Berkeley's. This was not due to the greater leniency of the British government, or to lack of ambition in the later Governors. But the Rebellion and the events following it, had weakened the loyalty of the people and shown them the possibility of resisting the King's commands. The commons, angered at the severity of the punishment inflicted upon the rebel leaders, and disappointed in the royal promise that their grievances should be redressed, regarded the government with sullen hostility. The wealthy planters resented what they considered Charles' ingratitude for their loyal support in the hour of need, and complained bitterly of his interference with their attempts to restore their ruined fortunes. Throughout Berkeley's administration their interests had seemed to be identical with those of the Governor, and they had ever worked in harmony with him. With the advent of Colonel Jeffreys, however, they had been thrown into violent opposition to the executive. Their success in thwarting the policies of the Lieutenant-Governor, and in evading and disobeying the King's commands gave them a keen appreciation of their own influence and power. They were to become more and more impatient of the control of the Governors, more and more prone to defy the commands of the English government.

The awakened spirit of resistance bore rich fruit for the cause of liberty. The chief difficulty heretofore experienced by the commons in defending their rights was the lack of intelligent and forceful leaders. These they now secured through the frequent quarrels of the wealthy planters with the Governors. More than once Councillors, suspended from their seats for disobedience, came forward as leaders in the struggle to preserve the rights of the people. In this capacity they rendered services of the highest importance. Strangely enough some of the leading spirits of the old Berkeley party became, by their continued opposition to the executive, champions of representative government in the colony. Had it not been for the active leadership of Robert Beverley and Philip Ludwell the cause of liberty might well have perished under the assaults of Charles II and James II.

The House of Burgesses was gradually becoming more representative of the people. The intimidation of voters practiced by the loyal party immediately after the Rebellion could not be continued indefinitely. As the terror inspired by Berkeley's revenge upon the rebels began to wane, the commons insisted more upon following their own inclinations at the polls. Moreover, the incessant quarrels of the Governors with the members of the aristocracy made it impossible for any clique to control again the electoral machinery. As the sheriffs and justices were no longer so closely allied with the executive as they had been in the Restoration period, false returns of Burgesses and other electoral frauds were apt to be of less frequent occurrence.

Thus, during the years immediately following the Rebellion, forces were shaping themselves which were to make it possible for the colony to resist those encroachments of the Crown upon its liberties that marked the last decade of the rule of the Stuart kings, and to pass safely through what may well be called the Critical Period of Virginia history.

CHAPTER VIII

THE CRITICAL PERIOD

For some years after the Restoration the administration of English colonial affairs had been very lax. The Council of Plantations, which had served as a Colonial Office during the period from 1660 to 1672, had done little to control the Governors or to supervise and direct their policies. With the exception of one list of questions sent to Virginia in 1670, they had left Sir William Berkeley almost entirely to his own devices. September 27, 1672, the Council of Plantations was united with the Board of Domestic Trade to form the Council of Trade and Plantations. This new arrangement seems not to have been productive of good results, for in December, 1674, after the fall of the Cabal ministry, it was discontinued and the direction of colonial affairs entrusted to the King's Privy Council. This important body, finding its new duties very onerous, created a committee of twenty-one members, to whom the supervision of trade and plantations was assigned. In this way the King's most trusted ministers were brought into close touch with colonial affairs. We find now such prominent statesmen as Secretary Coventry, Secretary Williamson and Sir Lionel Jenkins carrying on extensive correspondence with the Governors, becoming interested in all their problems and needs, and demanding copies of all journals of Assembly and other state papers.[1]

This closer intimacy with the colonial governments led inevitably to a feeling of intolerance for local autonomy and for representative institutions, and to a determination to force upon the colonists a conformity with the policies and desires of the English government. Charles II and James II, instituted, in the decade preceding the English Revolution, a series of measures designed to curb the independence of the

[1] Osg., Vol. III, pp. 280, 281.

colonists. Some of the Assembly's long-established and most important rights were attacked. Many of its statutes were annulled by proclamation; its judicial powers were forever abolished; its control over taxation and expenditure was threatened; the privilege of selecting the Assembly clerk was taken from it; while even the right to initiate legislation was assailed.

The intolerant mood of the King and Privy Council is reflected in the instructions given Lord Culpeper upon his departure for Virginia. They included orders depriving him of the power, exercised freely by all former Governors, of calling sessions of the Assembly. "It is Our Will and pleasure," Charles declared, "that for the future noe General Assembly be called without Our special directions, but that, upon occasion, you doe acquaint us by letter, with the necessity of calling such an Assembly, and pray Our consent, and directions for their meeting."[2]

Even more dangerous to the liberties of the people was the attempt to deprive the Assembly of the right to initiate legislation. "You shall transmit unto us," Culpeper was commanded, "with the advice and consent of the Council, a draught of such Acts, as you shall think fit and necessary to bee passed, that wee may take the same into Our consideration, and return them in the forme wee shall think fit they bee enacted in. And, upon receipt of Our commands, you shall then summon an Assembly, and propose the said Laws for their consent."[3]

Most fortunately neither of these instructions could be enforced. The great distance of England from Virginia, and the time required to communicate with the King, made the summoning of the Assembly and the initiation of legislation without the royal assent a matter of absolute necessity. Lord Culpeper, with his Majesty's especial permission, disregarded these orders during his first visit to the colony, and later, to his great satisfaction, the Committee of Trade and Plantations "altered their measures therein".[4]

Culpeper was directed to secure in the colony a permanent

[2] P. R. O., CO5-1355-334; McD., Vol. V, p. 302.
[3] P. R. O., CO5-1355-313, 334.
[4] P. R. O., CO5-1355-334; McD., Vol. V, p. 302.

revenue for the King. It was rightly judged that the representatives of royal authority could never be entirely masters of the government while they were dependent for their salaries upon the votes of the Assembly. Sir William Berkeley, it is true, had rendered his position secure by obliging all "the men of parts and estates", but similar methods might be impossible for other Governors. The King and Privy Council did not, however, attempt to raise the desired revenue by imposing a tax upon the people without their own consent. An act levying a duty of two shillings a hogshead upon all tobacco exported from Virginia was drawn up by the Attorney-General for ratification by the Assembly.[5] The consent of the King in Council was duly received and the bill, with an act concerning naturalization and another for a general pardon, were sent to Virginia by Lord Culpeper. "These bills," the King told him, "we have caused to be under the Greate Seale of England. and our will is that the same . . . you shall cause to be considered and treated upon in our Assembly of Virginia."[6]

The revenue bill was quite similar to an act of Assembly still in force, which had imposed a duty upon exported tobacco, but an all-important difference lay in the disposal of the funds thus raised. The former statute had given the proceeds of this tax to the Assembly, "for the defraying the publique necessary charges",[7] but the new act was to grant the money "to the King's most excellent Majesty his heires and Successors for ever to and for the better support of the Government".[8]

In order to carry out these new designs for the government of the colony, the King ordered Lord Culpeper to prepare to sail at once. The Governor, however, was most reluctant to leave the pleasures of the court for a life in the American wilderness. His departure had already been long delayed, more than two years having elapsed since Charles had told the colonists to expect his speedy arrival. Yet he still delayed and procrastinated. On the third of December, 1679,

[5] P. R. O., CO5-1356; CO391.2-276, 325, 283 to 285.
[6] P. R. O., CO1-43-165.　　　　[7] Hen., II, p. 133.
[8] P. R. O., CO5-1376; Hen., Vol. II, p. 466.

an order was issued giving his Lordship "liberty to stay in Towne about his affaires until Monday next, and noe longer, and then to proceed forthwith" to the Downs, where "the Oxford frigat" was waiting to convey him to Virginia.[9] But as he still lingered in London, the Captain of the frigate was ordered to sail up the Thames to take him on board.[10] No sooner had he left his moorings, however, than Culpeper, probably in order to gain time, hastened away to the Downs. This so aroused the King's anger that he was pleased to direct one of his principal secretaries to signify by letter to Lord Culpeper his high displeasure at his delay and neglect of duty, and that his intentions were to appoint another Governor of Virginia unless he embarked as soon as the frigate returned to the Downs.[11] But now adverse winds set in, and Culpeper, with the tobacco fleet which had waited for him, was unable to sail until February 13, 1680.[12]

He arrived off the capes May the second, and eight days later took formal possession of his government. Immediately the Councillors and other leading planters flocked around him, eager to secure his support against the old rebellious party. Nor was their presentation of their cause ineffectual in winning the Governor's sympathy. "All things," he wrote Secretary Coventry, "are . . . far otherwise than I supposed in England, and I beleeve ye Council, at least I have seen through a mist."[13] It was to be expected then, that in settling the dispute that had so long troubled the colony he would favor the Berkeley faction. And this, so far as the King's commands would permit, he seems to have done. The wealthy planters expressed their satisfaction with his measures, and the commons, if they disapproved, feared to reveal their resentment. "His Excellency," wrote Colonel Spencer, "has with soe great prudence settled all the Affairs of the Country that our late different Interests are perfectly united to the general satisfaction of all his Majesty's Subjects in this colony."[14]

The Berkeley party was deeply displeased at the King's

[9] P. R. O., CO5-1355-372.   [10] P. R. O., CO5-1355-375.
[11] P. R. O., CO5-1355-375, 376.   [12] P. R. O., CO5-1355-378.
[13] P. R. O., CO5-1355-385.   [14] P. R. O., CO5-1355-384.

command to exclude Colonel Philip Ludwell from the Council. Recognizing in the order the influence of Colonel Jeffreys and the other commissioners, they assured the Governor that it had been secured by false representations. The Councillors declared "that they were very sencible of ye want of that Assistance they for many Years" had had from Colonel Ludwell, "whose good abilities, Knowne Integrity and approved Loyalty" rendered him most necessary to his Majesty's service. They therefore earnestly requested "his Exceilency to Readmitt & Receive him to be one of ye Councill".[15] Culpeper yielded readily, and Ludwell was restored to his seat.

The Burgesses were chagrined at the order to oust Major Robert Beverley from all public employment. He was again the clerk of Assembly, for which office he was "their Unanimous Choyce", and his disgrace was regarded as a rebuke to the House.[16] Upon their earnest petition Culpeper consented that he should retain that important post in which he was soon to render signal service to the people and to incur again the anger of the King and his ministers.[17]

When the Assembly convened the Governor at once laid before it the Act of General Pardon, the Act of Naturalization and the Act for a Public Revenue. To the first and the second he obtained a prompt assent, but the third was strenuously resisted. The House of Burgesses was filled with gentlemen of the best families, men closely allied with the Council in position and interest, yet they were unwilling to permit any part of the public revenue to pass out of the control of the people.[18] "The House," they declared, "doe most humbly desire to be Excused if they doe not give their approbacon of his Majesties bill."[19] And so determined were they, that when the matter was again brought before them by the Governor they refused even to resume the debate.[20]

[15] P. R. O., CO5-1376-265.   [16] Jour. H. of B., 1680, p. 1.
[17] Jour. H. of B., 1680, p. 7.
[18] Among the Burgesses were Captain Wiliiam Byrd, Major Swann, Benjamin Harrison, Colonel Ballard, Colonel Mason, Colonel John Page, Colonel Matthew Kemp, William Fitzhugh, Isaac Allerton, John Carter and Captain Fox. P. R. O., CO5-1376-321.
[19] Jour. H. of B., 1680, pp. 13, 14.   [20] Jour. H. of B., 1680, p. 27.

But Culpeper, fearful of the King's displeasure, and uneasy for the payment of his own salary, made strenuous efforts to secure the passage of the bill. He did not scruple to resort to bribery and intimidation to force obedience from the stubborn Burgesses. We have the testimony of the Governor himself to one notorious case of the misuse of the patronage. Among the leaders of the House of Burgesses was Isaac Allerton, a man of wealth and education, and an excellent speaker.[21] "He did assure me," Culpeper reported to the Privy Council, "of his utmost services in whatsoever the King should command him by his Governor, particularly as to a further Bill of Revenue for the support of ye Government, And I did engage to move his Majesty that hee should bee of the Council . . . though not to be declared till after the Session of next Assembly, when I am sure he can bee as serviceable if not more than any other person whatsoever."[22] This bargain was faithfully kept and in time Allerton, for thus betraying his trust, received his seat in the Council.[23]

Nor did Lord Culpeper hesitate to intimidate the Burgesses by threatening to demand the payment of all arrears of quitrents. This tax, although belonging to the King from the first settlement of the colony, had not, for many years, been duly collected. It was now rumored, however, that the Privy Council intended, not only to enforce for the future a strict payment, but to demand a settlement for the accumulated arrears. In 1679 Sir Henry Chicheley had forwarded to his Majesty a petition from the Assembly asking relief from this great burden. If this be not granted, he wrote, the payments which have been so long due and amount to so vast a sum, will fall heavily upon all, but especially upon the poor.[24] Culpeper, knowing well the anxiety of the Burgesses upon this point, told them that if they expected the King to grant their petition, they must yield to his desire for a royal revenue in the colony.

Calling the Assembly before him, he urged them to resume their debate. "It looks," he said, "as if you could give noe reasons or as if you were affraid to be convinced. . . . I desire

[21] P. R. O., CO5-1356-125.   [22] P. R. O., CO5-1356-125, 126.
[23] P. R. O., CO5-1356-265.   [24] P. R. O., CO5-1355-361.

you to lay aside that irregular proceeding . . . and resume the debate." The Council, he added, had given their unanimous consent to the bill. "Consider the affaires of the Quitt Rents, Consider the King's favour in every thing you may aske even to a cessacon . . . and reflect if it be tante for you not to concurr in a thing that, I am assured, ye King . . . judges his owne and will soe use it and the more fully then if this Act pass."[25]

Thus threatened, the Burgesses finally yielded, and the bill became law. But they insisted upon adding to it two provisos: that the former export duty upon tobacco be repealed, and that the exemption of Virginia ship owners from the payment of the tax, which had been a provision of the former law, should be continued.[26] When some months later the matter came before the Committee of Trade and Plantations, their Lordships expressed much dissatisfaction at these amendments, declaring that the bill should have passed "in Terminis". Since, however, the first proviso in no way changed the sense of the act, and had been added only to prevent a double imposition, they recommended that it should be continued. But the second was declared null and void by order of the King, as "irregular and unfit to be allowed of".[27]

Lord Culpeper, immediately after the dismissal of the Assembly made ready to return to England. August 3, 1680, he read to the Council an order from the King granting him permission to leave the colony, and a few days later he set sail in *The James*.[28] The government was again left in the hands of the infirm Chicheley.[29]

Culpeper, upon his arrival in England, told the King that all was well in the colony, that the old contentions had been forgotten, and the people were happy and prosperous. But this favorable report, which was made by the Governor to palliate his desertion of his post, was far from being true. There was, as he well knew, a deep-seated cause of discontent in Virginia, that threatened constantly to drive the people again into mutiny

[25] Jour. H. of B., 1680, p. 32. [26] Jour. H. of B., 1680, p. 36.
[27] P. R. O., CO5-1355-388 to 394.
[28] P. R. O., CO5-1355-380; CO5-1376-286.
[29] P. R. O., CO5-1355-396.

and disorder. This was the continued low price of tobacco. In the years which had elapsed since Bacon's Rebellion, the people, despite their bitter quarrels, had produced several large crops, and the English market was again glutted. "What doth quite overwhelm both us and Maryland," complained the colonists, "is the extreme low price of our only commodity . . . and consequently our vast poverty and infinite necessity."[30] The Burgesses, in 1682, spoke of the worthlessness of tobacco as an "ineffable Calamity". "Wee are," they said, "noe wayes able to force a miserable subsistance from the same. . . . If force of penne, witt, or words Could truely represent (our condition) as it is, the sad resentments would force blood from any Christian Loyall Subjects heart."[31] Some months later the Council wrote, "The people of Virginia are generally, some few excepted, extremely poor, . . . not being able to provide against the pressing necessities of their families."[32] That the Privy Council was aware, as early as October, 1681, that these conditions might lead to another insurrection, is attested by a letter of the Committee of Trade and Plantations to Lord Culpeper. "We are informed," they wrote, "that Virginia is in great danger of disturbance . . . by reason of the extreme poverty of the People, occasioned by the low price of tobacco which, tis feared may induce the servants to plunder the Stores of the Planters and the Ships arriving there and to commit other outrages and disorders as in the late Rebellion."[33]

This universal distress created a strong sentiment throughout the colony in favor of governmental restriction upon the planting of tobacco. Unless something were done to limit the annual crop, prices would continue to decline. Many merchants, who had bought up large quantities of tobacco in England with the expectation that its value would eventually rise, "fell to insinuate with the easiest sort People how advantageous it would bee . . . if an Act of Assembly could be procured to cease planting tobacco for one whole year".[34]

[30] P. R. O., CO5-1355-408.   [31] Jour. H. of B., April 1682, p. 4.
[32] P. R. O., CO5-1356-179.   [33] P. R. O., CO5-1356-1, 2.
[34] P. R. O., CO5-1356-177.

When, in the spring of 1682, it became apparent that another large crop must be expected, an almost universal demand arose for the immediate convening of the Assembly for the passage of a law of cessation.

The Councillors, although themselves in favor of some restraint upon the huge output, advised the aged Deputy-Governor not to consent to a session at this juncture.[35] But Chichcley, persuaded, it was claimed, by the insistent arguments of Major Beverley, yielded to the desires of the people, and upon his own responsibility, issued writs summoning the Burgesses to convene at Jamestown, April 18, 1682.[36] Five days before the date of meeting, however, a letter arrived from the King, expressly forbidding an Assembly until November the tenth, when, it was hoped, Lord Culpeper would have returned to his government.[37] The letter also informed the Deputy-Governor that two companies of troops that had remained in Virginia ever since the Rebellion, could no longer be maintained at the expense of the royal Exchequer. Since many of the Burgesses were already on their way to Jamestown, Sir Henry decided to hold a brief session, in order to permit them, if they so desired, to continue the companies at the charge of the colony.[38] But he expressed his determination, in obedience to the King's commands, to forbid the consideration of any other matter whatsoever.

The Burgesses met "big with expectation to enact a Cessation".[39] The appeals of their constituents and the smart of their own purses made them desperately resolute to give the country relief from the present depressing conditions. When they learned that after all their session was to be in vain, and that they were to be allowed to vote only on the matter of continuing the companies, they were deeply concerned and angered. Addressing the Deputy Governor, they declared themselves overwhelmed with grief at the expectation of adjournment. They had, from all parts of the drooping country, passionately wended their way to Jamestown, to attend this Assembly, upon

[35] P. R. O., CO5-1356-73.

[36] P. R. O., CO5-1356-73, 156; Jour, H. of B., April 1682.

[37] P. R. O., CO5-1356-11, 12, 68, 72.

[38] P. R. O., CO5-1356-8.   [39] P. R. O., CO5-1356-68.

which the "last expiring hopes" of the "miserably indigent poor Country" were reposed. Should they be compelled to return to their homes, having accomplished nothing, the people would be struck with amazement, "like an unexpected death wound".[40]

The Deputy Governor, not daring to disobey the King, ignored their appeal, and bade them decide without delay whether or not they would continue the two companies. But the Burgesses would give no definite answer upon this matter, hoping by a policy of delay to win, in the end, Chicheley's consent to the cessation. After seven days of fruitless bickering Sir Henry, in anger at their obstinacy, prorogued the Assembly to November the tenth.[41] Before their dismissal, however, the Burgesses, in order to show that they had not been remiss in endeavoring to secure relief for the people, voted that the journal of their proceedings should be read publicly in every county.

Nor had they misjudged the desperate humor of the people. When it became known throughout the colony that the Assembly had done nothing to restrict the planting of tobacco, the anger of the poor planters could not be restrained. Some bold spirits proposed that the people should assemble in various parts of the country, and, in defiance of law and order, cut to pieces the tobacco then in the fields. If the King would not permit a cessation by law, they would bring about a cessation by force. A few days after the close of the Assembly, parties of men in Gloucester began the work of destruction. It required but little exertion to ruin the tender plants, and the rioters, passing from plantation to plantation, in an incredibly short time accomplished enormous havoc. Many men, filled with the contagion, cut up their own tobacco, and then joined the mob in the destruction of the crops of their neighbors.[42]

As soon as the news of this strange insurrection reached Jamestown, Chicheley dispatched Colonel Kemp to Gloucester with directions to muster the militia and to restore order by

[40] Jour. H. of B., April 1682, pp. 4, 5.
[41] Jour. H. of B., April 1682; P. R. O., CO5-1356-68.
[42] P. R. O., CO5-1356-65, 66, 67.

force of arms. This officer, with a troop of horse, fell upon one party of plant-cutters, and captured twenty-two of their number. "Two of the principal and incorrigible rogues" he held for trial, but "the rest submitting and giving assurances of their quiet and peacable behavior were remitted".[43] Other parties, intimidated by these vigorous measures, dispersed, and soon peace was restored throughout all Gloucester. But now news reached the Deputy-Governor "that the next adjacent county, being new Kent, was lately broke forth, committing the like spoyles on plants". And no sooner had the troops suppressed the rioters here than the disorders spread to Middlesex and other counties. It became necessary to issue orders to the commanders of the militia in each county to keep parties of horse in continual motion, to prevent the designs of the plant-cutters and arrest their leaders.[44] And then the rioters, who had at first carried on their work in the open day, "went in great companys by night, destroying and pulling up whole fields of tobacco after it was well grown".[45] Not until August were the disorders finally suppressed.

These troubles, coming so soon after Bacon's Rebellion, caused great apprehension, both to the colonial government and to the Privy Council. "I know," wrote Secretary Spencer, "the necessities of the inhabitants to be such . . . their low estate makes them desperate. . . . If they goe forward the only destroying Tobacco plants will not satiate their rebellious appatites who, if they increase and find the strength of their own arms, will not bound themselves."[46] And, although the actual rioters were "inconsiderable people", yet it was thought they had been instigated by men of position and wealth.[47]

Grave suspicion rested upon Major Robert Beverley.[48] It had been the importunities of "the over-active Clerk" that had persuaded Chicheley, against the advice of the Council, to convene the Assembly. It was he that had been the most industrious advocate of a cessation, that had fomented the disputes in the Assembly, that had most strenuously opposed

[43] P. R. O., CO5-1356-70.
[45] P. R. O., CO5-1356-178.
[47] P. R. O., CO5-1356-178.
[44] P. R. O., CO5-1356-71.
[46] P. R. O., CO5-1356-71.
[48] P. R. O., CO5-1356-74.

adjournment.   And it was he, the Council believed, that had "instilled into the multitude . . . the right of making a Cessation by cutting up Plants".[49]   Moreover, they thought it not improbable that he would lead the people into a new insurrection.   The rabble regarded him with veneration and love.   His activity in suppressing the Rebellion and his opposition to the county grievances of 1677 had been forgotten, and they saw in him now only the defender of the poor and helpless.   Were he to assume the rôle of a Bacon and place himself at the head of the commons, he might easily make himself master of the colony.   Although there was no evidence against him, "but only rudeness and sauciness", it was thought advisable to render him powerless to accomplish harm, by placing him under arrest.[50]   He was taken without resistance by Major-General Smith, "though to his own great loss of 2 or 300 pounds, by the Rabbles cutting up his Tobacco plants within two days after out of Spight".[51]

Beverley was kept in strict confinement on board an English ship, the *Duke of York,* where for the time, he was safe from rescue by the people.   But so fearful was the Council that he might plot for a general insurrection, that they issued orders forbidding him to send or to receive letters, and permitting him to speak only in the presence of the captain of the ship.[52]   Even these harsh measures did not reassure them, and it was decided to send him to the Eastern Shore, where the people were most loyal to the government, and where rescue would be impossible.[53]   As preparations were being made to effect his transfer, he escaped from the custody of the sheriff, and returned to his home in Middlesex.   But he was soon recaptured, and conveyed to Northampton.   Here, despite all the efforts of his friends and his own violent protests, he was kept in confinement for months.   In the fall he applied for a writ of habeas corpus, but this was denied him under the pretext that the whole matter had been referred to the King, and was no longer within the jurisdiction of the Deputy-Governor

[49] P. R. O., CO5-1356-74.   [50] Hen., Vol. III, p. 543.
[51] P. R. O., CO5-1356-156.   [52] Hen., Vol. III, p. 544.
[53] Hen., Vol. III, p. 546.

and Council.[54] Since, however, all fear of a rebellion was now passed, he was permitted, upon giving bail to the sum of £2,000, to return to his home. But he was still restricted to the counties of Middlesex and Gloucester, was declared ineligible to public office and was forbidden to plead as an attorney in any colonial court.[55]

When the Privy Council learned of the plant-cutting in Virginia, they ordered Lord Culpeper "to repair to the Government with all possible speed, in order to find out, by the strictest enquiry, the abbetors and instruments of this commotion". And since they too were fearful of a new insurrection, they gave directions "that some person who shall be found most faulty may be forthwith punished".[56] "After which," the Privy Council advised, "and not before the Governor may be directed to consider of and propose, with the advice of the Council and the Assembly, . . . some temperament in relation to the Planting of Tobacco and raising the price of that commodity."[57]

Culpeper left England in October, 1682, upon "the Mermaid frigat", and, after a tedious and dangerous voyage of eleven weeks, arrived safely in Virginia. He was resolved that the persons responsible for the plant-cutting should be brought immediately to trial, and punished with the utmost rigor of the law. The strictest inquiry was made into the conduct of Major Beverley, and had there been evidence sufficient to convict him, the unfortunate Clerk would undoubtedly have suffered death upon the gallows. But since only the most trivial offenses could be adduced against him, Culpeper was forced to turn elsewhere for the victims demanded by the English government.

So the prosecution was now directed against some of the actual plant-cutters. In this, however, Culpeper found himself greatly embarrassed by Chicheley's previous treatment of the matter. The Deputy-Governor had, some months before, issued pardons to many of the chief offenders, and had permitted the others to give bail, thus treating their crime as "Ryot and noe more", and making the affair seem "as slight

[54] Hen., Vol. III, pp. 546, 547. [55] Hen., Vol. III, p. 547.
[56] P. R. O., CO5-1356-76. [57] P. R. O., CO5-1356-76, 77.

as possible to the people".[58]   But Culpeper, despite this action
of Sir Henry, ordered the arrest of four of the most notorious
plant-cutters and charged them with high treason.   Their trial
created great excitement throughout the colony, but "despite
the high words and threats" of the rabble, three of them were
convicted.   Two were executed—Somerset Davies at Jamestown, and Black Austin "before the Court-house in Glocester
county, where the Insurrection first broke out".[59]   The third
was pardoned by the Governor.   "Hee was extremely young,"
Culpeper wrote, "not past 19, meerely drawn in and very
penitent, and therefore . . . I thought fit to mingle mercy
with Justice and Repreeved him . . . to the end the whole
country might be convinced that there was no other motive in
the thing but purely to maintain Government."[60]

But although Culpeper was thus vigorous in punishing the
disorders of the poor people, he did nothing to remove the cause
of their turbulence—the low price of tobacco.   By an order in
Council of June 17, 1682, he had been directed to grant a
cessation, should it seem expedient, and had been given a letter
from Secretary Jenkins to Lord Baltimore, requiring the co-
operation of Maryland.[61]   But, upon finding the colony in
peace and quiet, and the Assembly busy with other concerns,
he "took advantage thereof", and kept secret this unexpected
concession.   Culpeper pretended to believe that the desired
cessation would be of no real benefit to the planters, but it is
clear that he was consciously betraying the colony to the greed
of the royal Exchequer.[62]   "I soe encouraged the planting of
tobacco," he reported to the Privy Council ,"that if the season
continue to be favorable . . . there will bee a greater cropp
by far than ever grew since its first seating.   And I am confident that Customs next year from thence will be £50,000 more
than ever heretofore in any one year."[63]   Immediately after, he
declared that he well knew "that the great Cropp then in hand
would most certainly bring that place into the utmost exigen-

[58] P. R. O., CO5-1356-157.
[60] P. R. O., CO5-1356-159.
[62] P. R. O., CO5-1356-164.

[59] P. R. O., CO5-1356-158.
[61] P. R. O., CO5-1356-76, 77, 163.
[63] P. R. O., CO5-1356-164.

cies again", and he promised to be prepared to quell the disturbances that would result.[64]

Before Lord Culpeper left England an order had been delivered to him "commanding that noe Governour of his Majesty's Plantations, doe come into England from his Government", without first obtaining leave from the King.[65] But so loath was he to remain long in Virginia, that as soon as he had dispatched the business of the April court, he once more set sail for England. "I judged it a proper time," he said, "to make a step home this easy quiet year, not out of any fondness to bee in England, . . . but for the King's service only."[66]

But Charles and the Privy Council were weary of Culpeper's neglect of duty. They decided to rid themselves of so untrustworthy an officer and to appoint in his place a man that would remain in the colony and carry out their wishes and policies. An inquisition was held upon his conduct, and his letters patent as Governor-General were declared void[67] On the 28th of September, 1683, a commission as Lieutenant- and Governor-General of Virginia was granted to Lord Howard of Effingham.[68]

Few British colonial Governors are less deserving of respect than Thomas Lord Culpeper. He was insensible of any obligation to guard the welfare of the people of Virginia, and was negligent in executing the commands of the King. He seems to have regarded his office only as an easy means of securing a large income, and he was untiring in his efforts to extort money from the exhausted and impoverished colony. Sir William Berkeley's salary as Governor had been £1,000, but Culpeper demanded and received no less than £2,000.[69] In addition, he was allowed £150 a year in lieu of a residence, received pay as captain of infantry and claimed large sums under the provisions of the Arlington-Culpeper grant.

Nor did he scruple to resort to open fraud in satisfying his greed. There were, in 1680, two companies remaining in

[64] P. R. O., CO5-1356-164, 169.   [65] P. R. O., CO5-1356-87.
[66] P. R. O., CO5-1356-168, 169.
[67] P. R. O., CO5-1356-188, 239, 244, 114.
[68] P. R. O., CO5-1356-188.
[69] P. R. O., CO5-1356-56, 145, 146.

Virginia of the troops sent over to suppress Bacon's Rebellion. Having received no pay for many months, the soldiers were discontented and mutinous.[70] The Privy Council entrusted to Culpeper, upon his first departure for the colony, money to satisfy them, and to compensate the householders with whom they had been quartered.[71] At this period, as always in the seventeenth century, there was a great scarcity of specie in Virginia. But there circulated, usually by weight, various foreign coins, the most common of which was the Spanish piece of eight, about equal in value to five shillings in English money. My Lord, upon his arrival, industriously bought up all the worn coins he could secure, arbitrarily proclaimed them legal tender at the ratio of six shillings to one piece of eight, and then paid the soldiers and the landlords. This ingenious trick probably netted him over £1,000. Later he restored the ratio to five to one, so that he would lose nothing when his own salary became due. Of such stuff were some of the Virginia colonial governors.[72]

But Culpeper's many defects were not wholly unfortunate for the colony, for they rendered him unfit to carry out the designs of the King. His frequent absences from his government made it impossible for him to become thoroughly acquainted with conditions in the colony, or to bind the wealthy to him by a judicious use of the patronage. He was too weak, too careless to pursue a long continued attack upon the established privileges of the people.

It boded ill, therefore, for Virginia, when he was removed, and a commission granted to Lord Howard. The new Governor was well fitted for the task of oppression and coersion. Unscrupulous, deceitful, overbearing, resentful, persistent, he proved a dangerous foe to the representative institutions of the colony, and an able defender of royal prerogative. Had he not encountered throughout his entire administration, the united and determined resistance of the Burgesses, he might have overthrown all constitutional government. Well it was for Virginia that at this moment of imminent danger, the Bur-

[70] P. R. O., CO5-1376-287.
[71] P. R. O., CO1-42-152; CO391.2-276.
[72] Beverley.

gesses should have been so conscious of their duty and so resolute in executing it. They were still, as in most periods of colonial history, men of high social position, but they represented, not their own class, but the entire colony. And they were ever watchful to guard the interests of the commons.

Effingham took the oath of office in England, October 24, 1683,[73] and a few months later sailed for the colony.[74] No sooner had he set foot in Virginia than the struggle with the Burgesses began. The session of Assembly of April, 1684, was filled with their bitter disputes.

Consternation reigned in the House when Lord Howard produced an instruction from the King forbidding appeals from the inferior courts to the Assembly.[75] As early as October, 1678, Colonel Francis Moryson had advised the Privy Council to abolish the judicial powers of the Assembly, claiming that they were the source of the great influence and "arrogancy" of that body.[76] Their Lordships did not awaken at once to the importance of this matter, but before long they became convinced that Moryson was right. Accordingly Lord Culpeper, in his commission of 1682, was directed to procure the immediate repeal of all laws "allowing appeals to the Assembly".[77] But Culpeper, interested only in securing money from the Burgesses, failed to put this instruction into operation. "As to what concerns Appeals," he declared, "I have never once permitted any one to come to the Assembly, soe that the thing is in effect done. But having some thoughts of getting a Revenue Bill to pass, I was unwilling actually to repeal ye Laws relating thereunto till the next session of Assembly should be over, well knowing how infinitely it would trouble them."[78]

But Effingham had no such scruples, and told the Burgesses plainly the commands he bore from the King.[79] The House, in great dismay, requested the Governor and the Council to join them in an address to his Majesty, imploring him to restore a privilege which had so long been enjoyed "according to ye

[73] P. R. O., CO5-1356-244, 245.   [74] P. R. O., CO5-1356-248.
[75] Jour. H. of B., 1684, pp. 23, 24.   [76] P. R. O., CO1-42-138, 139.
[77] P. R. O., CO5-1356-53.   [78] P. R. O., CO5-1356-142.
[79] P. R. O., CO5-1356-22.

Laws and antient Practice of the Country".[80]   But Lord
Howard replied coldly, "It is what I can in noe parte admitt
of, his Majesty haveing been pleased by his Royal instruccons
to direct & command that noe appeales be open to the General
Assembly."[81]

Nor did the Assembly ever regain this important power.
As late as 1691 we find the agent of the Burgesses in England
asking in vain for the restoration of the right of appeals.[82]
The change threw into the hands of the Governor and Council
extraordinary power over the judiciary of the colony.   The
county justices, who sat in the lower courts, were the appointees of the Governor, and could not effectually resist his will.
Moreover, as appeals lay from them to the General Court,
they were powerless before the decisions of the superior tribunal.   Thus the judiciary of the colony lost its only democratic
feature.

The Burgesses, undismayed by their defeat in this matter, at
this same session entered a vigorous protest against the King's
right to annul acts of Assembly.   During Berkeley's administration his Majesty had seldom exercised this power, but of
late many acts had been repealed by proclamation without the
consent or knowledge of the Assembly.   This, the Burgesses
claimed, was an unwarranted infringement upon the privileges granted them "by sundry Comissions, Letters and
Instructions", that was most destructive of their cherished
liberties and rights.   And they demanded that henceforth
their statutes should have the force of law until they had been
"Repealed by the same Authority of Generall Assembly".[83]
But they received no encouragement from the Governor.
What you ask, he told them, "is soe great an entrenchment
upon ye Royall authority that I cannot but wonder you would
offer at it".[84]

Thereupon the House determined to appeal directly to the
King, petitioning him not only to give up the right of repealing laws by proclamation, but to permit the continuation of
appeals to the Assembly.   Since the Governor refused to

[80] Jour. H. of B., 1684, p. 37.   [81] Jour, H. of B., 1684, p. 42.
[82] Justice in Va., p. 25.   [83] Jour. H. of B., 1684, p. 114.
[84] Jour. H. of B., 1684, p. 159.

transmit their address to his Majesty, they forwarded copies to Secretary Jenkins by two of their own members—Thomas Milner and William Sherwood.[85]

This address received scant consideration from the King and the Privy Council. "Whereas," James II wrote Effingham in October, 1685, "it hath been represented unto us by our Committee for Trade and Plantations, that they have received from some unknown persons a paper entitled an address and supplication of the General Assembly of Virginia . . . which you had refused to recommend as being unfit to be presented. . . . Wee cannot but approve of your proceedings. . . . And wee doe further direct you to discountenance such undue practices for the future as alsoe the Contrivers and Promoters thereof."[86] For their activity in this matter Sherwood and Milner "in ye following year were both turned out of all imployments to their great damage and disgrace".[87]

In the spring of 1685 Effingham received notification from the Privy Council of the death of Charles II and the accession of the Duke of York as James II.[88] He replied a few days later, "I have, with the greatest solemnity this place is capable of proclaimed his Majesty King James II in all the considerable places of this colony, where the great Acclamations and Prayers of the People gave a universal Testimony of their Obedience."[89] Despite these outward manifestations of joy, the people were by no means pleased to have a Roman Catholic monarch upon the English throne. When news reached Virginia that the Duke of Monmouth was in open rebellion, and had gained important successes over his Majesty's forces, there was grave danger that the commons of the colony might espouse his cause.[90] Many were so emboldened, wrote Effingham, "that their tongues ran at large and demonstrated the wickedness of their hearts, till I secured some and deterred others from spreading such false reports by my Proclama-

---

[85] P. R. O., CO5-1356-299, 301.
[86] P. R. O., CO5-1357-58.
[87] McD., Vol. VII, p. 88.
[88] P. R. O., CO5-1356-316.
[89] P. R. O., CO5-1356-328.
[90] P. R. O., CO5-1357-79, 80, 95, 96; Jour. H. of B., 1685, p. 49.

tion".[91] The defeat and execution of the Duke of Monmouth for a time ended all thought of resistance to the King.

But Effingham found the people sullen and discontented and the Burgesses more stubborn than ever. The session of Assembly of 1685 was, perhaps, the most stormy ever held in Virginia. The House made a strenuous and successful resistance to a vigorous attempt to deprive it of its control over taxation. In 1662, when the Assembly was dominated by Sir William Berkeley, an act had been passed empowering the Governor and Council to levy annually for three years a tax of not more than twenty pounds of tobacco per poll.[92] In 1680 the Council had requested Lord Culpeper to represent to the King the disadvantages of leaving taxation entirely in the hands of the Assembly, hoping that his Majesty would by proclamation revive the law of 1662.[93] The greatest item of expense to the government, they argued, arose from the Assembly itself, "ye charge of which hath been too often found to be twice as much as would have satisfied all publiq dues".[94] The matter was presented to the consideration of the Burgesses in 1680, but was lost in the committee room.[95]

The King and Privy Council, although they approved of the levy by the Governor and the Council, did not venture to grant them that power by royal proclamation. They instructed Lord Howard, however, in his commission of 1683, to propose for passage in the Assembly a law similar to that of 1662.[96] Accordingly, in 1684, Effingham placed the matter before the Burgesses and told them that it was the King's desire that they give their consent. But they ignored his message, and the Governor could not press the matter at that time. In the next session, however, he became more insistent. "I must remind you," he told the Burgesses, "of what was omitted in ye last Assembly . . . that a Law may passe whereby His Majesty's Governor with ye advice of ye Council may be empowered to lay a levy."[97] But the Burgesses

[91] P. R. O., CO5-1357-80.
[92] Hen., Vol. II, p. 24; P R. O., CO5-1376-281.
[93] P. R. O., CO5-1376-281.
[94] P. R. O., CO5-1376-281; CO5-1356-101.
[95] P. R. O., CO5-1376-362.   [96] P. R. O., CO5-1356-267.
[97] Jour. H. of B., 1685.

would not yield. "The House," they replied, ". . . do humbly signifye to your Excellency, that they can noe waies concede to or comply with that proposition, without apparent and signal violation of ye great trust with them reposed."[98] And when Effingham urged them to reconsider their action, they passed a resolution unanimously refusing to relinquish this their greatest privilege.

After the prorogation of the Assembly, Lord Howard wrote home his complaints against the stubborn Burgesses. "Your Lordships," he said, "will . . . find their total denyal that the Governor and Council should have any power to lay the least Levy to ease the necessity of soe frequent Assemblys. . . . This was propounded by mee to them before his Majesty's Instructions came to my hand that I should, . . . but nothing would prevail nor I beleeve will, unless his Majesty's special command therein."[99]

A long and acrimonious quarrel occurred over the quit-rents. Because of the lack of specie in the colony, it had always been necessary to collect this tax, when it was collected at all, in tobacco. In March, 1662, the Assembly had passed a law fixing the rate of payment at two pence a pound, which was then not far from the current price. But the decline in value of the commodity which had occurred since 1662, had resulted in a great diminution in the tax.

In July, 1684, the King wrote Effingham that he had taken over all the rights of Arlington and Culpeper to the quit-rents, and announced it his intention to use them for the support of the Virginia government. He directed the Governor to secure the repeal of the law of 1662 and to forbid all payments in tobacco. "You must . . . impower," he wrote, "the Officers of our Revenue to collect (them) . . . according to ye reservation of 2s per every hundred acres . . . to be paid in specie, that is in Mony."[100]

As tobacco sold, in 1684, at a half penny a pound, this order, had it been put into operation, would have quadrupled the value of the quit-rents, and increased materially the burdens

[98] Jour. H. of B., 1685.   [99] P. R. O., CO5-1357-85.
[100] P. R. O., CO5-1356-282.

of the planters. The Burgesses, in alarm, petitioned the Governor to allow the old arrangement to continue, declaring that the lack of specie made it impossible to comply with the King's order. And they refused to repeal the law of March, 1662.

Displeased at their obstinacy, the King, in August, 1686, nullified the law by proclamation. "Being now informed," he declared, "that several persons goe about to impede our Service . . . by imposing bad tobacco upon our collectors at the rate of 2d per llb, under pretence of an Act of Assembly of March 30, 1662, . . . Wee have thought fit to Repeal the said Act."[101]

Even then the Burgesses resisted. At the session of 1686 they petitioned on behalf of all the freeholders of the colony that the quit-rents should be paid as formerly. To make payment in specie, they declared, would not only be ruinous, but utterly impossible.[102] So angered were they and so determined not to obey, that Effingham found it expedient to consent to a compromise. It was agreed that the tax should be collected in tobacco as before, but at the rate of one penny per pound, which, as Effingham said, was not ad valorum. Thus the only result of this long quarrel was to double the value of the quit-rents, and to add greatly to the burdens of the impoverished and discontented people.[103]

Even more bitter was the contest over the so-called Bill of Ports. This measure was designed to remedy the scattered mode of living in Virginia, by appointing certain places as ports of landing and shipment, and confining to them all foreign trade. Throughout the seventeenth century almost all shipping was done from private wharves. The country was so interspersed with rivers, inlets and creeks, deep enough to float the largest vessels, that ports were entirely unnecessary. Each planter dealt directly with the merchants, receiving English manufactured goods almost at his front door, and lading the ships with tobacco from his own warehouse. This system, so natural and advantageous, seemed to the English Kings, and even to the colonists, a sign of unhealthful con-

---

[101] P. R. O., CO5-1357-113.　　　[102] Jour. H. of B., 1686, p. 17.
[103] Jour. H. of B., 1686, p. 37.

ditions. More than once attempts had been made to force the people to build towns and to discontinue the desultory plantation trade.

In 1679, Culpeper was ordered to propose a law in the Assembly requiring the erection of towns on each great river, to which all foreign trade should be confined. Accordingly, in 1680, a Bill of Ports was passed. "Wee are now grown sensible," wrote Secretary Spencer, "that our present necessities, and too much to be doubted future miseries, are much heightened by our wild and rambling way of living, therefore are desirous of cohabitation, in order whereunto in ye late Assembly an Act was made appointing a town in every County, where all Goods imported are to be landed, and all Goods exported to be shipt off. And if this takes effect, as its hoped it may, Virginia will then go forward which of late years hath made a retrograde motion."[104]

But this attempt ended in dismal failure. In 1681, when the shipmasters came to the appointed ports, they found that no shelter had been constructed for their goods. Thinking the law nullified, or not yet in operation, they traded as usual from private wharves. For this breach of the law, some of them were prosecuted in the colonial courts, to their own great loss and to the inconvenience of many of the planters.[105] Loud wrangling and bitter animosities resulted throughout the colony, and at length the King was compelled to suspend the law.[106]

In the Assembly of 1685 it was proposed to enact another Bill of Ports. Accordingly an act was drafted in the House of Burgesses and, in due time, sent up for the approval of the Council. The upper house, after making several alterations, consented to the bill and returned it to the Burgesses. The latter agreed to most of the changes, but struck out a clause restricting the towns to two upon each river, and added an amendment permitting one port to a county.[107] The Council in turn yielded, but inserted a new clause, "That there should bee ffees ascertained on Goods exported and imported for the

[104] P. R. O., CO5-1355-383.   [105] P. R. O., CO5-1356-177.
[106] P. R. O., CO5-1356-4.   [107] P. R. O., CO5-1407-310, 282.

support of those Officers which should bee obliged to reside in those Ports".[108]   As "there was noe room in ye margint to write ye alteration . . . it was wrote in a piece of paper and affixt to ye Act".[109]   When the bill came back to the House, Major Robert Beverley, who was again the clerk of the Assembly, acting it would seem upon his own initiative, tore off the paper containing this amendment. The bill then came before the House apparently assented to without change and was returned by them for the signature of the Governor and the Councillors. Neither Effingham nor any of the Council noticed the omission, and thinking their amendment had been accepted, signed the bill.[110]   Thereupon it was engrossed, and sent up for the final signature of the Governor. But Effingham in reading the engrossed copy, discovered the omission, and refused to affix his name to the bill, claiming that it "was not engrost as assented to" by him and the Council.[111] "To which," wrote the Governor, "they sent mee word that the Bill could admit of noe alteration or amendment after it was attested by the Clerk of the General Assembly as assented to, and that it had by that the force of a Law. . . . I sent them word again that though any bill was assented to by mee and the Council, yet if I should afterwards perseive it would prove prejudicial . . . I had power to refuse the signing of it by vertue of His Majesty's negative voice. . . . But all would not persuade them out of their obstinacy, nay tho' I offered to lay that Bill aside till His Majesty's pleasure should bee known therein; And to sign all the others. . . . But nothing would please them but Invading, if not destroying, His Majesty's Prerogative." The Burgesses declared that they did not contest the Governor's right to the veto, but contended that when once he signed a bill, "it could not faile of having ye force of a Law".[112]   Effingham, they complained, was claiming a "double negative Voice". So angry did they become that they refused to apportion the levy for defraying the public charges, and after many days of bitter contention the Governor was forced to prorogue them.

[108] P. R. O., CO5-1357-89.   [109] P. R. O., CO5-1407-310.
[110] P. R. O., CO5-1357-89.   [111] P. R. O., CO5-1357-89.
[112] Jour. H. of B., 1685.

"I did not disolve them," he wrote the Privy Council, "for these reasons. Because if his Majesty shall think fitt to have them dissolved, it will bee soe great a rebuke to them, when done by his Majesty's special command, that I hope it will deter them for the future to bee soe obstinate and peevish."[113] Accordingly, in August, 1686, the King wrote the Governor, "Whereas, we have been informed of ye irregular and tumultuous proceedings of the House of Burgesses of Virginia, at their late meeting, the members thereof having . . . presumed so far as to raise contests touching ye power of ye Negative Voice . . . which wee cannot attribute to any other Cause then the disaffected & unquiet Dispositions of those Members. . . . Wee have thought fitt hereby as a mark of our displeasure . . . to Charge . . . you forthwith to Dissolve the present Assembly."[114]

When this order reached Virginia the Assembly was again in session. "After I had passed the Acts," wrote Effingham, "I ordered His Majesty's Letter to bee publickly read to them, and then Dissolved them . . . and told them they were the first Assembly which had been soe dissolved and I hoped they would bee the last that should deserve it. I ordered copies of his Majesty's Letter to bee sent to the several County-Courts, that all the Inhabitants might know how displeasing such proceedings were to his Majesty."[115] "And now," he added, "the public debts being paid, . . . I shall not for the future have soe frequent Assemblys."[116]

More damaging to the Burgesses than this rebuke was the loss of the right to elect their own clerk. "I was severely angry with their Clerk," declared Effingham, "that he durst omit ye least clause, especially soe material an one . . . I sent to the Assembly to make him an example for it, But they rather maintained him."[117] Some months later the King sent orders that Beverley be tried for defacing the records and that he be once more deprived of all offices. Probably because of his great popularity, Beverley was never brought to trial, but

[113] P. R. O., CO5-1357-93.   [114] P. R. O., CO5-1357-119.
[115] P. R. O., CO5-1357-127.   [116] P. R. O., CO5-1357-133.
[117] P. R. O., CO5-1357-92; McD., Vol. VII, p. 222.

he was forced to relinquish his lucrative governmental posts.[118] In May, 1686, Nicholas Spencer wrote the Committee of Trade and Plantations, advocating the appointment of the clerk by the Governor. "I . . . beg leave to present," he said, "how necessary it is . . . that the clerk of the House . . . bee commissionated by his Majesty's Governour . . . and that his salary be appointed unto him out of his Majesty's revenue. This will take off his dependency on his great masters the House of Burgesses, and leave noe room for designed omissions."[119] Nothing loath, the King, in August, 1686, wrote Lord Howard, "Wee . . . require you . . . upon the Convening of the Assembly to appoint a fit person to execute the Office of Clerk of the House of Burgesses, & not to permit upon any pretense whatsoever any other person to execute ye said Office but such as shall bee soe chosen by you."[120]

Accordingly, at the session of April, 1688, the Governor, with the approbation of the Council, appointed Captain Francis Page as clerk of the House.[121] The Burgesses could but yield, but they told Effingham that the clerk was still their servant and ought to take the usual oath of secrecy. "I do declare," replied the Governor, "it was never my intention nor my desire that the Clerk should be as a spy upon your Actions and to declare to me your private Debates." It was therefore agreed that he should take the following oath: "You shall keep secret all private Debates of the said House of Burgesses."[122] Despite this, it was quite evident that the House was no longer to be master of its own clerk, and that he was to be in the future, to some extent at least, an emissary of the enemy seated in their midst.

The resolute and vigilant defense of the constitutional rights of Virginia made by the House in this the critical period of her history is deserving of the highest praise, because it was made in the face of vigorous personal attacks by Effingham upon the most active of the members. Every Burgess that voted against the measures proposed by the King or advocated by his Gov-

[118] Sains., Vol. XV, p. 30.
[120] P. R. O., CO5-1357-119.
[122] Jour. H. of B., 1688, p. 17.

[119] McD., Vol. VII, p. 229.
[121] Jour. H. of B., 1688, p. 1.

ernor, exposed himself not only to removal from office, but to active persecution. As we have seen, Mr. William Sherwood and Colonel Thomas Milner, for forwarding to the Privy Council the address of the Burgesses in 1684, had been dismissed from office.[123] "In ye year 1686 Mr. Arthur Allen & Mr. John Smith, who were Burgesses in ye year 1685, were turned out of all imployment Civill & Military to Mr. Allen's great damage, he being a surveyor of land at that tyme."[124] I have displaced Allen, wrote Effingham, because he was "a great promoter of those differences between mee and the Assembly concerning the King's negative Voice . . . as not thinking it fitt that those who are peevishly opposite to his Majesty's interest should have any advantage by his favor".[125] "In the year 1688 Mr. William Anderson, a member of ye Assembly in that year was soon after the Assembly by the Governor's order and Command put in ye Common goale and there detained 7 months, without Tryal, though often prayed for, and several courts past in ye time of his imprisonment. Nor could he obtain ye benefit of habeas corpus upon his humble petition. . . . Mr. Charles Scarburgh, a member of that Assembly, alsoe was, soon after ye Assembly, turned out of all imployment and as a mark of his Lordship's displeasure, a command was sent to ye clerk of ye county to raze his name out of ye records as a Justice of Peace."[126] "From whence," it was declared, "the people conclude these severities are inflicted rather as a terrour to others than for any personall crimes of their owne, and is of such ruinous consequence that either the public or particular interests must fall, for if none oppose, the country must languish under the severity of the government, or fly into a mutiny to save themselves from starving. If any do appear more zealous in prosecuting the countries complaints they know what to expect. It being observable that

---

[123] Sains., Vol. IV, p. 254.   [124] McD., Vol. VII, p. 26.

[125] McD., Vol. VII, p. 257. Some years later Effingham contradicted this statement. "They were not dismissed," he said, "from their imployments upon account of their proceedings in ye Assembly, but being Justices of Peace they oppenly opposed the King's authority in naming sheriffs by his Governour alledging that office ought to go by succession."

[126] McD., Vol. VII, pp. 437-441.

none has been thus punisht but those who were forward in the assembly to oppose the encroachments on the people, and promote the complaint to England, being out of hope of relief on the place."[127]

One is inclined to ask, when considering the incessant quarrels of the Governor and the Burgesses, why Lord Howard was less successful than Governor Berkeley had been in gaining an ascendency over the Assembly. During the Restoration Period the Burgesses had worked in entire harmony with Sir William, even when he advocated the oppressive measures that were so instrumental in bringing on Bacon's Rebellion. Effingham, on the other hand, found himself continually embroiled with the Assemblymen, and unable to force them into submission even with rebukes and persecution.

The explanation must be sought partly in the different characters of the two Governors. Berkeley was an abler man than Lord Howard, more tactful, more capable of utilizing the weapons at hand. His method of overwhelming the legislators with favors was more effective in winning their support than intimidation and threats. Moreover, Sir William, himself a Virginian by his long residence in the colony, carried out only his own policies, and by methods that did not openly assail the charter rights of the people. Effingham, on the other hand, was the instrument of the English King and his Councillors in an assault upon representative government in the colony. It was but natural that all classes, even the wealthy planters, should resist him with stubborn resolution. Nor was it possible for Effingham to control, as Sir William had done, the elections of Burgesses. The opposition of many sheriffs, whose duty it was to preside at the polls, to the administration, the greater vigilance of the House, and the independent spirit of the commons conspired to render the returns more accurate and the House more responsive to the will of the people. Finally, the poor planters found now, what they had lacked during the Restoration Period, cultured and able men to represent them in the Assembly. Without the aggressive leadership of Major Robert Beverley, Thomas Milner, Colonel Ballard, and other

[127] McD., Vol. VII, pp. 437-441.

prominent planters, the cause of the people might have been lost.

Even in the Council the commons had one staunch friend— Colonel Philip Ludwell. This restless man, who was unable to work in harmony with any Governor save Sir William Berkeley, sympathized with his old friends of the Green Spring faction in their resistance to Effingham. As early as 1684 he had aroused the Governor's suspicion by arguing in Council "for the undutiful Address which was sent to his Majesty",[128] and during the sessions of 1685 and 1686 it was thought that he was "an Instrument in Abbetting and formenting those Disputes & Exceptions the Assembly soe insisted on".[129]

Soon after, the Governor's distrust was heightened by two acts of favor shown by Ludwell to leaders of the opposition in the House of Burgesses. When ordered to oust Major Allen from his surveyor's place, he gave it to "Major Swan, one altogether as troublesom as the other & that only for the use of Allen". Upon receiving information that the King had declared Major Beverley "uncapable of any public imploy- ment . . . hee presently gives his Surveyor's place, the best in the Country to his Son".[130] In the spring of 1686 the Governor made one last attempt to win Ludwell over from the people's cause. "I did," he wrote, "on the death of Colonel Bridger . . . give him a collector's place, in hopes to have gained him by it."[131] But Ludwell, unaffected by this at- tempted bribery, continued his active opposition to the arbitrary and illegal conduct of the Governor. At last, during the ses- sion of Assembly of 1686, there occurred an open breach. "His Lordship flew into a great rage and told . . . Ludwell he had formerly made remarks upon him, and that if he did not look the better to himself he should shortly suspend him from the Council."[132] Early in 1687 this threat was put into effect,[133] and the troublesome Councillor was for the second time deprived of his seat. But this persecution, which the people believed to be directed against Ludwell for his support

[128] P. R. O., CO5-1357-130.
[129] CO5-1357-127.
[130] P. R. O., CO5-1357-129.
[131] P. R. O., CO5-1357-130.
[132] McD., Vol. VII, pp. 437-441.
[133] Sains., Vol. IV, p. 226; P. R. O., CO5-1357-127.

of their cause, brought him into great popularity throughout
the colony and made him the acknowledged leader of the opposition to the administration. In the elections for the Assembly of 1688 he was chosen by the freeholders of James City
county to represent them in the House of Burgesses.[134] Effingham, however, would not allow him to take his seat, producing
a clause from his commission which forbade suspended Councillors to become members of the Assembly.[135] Despite this
exclusion, Ludwell could and did, by conferences with individual members, influence the actions of the House and lead them
in their fight against the Governor.

The most important task that confronted the Burgesses when
they assembled in 1688 was to call the Governor to account for
many burdensome fees which he had imposed upon the people
by executive order. First in importance was "a fee of 200
pounds of tobacco for the Seal affixed to Patents & other public
instruments".[136] This the Burgesses considered a tax imposed without the authority or consent of the Assembly, and
consequently destructive of the most cherished rights of the
people. Moreover, it had, they claimed, deterred many from
using the seal and had greatly impeded the taking up of land.
They also protested against a fee demanded by the "Master
of the Escheat Office of £5 or 1000lbs tobacco", and to one of
thirty pounds of tobacco required by the Secretary for record-
ing surveys of land.[137] "This House," they declared, "upon
Examination of the many grievous Complaints . . . (have)
been fully convinced and made sensible that many unlawful
and unwarrantable fees and other dutyes have been, under
colour of his Majesty's Royal authority, unjustly imposed . . .
& that divers new unlawful, unpresidented & very burthensom
and grievous wayes & devises have been of late made use of
to the great impoverishing Vexing and utter undoeing of
many of his Majesties Subjects of this his Dominion."[138]

The Burgesses were also deeply concerned at an instance of
the unwarrantable use of the royal prerogative. In 1680 an

[134] McD., Vol. VII, pp. 437-441; Jour. H. of B., 1688, p. 13.
[135] P. R. O., CO5-1355-313; Jour. H. of B., 1688, p. 29.
[136] P. R. O., CO5-1357-218.   [137] Jour. H. of B., 1688, pp. 82, 83.
[138] Jour. H. of B., 1688, pp. 82, 83.

act had been passed concerning attorneys. Two years later, before the act had received the royal assent, it had been repealed by the Assembly. Later the King, by proclamation, had made void the act of 1682, and the Governor had insisted that this revived the law of 1680. Against this, the Burgesses in 1688 entered a vigorous protest. "A Law," they declared, "may as well Receive its beginning by proclamation as such revivall. . . . Some Governor may be sent to Govern us who under the pretense of the liberty he hath to construe prerogative and stretch it as far as he pleaseth may by proclamation Revive all the Lawes that for their great Inconveniences to the Country have been Repeal'd through forty years since."[139]

The Burgesses drew up a long paper, setting forth their many grievances, with the intention of presenting it to the Governor. They first, however, requested the Council to join them in their demand for redress. This the Council with some sharpness, refused to do. We are apprehensive, they replied, that the grievances "proceed from petulent tempers of private persons and that which inclines us the rather so to take them is from the bitterness of the Expressions".[140] Judging the Governor's temper from this reply of the Councillors, the Burgesses relinquished hope of redress from the executive and determined to petition the King himself. An humble address was drawn up, entrusted to Colonel Philip Ludwell and delivered by him at Windsor, in September, 1688, into the hands of James II. Before it could be considered, however, William of Orange had landed in England and King James had been overthrown.[141]

In the meanwhile a crisis in Virginia had been approaching rapidly. The people felt that their religion, as well as their liberties, was menaced by the rule of James II. In 1685, the King had directed Effingham "to permit a Liberty of Conscience to all persons", that would "bee contented with a quiet and peaceable enjoyment of it, not giving offence or scandal".[142] The people of Virginia understood well enough that this order was dictated, not by considerations of liberality, but

---

[139] Jour, H. of B., 1688, p. 50.
[141] P. R. O., CO5-1357-248.

[140] Jour. H. of B., 1688, p. 116.
[142] P. R. O., CO5-1357-38, 39.

by James' determination to favor the Catholic church. The feeling of uneasiness was increased when, in 1688, Effingham, declaring it no longer necessary for the Burgesses to take the oaths of allegiance and supremacy, admitted a Catholic to the Assembly.[143]

In October, 1688, James sent word to the Governor of the impending invasion of the Prince of Orange and commanded him to place Virginia in a posture of defense.[144] Immediately the colony was thrown into the wildest excitement, and, for a time, it seemed probable that the people would attempt the expulsion of Effingham. "Unruly and unorderly spiritts," the Governor afterwards testified, "laying hold of the motion of affairs, and that under the pretext of religion, . . . betook themselves to arms."[145] Wild rumors spread through the colony that the Papists of Maryland were conspiring with the Senecas to fall upon Virginia and cut off all Protestants in a new Saint Bartholomew's Eve.[146] The frontiersmen along the upper courses of the Rappahannock and the Potomac "drawing themselves into parties upon their defense", were "ready to fly in the face of ye government. Soe that matters were . . . tending to a Rebellion." However, the news of William's easy victory and the flight of James restored quiet to the colony. On February the nineteenth, 1689, the Privy Council wrote the Governor that William and Mary had ascended the throne of England,[147] and a few weeks later their Majesties were proclaimed at Jamestown with solemnity and thanksgiving.[148]

The Glorious Revolution was a victory for liberty even more important to Virginia than to England. It brought to an end those attacks of the English government upon the representative institutions of the colony that had marked the past ten years. It confirmed to the people the rights that had been guaranteed them, through a long series of patents dating back as far as 1606, and rendered impossible for all time the illegal oppressions of such men as Harvey, Berkeley, Cul-

---

[143] Jour. H. of B., 1688, p. 8; McD., Vol. VII, pp. 437-441.
[144] P. R. O., CO5-1357-229.   [145] McD., Vol. VII, p. 316.
[146] McD., Vol. VII, p. 316.   [147] P. R. O., CO5-1357-236.
[148] Sains., Vol. IV, p. 215.

peper and Effingham. Other Governors of despotic disposition were yet to rule Virginia—Nicholson, Andros, Dunmore —but it was impossible for them to resort to the tyrannical methods of some of their predecessors. The English Revolution had weakened permanently the control of the British government over the colony, and consequently the power of the Governor.

The advance of liberalism which was so greatly accelerated both in England and in America by the events of 1688 was halted in the mother country in the middle of the eighteenth century. But Virginia and the other colonies were not greatly affected by the reaction upon the other side of the Atlantic. Here the power of the people grew apace, encountering no serious check, until it came into conflict with the sullen Toryism of George III. Then it was that England sought to stifle the liberalism of the colonies, and revolution and independence resulted.

The changed attitude of the Privy Council towards Virginia was made immediately apparent by the careful consideration given the petition of the Burgesses. Had James remained upon the throne it is probable that it, like the address of 1684, would have been treated with neglect and scorn. But William received Ludwell graciously, listened to his plea "on behalf of the Commons of Virginia", and directed the Committee of Trade and Plantations to investigate the matter and to see justice done.[149]

Effingham, who had been called to England upon private business, appeared before the Committee to defend his administration and to refute Ludwell's charges. Despite his efforts, several articles of the petition were decided against him, and the most pressing grievances of the people redressed. The "Complaint touching the fee of 200lbs of tobacco and cask", it was reported, "imposed by my Lord Howard for affixing the Great Seal to Patents . . . in regard it was not regularly imposed . . . the committee agree to move his Majesty the same be discontinued".[150] Similarly their Lordships declared in favor of abolishing the fee of thirty pounds of tobacco

[149] P. R. O., CO5-1357-247, 248.   [150] Sains., Vol. IV, pp. 233, 234.

required for registering surveys. The article touching the revival of repealed laws by proclamation was referred to the consideration of the Attorney-General and the Solicitor-General. These officers gave it as their opinion that his Majesty did have the right, by repealing acts of repeal, to revive laws, but the committee agreed to move the King that the Act of Attorneys should be made void by proclamation.[151]

This was a signal victory for the Burgesses, but Ludwell, who had personal scores to settle with the Governor, did not let matters drop here. After the lapse of several months he appeared once more before the Committee with charges against Effingham of misgovernment and oppression.[152] Referring to the quarrel over the Bill of Ports, in 1685, he accused him of exercising "two negative voices". He complained bitterly of his attacks upon those Burgesses that had opposed him in the Assembly, and of his abuse of the power of suspending Councillors. The money arising from fort duties, he said, which had formerly been accounted for to the Assembly, had, during Effingham's administration, "been diverted to other uses". The Governor had established new courts of judicature contrary to the wishes of the people.

These persistent attacks of Ludwell resulted in another victory, for the Committee decided that Effingham should no longer rule the colony. He was not displaced as Governor-General, but he was commanded to remain in England, and to leave the control of the administration to a Lieutenant-Governor. This, doubtless, was not unsatisfactory to Lord Howard, for he retained a part of his salary and was relieved of all the work and responsibility of his office. The Lieutenant-Governorship was given to Captain Francis Nicholson.[153]

Thus the colony emerged triumphant from the Critical Period. It is true the House of Burgesses had lost many privileges—the right to elect its own clerk, the right to receive judicial appeals, the right to control all revenues,—but they had retained within their grasp that all-important power—the levying of general taxes. And they had gained greatly in

[151] Sains., Vol. IV, p. 243.   [152] Sains., Vol. IV, p. 246.
[153] Sains., Vol. IV, p. 254.

political experience. Long years of watchfulness, of resistance to encroachments upon their rights, had moulded them into a body that the most cunning executive could neither cajole nor intimidate. Unmindful of the anger of Governors, the rebukes of Kings, of personal loss, even of imprisonment, they had upheld the people's rights. And their descendants were to reap the reward of their faithfulness. The traditions of ability, probity and heroism established by the men of the Critical Period made possible that long and honorable career of the House of Burgesses and the important rôle it was to play in winning independence for America.

INDEX

Abigall, brings contagion, 46.
Accomac, see also Eastern Shore, 80;
Berkeley flees to, 171; expedition
against, 176, 177; 182; 184; 186;
195; 197.
Adam and Eve, ship, captures Bacon,
163; 177; 203.
Adams, Peter, excepted from pardon,
202.
Admirall, ship, 128, 129.
Allen, Arthur, 251, 253.
Allerton, Isaac, 229; corrupt bargain
of, 230.
Anderson, William, 257.
Annelectons, aid in Susquehannock
defeat, 160.
Apachisco, negotiates peace, 26.
Appomatocks, expedition against, 52.
Appomattox, river, 21.
Archer, Gabriel, admitted to Council,
tries to establish a parliament, 6;
8; helps depose Smith, 10.
Argoll, Samuel, 19; enforces laws, 23;
captures Pocahontas, 25.
Arlington, Earl of, grant to of Virginia, 123, 124; yields his rights,
125; 145; 245.
Arnold, Anthony, excepted from pardon, 202; hanged, 204.
Assembly, General, attempt to establish, 6; early desire for, 8; describes tyranny of Governors, 24;
established, 1619, 36; convenes,
37; legislative powers of, 38; control over taxation, 39; judicial
functions of, 40; Council the upper house of, 41; 42; describes
Indian war, 51; supports Company, 60; 61; saved, 62; restored,
63; 64; Harvey usurps powers of,
72; 73; refuses tobacco contract,
74; 76; Council summons, 1636,
77; elects West Governor, 78; 79;
86; opposes revival of Company,
88; 91; persecutes Puritans, 92;
acknowledges Charles II, 95; de-
fies Parliament, 98; surrenders,
100; 102; Northampton petitions,
104; 105; 106; 107; 108; contest
in, 109; elects Berkeley Governor,
110; Berkeley addresses, 111;
112; 115; encourages manufacture, 119; 122; protests to King,
124; 125; 133; 134; Long Assembly, 135; 136; 137; 138; 140;
143; erects forts, 151, 152; hatred
of, 153; Berkeley dissolves, 1676,
158, 159; Bacon elected to, 162;
163; Bacon threatens, 168; liberal
laws of, 169, 170; Bacon summons, 173; interrupted, 178; 204;
supports Berkeley, 206, 207; protest of, 1677, 214; session of October, 1677, 218, 219; session of
1679, 222; rights of attacked, 226;
session of 1682, 233; appeals to
forbidden, 241, 242; petition of
242, 243; quarrels with Effingham
over, taxation, 244, 245; quit-rents,
245, 246, veto power, 246, 247, 248,
249, the clerk, 249, 250.
Austin, Black, executed, 238.

Bacon, Nathaniel, the rebel, 123; ac-
cuses Burgesses, 133, 134; describes abuses of the rich, 135;
Berkeley jealous of, 144; 145;
character of, 154; becomes leader
of rebels, 155; prepares to attack
Indians, 156; attacks Indians, 157;
proclaimed a rebel, 158; pursues
Susquehannocks, 159; visits Oc-
caneeches, 160; battle with Occaneechees, 161, 162; elected
Burgess, 162; captured, 163; pardoned, 164; flees from Jamestown, 165; seizes Jamestown, 166;
demands commission, 167; new
demands of, 168; secures liberal
laws, 169, 170; prepares new Indian expedition, 171; marches
against Berkeley, 171; resolves to
defy King, 172; forces oaths on
prominent men, 173; attacks
Pamunkeys, 174, 175; marches on
Jamestown, 178, 179; repulses

DATE DUE

SEP 27 '65			
OCT 8 '65			
OCT 7 '66			
DEC 6 '72			
			PRINTED IN U.S.A.

GAYLORD